BEFORE AND AFTER THE GLOBAL CRISIS

BEFORE AND AFTER THE GLOBAL CRISIS

TT Ram Mohan

GYAN

ISBN: 978-81-212-1175-8

₹ 990/-

First Published 2013

Printed by

Gyan Publishing House
23, Main Ansari Road
Daryaganj, New Delhi-110002
Phones: 23282060, 23261060
Fax : 91-11-23285914
E-mail: books@gyanbooks.com

Laser Typesetting : Awadhesh Computers, Delhi
Printed at: G. Print Process, Delhi

Cataloging in Publication Data- -DK
Courtesy: D.K. Agencies (P) Ltd. <docinfo@dkagencies.com>

Mohan, TT Ram, 1956-
Before and after the global crisis / TT Ram Mohan.
p. cm.
Articles; previously published.
ISBN: 9788121211758

1. India-Economic policy-1991- 2. Banks and banking-India. 3. Global Financial Crisis, 2008-2009. 4. Banks and banking, International. 5. Corporate governance. I. Title.

DDC 330.954 23

To Jayashree

who endured much but never faltered in her support

Contents

Preface

It is nearly six years since the global economic crisis erupted. The crisis has stretched out for longer than most people had thought. The downturn in some parts of the world, notably Europe, has turned out to be more severe than expected. India's growth story has unravelled in a way that we could not have imagined during the boom period of 2004-08. The crisis and its impact on India have been written about extensively.

This book brings together a selection of my writings during the period 2004-12. It thus spans years on either side of the crisis, although it leans more towards the post-crisis period. Most of these pieces are from my fortnightly column in the *Economic Times*. A few are from the *Economic and Political Weekly*. The pieces from *EPW* carry the name of the journal below; the rest may be presumed to be from *ET*. The articles have been broken up into five broad themes: *Indian Economy, Indian Banking, World Economy, Management and Governance,* and *Indian Polity*. Under each theme, the articles appear in chronological order.

The diversity of themes covered is intentional. As my column in the *Economic Times* evolved over the years, I thought it necessary to range over different subjects order to retain the interest of the reader. If I wrote about the Indian economy in a given week, I would try to write about the world economy in another; then, it would be a piece on banking. From time to time, I wrote on management subjects, and was pleasantly surprised at the response from readers. The occasional political piece would be thrown in, just to inject variety. Most of the time, I tried to find a news peg on which to hang an article, as befits a newspaper column. At the same time, I tried to create room for the occasional academic or research-related article.

All journalism is instant history. It has the virtue of immediacy but lacks the perspective and detachment of the historian. This collection of articles is not meant to be a systematic chronicle of events under the different heads covered. It is merely a snapshot of events and policy issues in the themes covered. The articles are not meant to be read at one shot or in sequence. The reader may prefer to take them in small doses and dip into whatever topics and titles that catch her fancy.

****

It is not possible for me to summarise here the many ideas I have presented over the years. I will content myself with highlighting a few. One that stands out in the section on the *Indian Economy* is optimism about India's growth prospects. In today's environment, it may appear that I got carried away by the India Shining years or failed to grasp the extent to which India's growth acceleration was linked to the global boom. Certainly, like many others, I have been surprised at the extent of the slowdown in 2011-12 and 2012-13. During the economic boom, who could have imagined that the growth rate would fall to 5 per cent!

However, it is important that we do not swing to the other extreme and become unduly pessimistic about India's growth prospects. A combination of external and internal factors has caused the deceleration in growth over the past two years. One is the global environment, especially the flaring up of the Eurozone crisis.

Among the internal factors are: judgements or orders of the Supreme Court that have adversely impacted certain sectors of the economy (telecom and mining); the political controversy that erupted over the CAG reports on 2G licenses and coal blocks to private companies and that has had the effect of slowing down decision making in the bureaucracy; and the Anna Hazare agitation against corruption in 2011 which proved disruptive of Parliament and again contributed to a fear psychosis in the bureaucracy. According to the RBI, India's growth potential is around 7.5 per cent. If we have not achieved this growth rate, it is mainly because of stalled projects and their impact on corporates and the banking sector. This is not a structural issue.

A major factor dampening growth has been the incidence of high inflation for several years running and which has, among other things, impacted in a big way on the current account deficit by causing huge imports of gold. How monetary policy should respond to the challenge posed by low growth and high inflation has been greatly debated in the last couple of years. One issue in the debate, which I touch upon, is whether we have to reconcile ourselves to a relatively higher rate of inflation in the medium-term, say 6 per cent, instead of the RBI's comfort zone of 4-5 per cent or what is called the 'new normal' for inflation.

For India to find its way back to a growth trajectory of 8% in the face of these adverse factors will be quite a challenge. It will also not happen quickly. However, the structural factors that underpinned India's high growth earlier remain intact: high savings and investment rates, favourable demographics, the spread of the entrepreneurial culture. What strikes me when I look back on my writings of that period is how the predictions of economists can be unsettled by a host of unanticipated events.

****

The banking sector has been one of the strengths of the economy over the post-reform period. India's banking sector remained relatively unscathed during the early crisis years even as banks in the advanced economies were getting battered. Return to assets in Indian banking stayed at over 1 per cent in the period 2008-12. For the banking sector, it was almost as if the biggest crisis in the world economy since the Great Crash had never happened!

In 2007 and early 2008, just as the crisis was beginning to unfold, two reports of committees (headed by Percy Mistry and Raghuram Rajan) came out. The Percy Mistry was scathing in its criticism of banking policy. It advocated the government's exit from ownership of banks by 2014. It also faulted the RBI for being excessively conservative in its policies and it urged the RBI to move towards 'principle- based' regulation as distinct from 'rule-based' regulation. The financial crisis had erupted by the time the Rajan committee report came out. It was a little more cautious in advocating change in the banking sector.

My own view, reflected in the articles in this volume, has been that the RBI has got the policy framework for Indian banking in the post-reform period right, on the whole. The RBI's approach has been vindicated by what happened to banking systems elsewhere during the financial crisis and the Indian banking sector's own robustness in the face of a major global crisis. Think of where the Indian economy would be if the banking sector had been impacted as severely as the real sector. There is, of course, room for improvement, both in terms of the policy framework in the sector and the performance of public sector banks (PSBs), which still account for 70 per cent of the Indian banking system in terms of assets.

In terms of the policy framework, the major initiative on the part of RBI has been its decision to license new banks in the private sector. I have examined the case for this, in particular, the issue of issuing bank licenses to industrial houses, and am inclined to believe that letting in industrial houses is not such a great idea.

When it comes to improving the performance of PSBs, my sense is that the ministry of finance and the RBI haven't done enough. There are enormous human resource issues that need to be tackled. And the composition and functioning of bank boards leave much to be desired. I have also been sceptical about talk of bank consolidation or foreign ventures by PSBs. These are escapist exercises; there is so much to be done right under your nose that there is no need to try to grow bigger or venture abroad.

****

The global crisis has been the defining event of the past decade. There is now a rich literature on what caused the crisis and what policies might help contain its impact and expedite a recovery. It is a different matter that recovery has been slow in happening.

In my writings on the subject, three points stand out. While global macroeconomic imbalances were undoubtedly a key driver in the crisis, the collapse of banks undoubtedly represented a failure or regulation. Banks moved away from their traditional banking role and became more oriented towards investment banking. The focus on proprietary trading, financed by short-term funds in the capital market, left banks extremely vulnerable in a situation in which their investment in assets related to sub-prime loans plunged in value.

Secondly, while de-leveraging and the associated decline in economic growth were inevitable following the credit bubble, the downturn became more severe because of a major policy failure: the decision to allow Lehman Brothers to fail. This led to a significant drying up of funds and enhanced their losses on their asset portfolios. The major attempts to redesign regulation-the Basel 3 proposals, the Volcker Rule in the US, the Turner Report in the UK and a few others- are covered in my writings.

Thirdly, banks need to reinvent themselves in a number of ways. They need a lot more capital and will end up generating lower returns than in the past; they need a proper balance between banking and investment banking activities, even if this is not ordained by regulation; and they need to think through what is an appropriate size from the standpoint of risk management. On a different note, it makes sense for the advanced economies to have a smaller financial sector and one that is less glamorous. It will ensure that talent is not drawn away on the scale we have seen from other fields, including the real sector, academics and research.

The collapse of banks caused governments to bail out many by infusing taxpayer money. This caused public debt to soar in the advanced economies. High levels of public debt, it was widely supposed, were a developing country problem; advanced economies were said to be characterised by prudent fiscal policy and low levels of debt. The post-crisis period has turned this piece of conventional wisdom on its head.

High levels of debt and the fact that much of this debt is held by banks in Europe resulted in the Eurozone crisis in 2010, first manifested in the bail-out of Greece. That crisis, which is but an extension of the sub-prime crisis, is now proving obdurate and is posing a risk to the global economy. A global recovery hinges on a proper resolution of the Eurozone crisis. There have been bailout packages for Ireland, Greece, Spain, Portugal and Cyprus. I correctly predicted that the first package for Greece would be a failure as it caused most of the burden of adjustment to fall on the people of Greece. This is one drama that will play out over the next couple of years at least. It is hard to see how it can be resolved in an orderly way unless there is willingness on the part of the entire European Union- and indeed the world at large- to share the burden of adjustment.

****

For anybody at a business school, interest in the broader issues of management and governance is natural. I made it a point to comment on these matters whenever possible. I was pleasantly surprised to note that management-related themes often drew more responses from readers than articles on other topics.

The functioning of corporate boards is one theme that has interested me because of my involvement in various boards over the years. We have seen several initiatives in corporate governance in the past decade. Have they made boards more effective? The jury is out.

The significant change has been the appointment of 'independent directors'. These directors are supposed to act independently of management in safeguarding the interests of shareholders, including minority shareholders in family-managed enterprises in India. A fundamental problem remains unaddressed: how can we expect directors to be independent of management when they are beholden to management for appointing them and, often, rewarding them handsomely? Clearly, other stakeholders – institutional investors, minority shareholders, employees-need to have a say in the appointment of directors.

Another theme of interest to me is the role of CEOs. For all the talk of decentralisation and empowerment, most companies tend to be extremely CEO-centric, with a heavy concentration of powers in the office of CEO. There is little recourse against the arbitrary exercise of powers by the CEO. This is sought to be justified by the need to deliver performance. Yet, the corporate world in the post-crisis period is littered with the debris of financial firms that went under precisely because too much power was concentrated in one person. Peter Drucker once observed that the CEO should not be a person but a team of at least three persons. Clearly, companies have forgotten his dictum.

CEO succession is another prickly issue in the corporate world. CEO succession is rarely well-managed. Many, if not most, exits in the US and UK are abrupt, and the search for a successor far from orderly. And yet finding a successor is one of the basic tasks of any CEO. One test of a CEO's performance is how well the company does after he leaves. How many companies with successful CEOs would pass this test?

I have included a tribute to Ravi Matthai, the first full-time director of IIMA, who remains an iconic figure on the campus and in the world of management education. One of the things for which he is remembered- and one of the most important reasons for IIMA's pre-eminence, in my view- is the convention he put in place of a single term for the director. Matthai believed that organisations need change at the top as they evolve, as new situations need new approaches and styles of leadership. If only CEOs knew when to call it a day, without having to be shown the door!

The relationship between B-schools and business – and to what extent the former do add value to the latter-has been explored for long. The standard line is that if B-schools did not add value, they would not exist and they would not have proliferated. There is something to that.

However, when we ask in what ways B-schools actually contribute to business, we do not have satisfactory answers. Much of the research produced by B-schools is seen as esoteric and of little relevance to managers. As for the graduates of these schools, many firms think they are merely hiring smart people who have gone through an intensive process of selection and have survived a competitive two-year process. It is as if the MBA programme itself adds value

Whether B-schools actually equip their students with skills and techniques that enhance the effectiveness of business, with the exception of niche areas such as consulting and investment banking, is something that the corporate world questions all the time. Providing a persuasive answer remains a challenge for B-schools.

****

India's political environment has been turbulent with the ending of one-party rule in the 1980s and the emergence of coalition governments. Politicians themselves are seen by the public in poor light. They are seen as people who are hungry for power and the spoils of power. And yet it is this very political system and the set of politicians we have had that have created the environment in which India's economic profile has changed dramatically.

Governments in India have had to manage economic policy in one of the most challenging settings in the world. They have had to provide law and order in a large country riven by communal, caste and linguistic conflicts, ensure that the frontiers are safe while dealing with difficult neighbours in the west and the north, and manage the long-simmering problems in Kashmir, the North-East and the Naxalite areas of the country.

I am not a political scientist and do not write often on matters political. However, on the few occasions that I have expressed myself on the subject of Indian politics, the reader will notice that I have been kinder to Indian politicians than much of the intelligentsia.

It is not that I think Indian politicians are a superior breed. It is just that, given India's vibrant democracy, their job requires them to be responsive and to deliver at a level that is at least adequate to get re-elected. When political parties rally behind affirmative action or quotas, for instance, many call it 'vote-bank' politics; I prefer to think they are merely recognising the reality on the ground, which is that large sections of the electorate cannot be left behind in the economic race. 'Inclusion' may sound like a catch-phrase, and yet no political party can survive unless it grasps the imperative of inclusion in the Indian context.

****

My output over the years would not have been possible without the support of many people. At *ET*, I had very pleasant and fruitful interactions with a succession of op-ed editors: TK Arun (in two stints), Mythili Bhusnurmath, Bodhisatva Ganguly and M K Venu. TK, in particular, went out of his way to provide encouragement. At *EPW*, C Rammanohar Reddy, who has done a remarkable job of steering the journal after Krishna Raj, has been an indulgent presence.

I have also benefited from feedback from numerous readers. I must mention two. Dr K B L Mathur, a retired bureaucrat with a long association with the ministry of finance, would call after almost every article. He was lavish with his praise but did not hesitate to express criticism. Often, he would go over the main points of an article in detail, indicating where he agreed and where he disagreed. Jagan Mohan, a veteran banker and voracious reader of books, not only responded to many of my articles but gave me the benefit of his own insights.

My family helped me cope with the vicissitudes of life over the decade in which these articles were written. I must mention my mother, Padmini Vijayaraghavan (who made it a point to read all my articles, a remarkable achievement in a housewife with no particular expertise in these areas); my father, T T Vijayaraghavan; my brother, T T Krishnan; my in-laws, Susheela Narayan and N S Narayan; my wife, Jayashree, and my son, Nandu, both of whom know by now what it is to put up with a distracted and often irritable columnist.

I am grateful to all of them.

Finally, I must thank Gyan Publishing House, who approached me with the idea of bringing these articles out in the form of a book and extended every help in seeing the project through to completion.

T. T. Ram Mohan

Sept. 2013

PART-I

INDIAN ECONOMY

1

Macro Economy

A Commission Flawed at Birth

Finance minister P Chidambaram has sought to woo the business community by constituting an Investment Commission. The Commission, to be headed by Ratan Tata and with Deepak Parekh and A S Ganguly as its other members, has been given the task of boosting investment, domestic and foreign, in the country.

Assuming such a Commission is required at all, the government has got its composition terribly wrong. There is a serious conflict of interest in entrusting this task to businessmen. The conflict could be particularly acute in the case of foreign investors. This point may not be applicable to Mr Ganguly but it certainly holds for Mr Tata and Mr Parekh.

Mr Tata's business empire spans several industries that would interest foreign investors. Is it reasonable to expect Mr Tata to make out a strong case for investing in India to international firms in telecom, a sector in which his group has a significant presence? Is it fair to expect him to advise Chinese software firms to come in and tap Indian software talent so that they can give TCS a run for its money? Is it credible that Mr Tata will have a serious interest in asking Volvo to make a big investment in India when that would expose Tata Motors to greater competition?

In the event that Mr Tata does rise above his business interests in such instances, his shareholders would have some tough questions for him. He can please either the Indian government or his shareholders, not both. Mr Parekh's presence on the Commission raises similar concerns.

The possibility that the mandate given to the Commission may work against the business interests of its members is not the only cause for concern. There is also the possibility that the Commission's members might benefit from decisions the Commission takes. You have to wonder: if an investor became a client of HDFC Bank or IDFC, how would that sit with the competitors of these financial firms? If an international firm lured in by the Commission started sourcing its software from TCS or used VSNL as its telecom provider, would that not set tongues wagging?

The problem would be bad enough if the Commission were merely entrusted with the task of making a pitch to investors. But its mandate goes much further. As reported in the press, it will have the 'full authority' of the government and will be the 'government's face and voice'. This does place the members of the Commission in an invidious position. If they go ahead full throttle, people will want to know if their business interests are benefiting. If they tread warily - and with justification- that will be put down to lack of enthusiasm for foreign competition. They are damned if they do and damned if they don't.

Ideally, the Commission should have been headed by a politician with a clean image and a reputation for being pro-business. That would have given it the clout to follow through on commitments. If this was not feasible, there is no dearth of non-political talent of international stature and intimate knowledge of government processes. Two names that readily come to mind are Bimal Jalan and P C Alexander. Having businessmen on the Commission is a recipe for controversy and precisely the sort of paralysis in implementation the government is keen to avoid.

Putting businessmen on a Commission with such sweeping powers is a bad idea for another reason. It blurs the distinction between government and business. Those who affirm that government has no right to be in business must accept that businessmen should not be exercising governmental authority either. There are many reasons why this should not happen but the most compelling one, perhaps, is that violates the principle of accountability. Government is accountable to Parliament but the members of the Commission, while wielding governmental authority, are not.

The finance minister has a well-deserved reputation for being an impatient reformer. His eagerness to eliminate bureaucratic obstacles to investment is admirable but not the means he has chosen to deal with these. The answer to judicial delays is not setting up Kangaroo Courts or going in for summary executions-these methods more befit our northern neighbour for whose prowess in attracting FDI there is so much admiration in the country these days. It is reform of the judiciary.

So also the answer to bureaucratic delays is administrative reform, not bypassing administrative processes or creating structures with ill-defined accountability. The government has not distinguished itself by conferring on some of the tallest personalities in Indian business the prerogative of the harlot down the ages- to exercise power without responsibility.

December 16, 2004

Don't let China Give you a Complex

Few things give India's chattering classes such a complex as China's success in attracting FDI. Everybody "knows" the facts. We get around $3 bn in FDI, China gets more than $40 bn. We cannot shed our ideological blinkers about FDI and bureaucratic obstacles to FDI remain formidable.

The know-alls are wrong on both counts. The difference in FDI between China and India may not be as large as supposed. And China's greater receptivity to FDI is hardly the explanation for the difference that obtains.

India's measurement of FDI is not in accordance with international norms. The IMF counts earnings reinvested by foreign companies, proceeds of foreign equity listings and foreign subordinated loans to domestic subsidiaries as FDI. India does not. The IMF also includes portfolio investments in excess of 10 per cent in FDI. If India followed this practice, a big chunk of FII holdings would have to be categorised as FDI. Going by its norms, the IMF's estimate of FDI in India in 2001 was $8bn! (Sadhana Srivastava, *EPW,* February 15, 2003).

If India's FDI figure is under-estimated, China's FDI tends to be over-estimated. A big chunk of FDI in China is believed to be the result of "round-tripping"- domestic businessmen sending their money out and bringing it back to take advantage of the more liberal norms for FDI. Stripping away this element, FDI in China was estimated at $20 bn in 2000. As a percentage of GDP, the gap is even narrower- 1.7 per cent in India and 2 per cent in China.

Still, you might say, China does attract more FDI than we do. What explains its greater success? Ashok Guha and Amit Ray provide a fascinating analysis (in T N Srinivasan (ed), *Trade, Finance and Investment in South Asia*). For a variety of reasons, MNCs typically gravitate towards technology- and capital-intensive industries. They do not go into labour-intensive industries where developing countries have a comparative advantage. This means MNCs will invest in sectors catering to the domestic market and in infrastructure, not in the export-oriented industries.

MNC investment in China has conformed to this pattern. However, China also managed to attract large amounts of FDI into labour-intensive industries. These came from a quite different source- the Non-resident Chinese (NRC) spread over the entire East Asian region. In the sixties and seventies, the NRC had pioneered export-led industrialisation in all the East Asian economies except Korea.

By the end of the seventies, wages in the East Asian tigers had risen sharply, causing a shift towards capital-intensive techniques. This prompted a search for an alternative destination for low-cost manufacturing. China, with its abundant supply of cheap labour, was a natural choice but only because of the reservoir of capital and expertise available with the NRC.

The NRC were quick to grasp the opportunities presented by China's opening up to FDI in the early eighties. They knew their way around China and they understood the export markets. Equally important, they were in light manufacturing, businesses that involved small commitments and offered quick returns. Because MNCs venture into capital-intensive industries with long-gestation periods, they are slow to respond to a change in the economic regime.

The surge in FDI in the initial years in China was driven largely by the NRC. The share of NRC investment in FDI rose from 55 per cent in 1983-85 to 83 per cent in 1993 and declined thereafter. Ten years after liberalisation, MNC investment in China was just $4 bn, not much higher than India's in the same period. In other words, in terms of its ability to attract FDI from MNCs, India is not doing badly at all.

Overall FDI in India has been way below China's because the expatriate component in India has been nowhere near China's. NRIs are not as big a force in business as the NRC. Secondly, NRIs did not figure in the East Asian success story in light manufacturing and hence could not help India replicate China's success. It is the NRC factor, not any superior policy regime, that explains why China has done better on FDI.

What lesson does the comparison hold for India? It is futile to expect FDI flows to equal China's - we can only expect to match MNC investment in China. In 1997, 14 years after liberalisation, MNC investment in China totalled $13 bn. This is the figure we can reasonably expect in 2005-06, 14 years after we opened up to FDI. Going by the IMF's estimate of FDI of $8 bn for 2001, FDI should go up by under $5 bn in the next couple of years, not a great deal more. Stretching the FDI policy regime is unlikely to make a material difference. The UPA government might want to chew over that before it annoys the Left again.

February 10, 2005

Get Set for the Coming Boom

With growth set to touch 7 per cent in 2005-06, the trend rate is showing clear signs of acceleration over the rate achieved in the nineties. That is good news indeed. The news promises to get even better: there is every prospect now of the economy growing at 8 per cent in the medium term and not just the long term.

As in East Asia and later in China, growth has come from old-fashioned capital accumulation, not from increased productivity. In the nineties, investment peaked at 26.5 per cent in 1995-96 with a big rise in private corporate investment and fell sharply thereafter. That is why the high growth rate of the first half of the nineties could not be sustained.

Domestic investment has risen again from 22.6 per cent in 2001-02 to 26.3 per cent in 2003-04, fuelled by an increase in savings from 23.4 per cent to 28.1 per cent. Household savings have increased by 1.7 points. The bonus is a decrease in public sector dis-saving of 2.4 points. The decline in interest rates has helped rein in deficits at the centre and the states. It has also boosted PSU profits although price deregulation may have contributed more.

Private corporate investment, which has been the focus of most of the reforms, seems to have made no contribution to the rise in domestic investment- it declined marginally between 2002 and 2004. Of the increase in the investment rate of 3.7 percentage points, 1.6 points has come from the household sector. Public sector investment declined by 0.6 points. The greater part of the increase - of 2.8 points- is a puzzle at the moment. It is categorised as "errors and omissions".

FDI was 2.1 per cent of GDP in 2003-04 which means that total investment was 28.4 per cent. In 2002-03, it was 2.7 per cent of GDP, so a figure of 3 per cent of GDP for FDI appears attainable in the next year or two. That would place total investment within striking distance of 30 per cent. At this level of investment and given the continuing shift towards services, growth should easily exceed 7 per cent.

The recent rise in savings and investment thus transforms the outlook for growth but that is not the only reason for optimism. There has always been an issue of whether the services sector by itself can propel growth, given the weak linkages between services and the primary and secondary sectors on both the supply and demand sides.

The revival in manufacturing, in which the textile sector has been prominent, serves to allay such fears. The textile sector is a big employer, it has deep linkages with the primary sector and it will enhance domestic demand for IT services as well. The textile sector could well turn out to be the export story of this decade.

How do we know that the rise in savings is sustainable? Since the decline in interest rates has helped boost savings, what happens when the rate cycle turns? Fear not. First, it is unlikely that the weighted average interest rate on government borrowings will return to the level of the nineties. Secondly, interest rates have been shored up by the RBI's sterilising increases in money supply caused by its intervention in the foreign exchange market. The RBI wants to manage appreciation in the rupee because it is unsure whether the huge increase in FII flows is temporary or permanent.

The odds are that a big chunk of FII inflows is permanent. India has become a more attractive destination. Besides, America Inc does take cues from the political establishment, so India's growing closeness to the US augurs well for FII inflows. Once it is clear that higher inflows are here to stay, RBI's forex intervention and the associated sterilisation will decrease. This should mitigate any tendency towards an increase in interest rates.

Many fear that oil prices could spoil the growth outlook but they have caused little damage so far. They also hold out the prospect of an upside. On past showing, prices must fall in the medium term as consumers and producers respond to higher price levels. By the time this happens, however, the economy will have made major adjustments to high prices. So when oil prices decline, the economy stands to reap a windfall- the efficiency gains of each adjustment to high prices prove lasting.

At the end of the nineties, economists saw India's growth potential being limited by the absence of "reforms" in respect of fiscal policy, privatisation, FDI, labour laws. Then, some saw hope in the "demographic dividend"- the rise in the proportion of working people and the resultant increase in savings over the next 20 years. Recent performance suggests we may not have to wait that long. The fiscal problem is being tamed and the others are not material.

The Indian economy caught the world's attention in the nineties. We are now approaching a point where it is set to astonish the world.

September 22, 2005

A String of Positives

It is commonly believed that the reforms of the nineties ushered in a new era of high growth. This belief is not supported by rigorous analysis. The trend rate of growth in the nineties was not significantly different from that in the eighties. The Indian economy's performance over the past three years raises the prospect that the long-awaited breakthrough may have come. But this remains to be confirmed.

What we can point to with a measure of confidence is a string of positives that alters the long-term growth outlook. One that is cited very often is favourable demographics- the rising proportion of those who will constitute the working population. There are many others as well.

First, the combined fiscal measures of the centre and the states have been trending downwards since 2003-04. The received wisdom has been that, while the centre might be able to get a grip on its finances, the states faced disaster. Yet, the states will have contributed to the improvement in the period 2004-06. It is the centre's fiscal position that will worsen in 2005-06 thanks to the rural employment scheme and oil bonds. Still, the combined fiscal ratios for the centre and the states will decline in 2005-06 and there is every prospect this will continue.

The turnaround in the states is no small matter. Following the Fifth Pay Commission, the States' economies were said to have been wrecked. What was overlooked was that states were not adding to the numbers of employed. So, the effects of a pay rise could be digested over time. When economic growth touches 7 per cent, the fiscal problem looks increasingly tractable.

Another looming positive is the appreciation in the rupee. Never mind the depreciation we have seen lately. The BoP outlook points to an appreciation in the rupee over the long term. This has far-reaching implications. It will help keep inflation and interest rates low. It could lead to massive technological upgradation of Indian industry and a rise in productivity. It would facilitate overseas expansion on the part of Indian firms. And it could halt and even reverse the flight of talent that has occurred over the past several decades.

As we do not have capital account convertibility, the appreciation in the rupee will be managed. So, exporters will have time to adjust and can offset appreciation through higher productivity and scale economies- as indeed they have done over the past two years. Adapting to rupee appreciation after a decade and a half of depreciation will be a key challenge for Indian firms.

A third positive is the scope for improvement in the laggard states of the north and the east. These states are seen as hopelessly mired in caste politics and mis-governance. But, as V S Naipaul has observed, much of the disorder that one sees in these places has to do with new castes coming to terms with power. This is a transitory phase. Before long, democratic politics constrains those in power to get their acts together.

It has happened elsewhere. In the sixties, the DMK's ascension to power, a high watermark of caste and linguistic politics, was viewed with gloom. The gloom has turned out to be misplaced. Communism was said to have doomed West Bengal. The government there is now pulling out the stops to boost growth- and West Bengal is already the fastest-growing state in the country. So also in the laggard states, one can expect that pressures as much from the electorate as from insurgents will force governments to respond. Think of what land reforms, long suppressed, could accomplish.

Fourth, there is the improved efficiency and stability of Indian banking. Banking has proved the soft underbelly of many an experiment in liberalisation. Not so in India. The decline in interest rates in recent years helped recapitalise the banking system. Now, the system is well placed to take advantage of this good fortune- both by garnering more savings and by delivering more credit. With financial markets having developed as well, the financial system is geared to meet the demands of growth.

The rise in savings and investment in recent years has rendered a growth rate of 7-7.5 per cent eminently feasible. This is the effect of capital accumulation. Many of the positives listed above are about improvements in productivity. Together, they bid fair to lift the growth rate over 8 per cent.

Note that these positives have nothing to do with "reforms" such as cutting subsidies and raising user charges, privatisation, FDI and labour market policies. The reformers will argue that, with reforms, we could touch 10 per cent. But that is different from what they were saying earlier, namely, that you could not hope to touch 8 per cent without reforms.

December 15, 2005

Is Credit Growth a Concern?

Credit has grown at 30 per cent for the past two years- and promises to do so in the current year as well. The RBI has indicated that it would like to see credit growth slowing down to 20 per cent. What risks does rapid credit growth pose and how should policy makers respond?

The IMF's *World Economic Outlook* (WEO, April 2004) has a chapter on credit booms in emerging markets that sums up the issues. Credit can grow rapidly for three reasons: financial deepening, normal cyclical upturns and excessive cyclical movements. Only the last qualifies as a 'credit boom' that is potentially destabilising.

Credit typically grows faster than GDP as an economy develops-that is what financial deepening is all about. It can also grow faster than GDP because firms' investment and working capital needs fluctuate with the business cycle. The problem arises when asset prices get magnified. For instance, when stock prices shoot up, firms' net worth rises sharply. Banks may then be tempted to lend more. When asset prices collapse, banks find themselves in trouble.

The trick is to be able to distinguish a credit boom from healthy growth in credit. The WEO provides an empirical definition: a credit expansion is a boom when it exceeds the standard deviation of a country's credit fluctuations around trend by a factor of 1.75. The WEO also identifies a number of warning signs: a surge in capital inflows, a consumption or investment boom, a sharp rise in stock prices, a worsening of corporate leverage and an increase in banks' external borrowings.

How do we relate to these warning signs? The first three are in evidence in India but not the last two. External borrowings-whether of firms or banks- and a fixed rate regime are a lethal combination. That this is missing in India is reassuring. Further, while there is indeed a sharp rise in capital inflows, it is portfolio flows, not debt, that account for most of the rise.

The composition of credit is also important. Between 2000 and 2005, nearly a quarter of the increase in non-food credit was accounted for by retail credit, with 50 per cent of the retail credit increase being accounted for by housing loans. As a result, the share of retail credit in non-food credit rose from 15 per cent to 20 per cent. These figures, perhaps, understate the share of retail because small housing loans are included under 'priority sector'. As housing loans are a lot safer than other loans, it is not just aggregate credit growth we should look at. Within aggregate credit, the sustainability of household credit is a critical issue.

On household credit, the IMF's Global Financial Stability Report (September 2006) has an interesting chapter. Although household credit has grown rapidly in emerging markets in recent years, it remains low in relation to GDP. For emerging markets, the ratio of household credit to GDP averages 18 per cent; for emerging markets, the figure is 58 per cent. This difference is reflected in penetration rates for various segment: consumer credit, housing loans, credit cards.

However, these aggregate figures cannot be taken as an indication of borrowing capacity in emerging markets. Household credit is closely correlated with per capita GDP- it rises as per capita GDP rises. A better measure of borrowing capacity is the ratio of household credit to personal disposable income. On this India does very well- its ratio of 9.7 per cent is way below the average of 35 for emerging markets in 2004 and even lower the average for mature markets of 84.

Yet another measure of capacity to borrow would be household leverage. This ratio shows India in unfavourable light: its ratio of 60% for household liabilities to assets is the second highest among a sample of emerging and mature markets. This may not be a problem as lending to households is done against future income, not assets. Still, it is a revelation that the leverage of Indian households is worse than that of their American counterparts (under 40 per cent) who are said to have borrowed to the hilt.

In taking a view on rapid credit growth, it is important to track exposure to sensitive sectors such as real estate (which comprises loans to developers, not individuals), capital market and commodities. These sectors together accounted for just 3.5% of advances in the Indian banking sector in 2005.

In sum, it is easy to get carried away by aggregate figures on credit growth. We need to take into account the composition of credit- corporate versus retail, domestic versus foreign currency, sensitive versus non-sensitive- in judging whether there is an unsustainable boom. We must also look out for imbalances in the macro-economy. When we do so, the current surge in credit does not appear to warrant concern.

October 5, 2006

Much ado about Outward FDI

Tata Steel's impending takeover of Corus in the UK has created a buzz in the country. The sheer size of the deal is seen as a sign that Indian firms are now ready to take on the world. It is also seen as marking a trend towards large outflows of foreign direct investment (FDI). There has been endless talk of attracting FDI into the country. Suddenly, there is talk of outward FDI exceeding inward FDI!

Just to put things in perspective, a recent UNCTAD study shows that India is something of a laggard in the developing world when it comes to outward FDI (World Investment Report, 2006). Outward FDI of developing and transition countries has been rising fast since the late 1990s, reaching $133 bn in 2005. Outward FDI stock of this group of countries stood at $1.4 trillion in 2005 or 13 per cent of the world total. India does not figure even in the top 15.

Here are some salient facts from the study:

- As in the case of FDI flows from the developed world, most of the outward FDI from developing countries takes place through mergers and acquisitions- $90 bn out of the total of $130 bn in 2005.
- The aggregate figure for outward FDI is rather deceptive because it includes flows that occur wholly for financial reasons (such as offshore financial centers). If we exclude such flows, the total in 2004 comes down from $127 bn to $61 bn.
- The study gives figures separately for Hong Kong (China) and China. Hong Kong leads the pack in stock of outward FDI. Much of the FDI from Hong Kong is said to represent "round-tripping", money coming in from the mainland and going out as FDI. If we adjust for Hong Kong's FDI, developing country FDI is far less impressive than it appears.
- Almost all of the $61 bn of outward FDI was within developing and transition countries. In other words, outward FDI is a south-south phenomenon and it is also mostly intra-regional in character.
- Asian companies have dominated M&A deals, accounting for 60 per cent of the top 25 deals in the period 1987-2005.
- A better indicator of outward FDI performance is the ratio of FDI to the size of the economy- the study calls this the Outward FDI performance index. India ranks a lowly 88 in the world. Apart from Hong Kong, Singapore, Malaysia, Taiwan and even Panama and the Bahamas figure in the top 25.
- It is the services sector that dominates FDI from the developing world. Its share in the total stock is 81 per cent, higher than the services' share of 67% for the developed world's FDI. Services FDI from the developing world is not about IT. It is trade, construction, hotels, transport and storage and a category called 'business activities'.

As economies and their corporations grow, so does outward FDI. There is only one Indian company in the top 100 TNCs from the developing world. But this need not give us a terrible complex.

Neither growth in the asset size of domestic corporations nor the volume of outward FDI necessarily signifies global competitiveness. India has companies that are small in size and whose outward FDI is not large but that are globally competitive in software and IT services, pharmaceuticals, biotechnology, hotels and automotives.

Secondly, firms can be competitive in the sense of meeting global benchmarks without having a large overseas presence- like HDFC Bank, for instance. Thirdly, growth through mergers and acquisitions is suspect as the majority of these do not enhance shareholder value at the acquiring firm. It would be unwise, therefore, to use outward FDI fuelled by acquisitions as a measure of competitiveness or economic prowess.

Some of India's manufacturing companies may find it necessary to have a large overseas presence- say, in industries such as petroleum, chemicals and steel. For these companies, the acid test of competitiveness is the ability to make investments in the developed world rather than in the developing world. As we saw earlier, few TNCs from the developing world have been able to succeed in these terms. That is what makes the Tata offer for Corus impressive.

With the rise in foreign inflows (other than FDI) and exports, the Indian rupee is set to appreciate in the coming years. This will make overseas acquisitions easier for Indian companies. But making acquisitions is one thing, making a success of acquisitions is another. Beware of Indian companies that get carried away by the lure of headline-grabbing overseas acquisitions.

What of the talk of outward FDI exceeding inward FDI? Well, if it happens, it is likely to be a temporary phenomenon. FDI inflows into India are today extremely low in relation to the attractiveness of the Indian market ($7.8 bn in 2005-06). FDI inflows are bound to rise over time making the net FDI figure positive.

November 2, 2006

Loan Waiver Could be a Positive

The Rs 60,000 crore farm loan scheme is undoubtedly the centerpiece of the recent budget. Many see it as driven by the UPA's electoral calculations. They see it as inconsistent with Mr Chidambaram's reformist image and a huge setback to banking discipline. These are hasty judgements. Whatever the political calculations, the scheme could be a positive – provided it is handled with care.

Much of the criticism arises because the finance minister has left the details for later.

A key issue is how much of the write-off will be borne by the exchequer and how much will devolve on the banks. A sum of Rs 50,000 crore in loans outstanding from small and marginal farmers is to be waived. In respect of other farm loans, there will be one-time settlement with a rebate of 25%. This will cost Rs 10,000 crore.

Does the sum of Rs 50,000 crore refer to gross NPAs or net NPAs? (that is, sum outstanding after making provisions). If we are talking of gross NPAs, then banks will already have made provisions of, say, 30 per cent. The government can provide funds to help them write off the balance 70 per cent. This would involve a cost to the government of around Rs 35,000 crore. Banks' balance sheets would be cleaned up. This would be the best case scenario.

But this may be too much to hope for. The headline NPA figures are typically net NPA figures. This means that the full cost of the waiver of Rs 50,000 crore will have to be borne. By whom? Mr Chidambaram has not helped matters by promising banks "equivalent liquidity". So, it won't be capital equivalent to the write-offs of Rs 50,000 crore plus Rs 10,000 crore towards OTS relief? It does seem so.

It is suggested that the government may not provide capital to banks but will provide them bonds worth Rs 60,000 crore. In effect, NPAs will be substituted on the asset side by bonds. If, as indicated in media reports, the government were to make the bonds available in three instalments, the annual impact on the fiscal deficit would be under 0.4% of GDP. So there is no call for fiscal fundamentalists to panic. But how giving banks bonds constitutes "liquidity" is not clear.

A third – and dire– possibility is that a big chunk of the cost of

Rs 60,000 crore may have to be borne by the banks themselves. Bank capital will then be eroded and banks' ability to make fresh loans to farmers will be impaired. The government would address this problem–of lack of "liquidity"– by organising refinance for farm loans through Nabard or RBI at a concessional rate of interest. The government would bear the interest subsidy. This would enable banks to resume loans to disaffected farmers but only after incurring a huge cost on past loans themselves. This is the worst case scenario.

For the sake of the banking system, one sincerely hopes that the last option will not materialise and that government will bear most of the costs of the write-off. That would still keep recapitalisation costs in the Indian banking system in the post-reform period at 2 per cent of GDP, which is modest in relation to such costs elsewhere.

There are people who say it is not the costs to the exchequer that is the issue today. We can afford Rs 60,000 crore for a good cause. The issue is the weakening of credit discipline. Farmers will cheerfully default on loans hereafter in the knowledge that *sarkar* is there to waive loan dues.

This may seem self-evident but is not true for farmers any more than it is true for businessmen. To default is to be denied access to institutional credit, so there are built-in incentives for compliance. Incentives to default will be strong only if large loan waivers are frequent but that is hardly the case in India. Today, farmers with overdue payments are unable to get fresh loans and suffer in consequence. If farmers could get away with defaults, we would not need the present scheme.

Assuming the government bears most of the cost of the scheme, banks will be strengthened and fresh loans can commence. The share of institutional credit amongst farmers can rise from the present figure of 60% and the hold of money-lenders can be weakened. As several committees have pointed out. However, credit is only one element in agricultural growth. We need to create better conditions for credit absorption in the first place.

This means tackling a host of issues – investment in rural infrastructure, irrigation, research and extension services; generation of non-farm sources of income in rural areas; management of price risks for crops not covered by minimum support prices; better documentation of land records; and many others.

Today's buoyant revenue conditions have given the UPA government the courage to address one element in agrarian distress. It is up to future governments to follow up and address other elements. Provided the farm loan scheme does not impose a big cost on the banking system, Mr. Chidamabaram may have succeeded in signaling a welcome shift in budgetary priorities.

November 2, 2006

Are FDI flows into India for Real?

Foreign capital is flooding the country. Our experience is by no means unique. There has been a surge of capital into emerging markets in recent years following the dramatic fall during the east Asian crisis of 1997-98. Official flows have been substituted by private flows; debt by equity.

But the Indian experience departs from that of emerging markets as a group in two respects. Net capital flows to emerging Asia and Latin America are off their highs of a decade ago, as the IMF's *Global Financial Stability Report* (September 2007) points out Gross flows are close to their historical highs but capital outflows too have risen sharply, hence net capital inflows are lower than their historical highs.

In India, however, both gross and net capital flows are higher than in the past. Secondly, in emerging markets as a whole, FDI contribution to total flows has declined. In India in contrast, FDI has overtaken portfolio flows for the first time in the post-reform period.

FDI in 2006-07 was an astonishing \$19.5 bn. Adjusted for a share swap transaction of \$3.1bn, FDI was \$16.4 bn. This is an extraordinary rise over the previous three years' average of \$6 bn. Net FDI in 2006-07 was \$7.9 bn. This exceeded net portfolio flow of \$7bn, reversing the earlier pattern in which portfolio flows exceeded FDI.

In the nineties, the annual FDI target of \$10 bn seemed a distant dream. Of a sudden, it appears to have become a reality- and without the sort of sweeping reforms which many had thought vital. We have a puzzle here. What explains the sharp rise in FDI in recent years?

In the nineties, commentators harped on the many negative elements in the Indian environment: a restrictive FDI regime, high import tariffs, exit barriers for firms, stringent labour laws, poor infrastructure, centralised decision-making and a very limited scale of export processing zones.

We have seen some improvement since. Tariff barriers have come down, sectoral caps on FDI have been liberalised, some areas of infrastructure are doing better. But it is not as if there has been a dramatic change in the overall business environment. The World Bank's latest Doing Business ranks India a lowly 120 out of 178 countries surveyed.

Besides, poor governance as an explanation for low levels of FDI always presented problems: China's FDI regime is more restrictive than India's in some ways and the Chinese bureaucracy as exasperating and corrupt but this has not kept China from attracting FDI.

No, the explanation for the low level of FDI through the nineties and the recent surge must be sought elsewhere. FDI happens overwhelmingly through mergers and acquisitions (M&As), not through greenfield investment. In 2006, 77 per cent of FDI worldwide was through M&As. In emerging markets, M&A opportunities are related to privatisation. In these markets, there is thus a close link between FDI and privatisation. China's experience bears this out: the rise in China's FDI was linked to the sale of thousands of small Town and Village Enterprises (TVEs).

Since privatisation in India has taken place overwhelmingly through the issue of shares to financial institutions and not through sale of assets to firms, opportunities for FDI through the M&A route have been fewer in India. This, more than the other factors typically cited, might explain why, until recently, FDI has been disappointingly low in India compared to that in other emerging markets.

But, if this is true, how has FDI shot up in recent years? After all, privatisation has long ground to a halt. Partly, the rise in FDI reflects changes in accounting practices. India's FDI figures were understated until 2000-01 because these did not include reinvested earnings, as is the international practice. Reinvested earnings in 2006-07 were $3 bn.

But the material factor underlying the rise in FDI appears to be private equity which is categorised as FDI in official statistics.

Non-official agencies estimate private equity in 2006-07 at $8 bn. Adjusted for reinvested earnings and private equity, FDI in 2006-07 would be $5 bn, just half the target of $10bn. The steep rise in FDI is thus deceptive because it's not entirely about firm- or MNC-related FDI.

There is a difference between firm FDI and FDI through private equity. Firm FDI brings technology, export linkages with the parent firm and management. Private equity contributes mainly management. Hence, the BOP effects of the two types of FDI may be the same but not the contribution to the domestic economy.

Besides, private equity has a shorter time horizon- 5-7 years- than firm FDI, which is considered permanent in nature. Private equity partakes of the character of portfolio flows. If we were to classify private equity as portfolio investment, then India would fit into the emerging market pattern of portfolio investment being higher than FDI. The recent boom in FDI is thus something of a mirage.

March 6, 2008

Pay Commission Hike is only 13 per cent

Media reports have talked of a 'bonanza for babus' in the shape of a 40 per cent hike recommended by the Sixth Pay Commission (SPC). Many wonder whether government servants deserve such munificence. It is nothing of the kind. The pay hike recommended by the SPC is modest.

The correct way to estimate the average pay hike for central government servants is to see how much the government's wage bill goes up. The SPC estimates the annual gross impact of its recommendations to be Rs 9242 crore for the union government (excluding the Railways). Pay, allowances and pension of the union government amounted to Rs 68,290 crore in 2007-08. Hence the average increase in government compensation is 13.5 per cent.

The increase at the highest level- Grade A- is much larger, around 30-40 per cent. But grade A officers account for just 1 per cent of the total strength of government employees, so the increases at the highest levels have little impact on average compensation. The increase in compensation for the vast majority of government servants will be in the range of 10-13 per cent. Hardly the 'bonanza' the media has gone to town about.

Nobody needs to lose sleep over the fiscal impact of the SPC. The annual impact (including the Railways) amounts to Rs 12,561 crore. (This does not take into account possible savings of around Rs 4600 crore). Arrears amounting to Rs 18,060 crore are to be paid over two years or about Rs 9000 crore each year. The fiscal impact at the centre in 2008-09 is thus around Rs 21,000 crore- or about 0.4 per cent of GDP. This will taper off and become negligible over the next three years or so. The impact on the states is not likely to exceed 0.5 per cent of GDP either.

Compensation in Central Government as a proportion of revenue receipts has been falling over the years. It rose from 28 per cent in 1996-97 to 38 per cent in 1998-99 following the Fifth Pay Commission (FPC). It declined thereafter to an average of 24 per cent in the period 2005-07. The decline of 14 percentage points in the ratio over the past decade means that government has effectively been downsized by over a third, as the FPC had recommended. It may not be downsizing by asking people to leave. But, in financial terms, it is indeed downsizing.

The SPC recommends annual increments of 2.5 per cent. Add dearness allowance growth at 4.5 per cent. Add another 2.5per cent towards increase in manpower. That gives us growth in compensation of 9.5%. Revenue receipts are growing at 17 per cent. So the ratio of compensation to revenue will continue to decline in the years to come.

Once the ratio falls below the threshold by, say, 3 per cent, that could be the trigger for an increase in compensation that would take the ratio back to the threshold. This would have ensured that wage revisions in government take place sooner than 10 years and helped contain the demoralisation in government created by runaway growth in private sector compensation. The SPC has missed the opportunity for such a radical prescription. The improvements it proposes, while welcome, are timid-rising increments instead of fixed ones, allowances indexed to inflation, etc.

The SPC would like to bring into government the private sector concept of performance – related incentive schemes. This is not such a great idea. Measurement of performance is beset with problems in the private sector despite the existence of clear financial targets. In government, measurement of performance is even more difficult and highly susceptible to manipulation by politicians. In an era of the right to information, performance-based incentives will open the floodgates to litigation and paralyse the administration.

Besides, performance-related incentives in the private sector are mostly efficient at the top. This leads to huge disparities between the top and other levels but that is part of the accepted order of things. In government, where such large disparities are unacceptable, financial incentives do not make sense. Incentives must take other forms-accelerated promotion, prized postings, etc.

The SPC introduces the idea of market-based compensation on a contractual basis. But this can apply only to certain technical positions with clearly spelt out targets. It cannot apply to senior government positions in general. To do so would again open up opportunities for abuse by politicians and senior bureaucrats.

It is wise to stick to the principle that a government job spells lower pay than in the private sector, while having its own compensations in the form of job security, pension, variety and prestige. The best we can do is give civil servants the opportunity to encash their skills and experience in the private sector at some point in their careers. The SPC has two commendable proposals. One, collecting full pension without having to spend 33 years in government. Two, a generous severance package for those leaving after 15-20 years in service.

April 3, 2008

Keeping MNCs at Bay on Home Turf

MNCs have had far less success with the Indian market than most people had thought when the economy began to be opened up in the nineties. Many expected Indian firms to be wiped out because they lacked the scale, the products, the technology and the managerial capability.

The pessimists have been proved wrong- and not just in the Indian market. In a paper in the *Harvard Business Review* (March, 2008), Bhattacharya and Michael of the Boston Consulting Group, show that in a host of emerging markets, local firms are giving MNCs a run for their money. The authors list 50 homegrown champions in 10 emerging markets, with 21 having revenues of $1 bn in 2006.

India had a thriving private sector even in the days of socialism, so the success of Indian firms is not such a great surprise. The surprise is that local firms in China, Russia, Poland and Slovakia, where entrepreneurship had been long suppressed, have come into their own.

The Paper lists six reasons why MNCs haven't had as much luck as they had hoped. Two are particularly compelling. One is the tendency of MNCs to simply assume that emerging markets are behind developed markets by a few years and the two will resemble each other soon. Another is the quality of homegrown entrepreneurial and managerial talent.

MNCs thought they could simply push existing products and processes into emerging markets and wait for the volumes to grow. This was a big blunder. Local tastes and preferences are different and the challenge is to create products for markets that exist today, not the markets that will come into being tomorrow. Indigenous firms have figured this out quickly and have benefited hugely as a result.

C K Prahalad's famous prescription about tapping the bottom of the pyramid is part of the answer but it is not all of the answer. Catering to the local market is not just about creating cheaper products. It is also about creating customized products that address local tastes. Goodbaby, the Chinese market leader in baby products, is an excellent example: it has as many as 1600 items in 16 categories. Amul's success in coming up with ice-cream that use a variety of local flavours is another example.

The really big shock for MNCs in many emerging markets has been coming face to face with entrepreneurial and managerial talent of a high quality. Indian managerial talent is today well known and internationally celebrated but other emerging markets, it turns out, are not lagging behind.

The paper makes no mention of one common mistake many MNCs make in the initial years of their foray into a new market: flying in foreign expatriates from other parts of the firm. Very often, this has been an HRD disaster. Expats are not only expensive, they are unlikely to understand local markets as well as indigenous managers.

MNCs have realised their mistake and now see the value of hiring local talent but they find that local firms are doing a good job of attracting and retaining talent. When the Indian economy was opened up, many people confidently predicted that family-run businesses stood little chance of competing with MNCs because they would lose out in the most important area: people.

These predictions have been proved wrong. Family businesses have found ways to give professionals the freedom they look for. Odd as it may seem, it is in MNCs that professionals find themselves stifled, with local heads of product groups having to report to heads of worldwide operations located overseas. Local firms in emerging markets have also been able to offer better compensation through stock option schemes.

As a result, local firms have turned the tables on MNCs. Earlier, we saw Indian manufacturing firms luring away talent from MNCs. Of late, we are seeing this phenomenon even in the financial sector where one would expect foreign firms to score on sophistication. Relatively small Indian brokerage firms are now stealing talent from international investment banks!

Two interesting policy questions arise. One, if we accept that local entrepreneurs can better cater to the local market, is there a case for national champions? We need research on the extent to which the emergence of local champions can be ascribed to industrial policy and the gradual opening up to foreign competition.

Two, if local manufacturing firms have been able to hold their own against MNCs, can we expect similar success in the financial sector? The financial sector is different in many ways. It has issues of regulation that do not apply to other sectors. Secondly, clients require cross-border services and that is an area in which foreign firms have clear advantages.

Thirdly, in India, industrial houses that can take on foreign firms are barred from entering the banking sector. If we grant that the success of manufacturing is at least partly because of a long period of protection, is there a case for some more hand-holding in the financial sector?

May 1, 2008

'Small Ticket' Reform Helped India

The budget is a time for clichés. Through the Nineties, commentators informed us that 'it sends out a signal that reforms will continue'. Businessmen still find it prudent to commend the finance minister for 'striking a fine balance between growth and fiscal stability'.

The critics have their favourite line, 'What is sadly missing in the budget is "big ticket" reform'. This is one contention that has turned out to be completely misplaced. The success of the Indian economy is all about 'small ticket' reform.

One area in which 'small ticket' reform has clearly been a blessing for the economy is disinvestment of public sector undertakings (PSUs). Successive governments were panned for being pusillanimous on privatisation. Except for a brief period during the NDA regime, governments have preferred disinvestment, the sale of minority equity in PSUs, to privatisation, the transfer of control to private owners.

Critics of disinvestment made two points. One, PSUs would erode in value as long as they continued under government ownership; the longer the government hung on to them, the greater would be the loss to the exchequer. Two, prospective investors would pay more if PSUs were privatised instead of being disinvested.

As minister for disinvestment, Arun Shourie, attempted privatisation of PSUs. He became a hero to many votaries of reform. The mere promise of privatisation, it was claimed, had caused an appreciation in the value of listed PSUs of Rs 100,000 crore.

The critics have been proved resoundingly wrong. PSUs have appreciated in value over time, and beyond all expectations. So have public sector banks. (The government is not permitted to sell its equity in PSBs under the present statutes but that does not make a difference in conceptual terms).

"We have looked at the market capitalisation of 34 PSUs over 2001-11, a ten year period". The increase in value is a staggering Rs 632,000 crore, far greater than the increase in value of Rs 100,000 crore that Shourie is said to have created. The value of the government's shareholding in these PSUs has risen by over Rs 420,000 crore.

PSBs are an even bigger success story, going by the percentage increase in market capitalisation. The market cap of 14 listed PSBs increased by Rs 256,000 crore between 2001 and 2011. The value of the government's shareholding in these PSBs has risen by over Rs 138,000 crore.

Had the government gone down the privatisation route and sold off its stakes in PSUs in their entirety, the exchequer would have been considerably poorer. It is clear that the 'strategic sale' of PSUs, as privatisation was then called, would have been a bigger scam than the alleged 2G scam in telecom (where the benefits to the sector from the policies followed by successive governments have been enormous).

The number of listed PSUs has expanded beyond the 34 that is common to the two years considered, 2001 and 2011. Today, the value of 57 PSUs, including newly listed giants such as Coal India, is Rs 14,90,000 crore. The value of the government's shareholding in these PSUs is Rs 10,23,000 crore.

If, over the next five years, the government were to realise Rs 40,000 crore every year from disinvestment (which was the target for 2010-11), it would still be left holding shares worth Rs 823,000 crore. (We are not taking into account the value of government shareholding in 25 listed PSBs today, which is Rs 233,000 crore).

Nobody imagined that listed PSUs would provide the government the sort of cushion it enjoys today. They did not expect PSUs to perform as they did because they had a blinkered view of government ownership of commercial enterprises. They thought PSUs simply could not compete in a deregulated setting because government ownership is an obstacle to commercial performance.

We have discovered what many studies of privatisation elsewhere have highlighted: ownership matters less than competition. When PSUs are exposed to greater competition and subjected to market discipline by being listed on stock exchanges, their performance tends to improve. It is not true that our PSUs have done well only because they operate in regulated or monopolistic settings. There are PSUs that have done well in the face of competition, such as BHEL, BEL and NALCO.

It is contended that the sale of government assets cannot solve fiscal problems of a structural kind, it can only be a palliative. This is indeed true, but the sale of government assets helps manage the fiscal problem until the underlying structural problems are addressed. It spares the government the need to effect drastic adjustments in revenues and expenditure that could be politically unpopular or unfeasible.

The government is today well-placed to manage the fiscal deficit in the face of rising expenditure on various counts (subsidies, NREGA, etc) thanks mainly to buoyant revenues. In this year, the proceeds of spectrum sales of over Rs 100,000 crore has been an important factor in containing the deficit. Disinvestment can serve a similar purpose in the years to come. The trick is not to allow the fiscal problem to derail growth.

Disinvestment is a notable area of the success of 'small ticket' reform in India. We can point to several other areas where it has worked. The gradual movement towards full convertibility and the cautious approach towards foreign bank expansion helped stave off a banking crisis.

The phasing out of reduction in import duties over a long period gave Indian firms more time to adjust to competition and reduced the adverse impact on banks. The measured reduction in subsidies on petroleum and the reluctance to address other subsidies have ensured that economic progress was not derailed by popular unrest. One could go on. With sustained growth and rising incomes, it becomes easier for various constituencies to digest market-oriented policies. 'Small ticket' reform has served India well.

February 17, 2011

A 'New Normal' for Inflation?

The RBI's decision to clamp down on inflation through a 50 basis point increase in the repo rate has gone down surprisingly well in most quarters. In a different period, the RBI would have been roundly criticised for spoiling the Indian growth story so soon after the rebound from the financial crisis.

Not this time. Most people think that strong action was warranted given that the rate of inflation has remained high for over two years now- 10.2 per cent in 2009-10 and 9.0 per cent in 2010-11. Looking ahead, the upside risks from the two principal sources of inflation, oil and food prices, remain strong.

The RBI has felt the need to clamp down on the demand side even if inflation is primarily caused by supply-side factors. The RBI governor was quoted as saying, "We need to bring inflation down in order to sustain medium term growth even if that means sacrificing some growth in the short-term."

The RBI's move raises two important questions. One, what precisely is the growth potential of the economy in the medium-term? Two, what rate of inflation would be consistent with that growth rate?

There are indications of late that some of the euphoria about the emergence of an "Asian century" is fading. The President of the Asian Development Bank, Haruhiko Kuroda, warned recently that it was not "pre-ordained" that Asia would come to dominate the global economy. Asian economies could well fall into the "middle-income trap". This refers to countries that have grown out of poverty and can no longer compete with low-cost producers, but cannot also make the leap to an advanced economy.

Last September, the ADB's chief economist created a stir by suggesting that China's growth rate could fall to 5.5 per cent in the next 20 years. Here in India, optimism about growth accelerating to 9 per cent in the next couple of years and moving thereafter to 10 per cent has waned. The Planning Commission believes that growth in the Twelfth Plan will be 9-9.5 per cent, not 10 per cent, as thought earlier. The RBI projects growth for 2011-12 at 8-8.5 per cent.

But the reasons for the downward revisions in forecasts differ. The ADB sees governance as a big hurdle - things such as corruption, poor access to justice, income inequality. The Planning Commission thinks global uncertainties as well as inflation will drag down the growth rate. For the RBI, it is the persistence of high inflation that is the bugbear.

Tighter monetary policy in the current period is not a response to over-heating in the economy, as was the case in the run-up to the financial crisis. When the RBI says it will sacrifice growth in order to lower inflation, it is talking of the Phillips curve trade-off. The potential growth rate is higher but the RBI will deliberately keep growth below that level. This would imply that, in the RBI's view, the potential growth rate is closer to 9 per cent.

The Chairman of the PM's Council of Economic Advisors, C Rangarajan, thinks likewise. Rangarajan has pointed out that the investment rate currently exceeds 36 per cent and should be expected to rise to 38 per cent under favourable conditions. Assuming a capital-output ratio of 4:1, the growth rate should be in the range of 9-9.5 per cent. It follows that any slowing down of the growth rate must arise from deliberate compression of demand, aimed at lowering the inflation rate.

Is this an appropriate response? In a recent Paper, Mihir Rakshit finds that in 2006-10, inflation was driven primarily by oil prices and agricultural GDP. More crucially, excess demand or the output gap was irrelevant to inflation. (*EPW*, April 16-22). This is because, in the non-agricultural sector, prices of variable inputs do not respond to changes in demand.

Rakshit provides an explanation. Of the two variable inputs, oil and labour, oil price is autonomous and is determined by international prices. Wages don't respond to a rise in output, thanks to jobless growth and the rise of employment in the unorganised sector. For the same reasons, even food inflation does not cause an increase in wages and a wage-price spiral in the manufacturing sector. Rakshit concludes that "orthodox monetary (or fiscal) measures would be of little avail as non-inflationary devices".

The RBI's monetary policy statement clearly does not believe that this holds true in the present situation. It sees high input prices as translating into non-food manufacturing inflation on account of "strong underlying demand pressures". Why so now if it did not happen in 2006-10? Are we seeing this in a few sectors where capacity is fully utilised or is it a broader phenomenon? This needs explaining.

A more critical policy issue is the rate of inflation the RBI is now comfortable with. The RBI has said it expects inflation to moderate to 6 per cent by the end of the year. What if it doesn't and ends up at 7-8 per cent? Will we see a further compression of demand and a further lowering of the growth rate?

In other words, we need clarity as to whether the RBI is committed to its previous comfort level of inflation of 3-4 per cent or whether there is to be a 'new normal' for inflation. The Economic Survey thinks the latter- for structural reasons, inflation will be of a higher order than in the past.

If we simply accept that a higher level of oil prices is here to stay and that deregulation of oil prices will continue, a 'new normal' for inflation may become inevitable. Inflation expectations must be anchored accordingly. High levels of inflation do impose costs on the economy but so does lower growth. It is imperative to get the medium-run trade-off right.

May 12, 2011

Can Services-led Growth Continue?

The services sector is largely responsible for the Indian growth miracle. Few had anticipated this when economic reforms were rolled out two decades ago. It is one of many aspects in which the Indian growth story has not conformed to the text.

Can growth in services continue at the same pace? And can a services-dominated economy generate enough jobs? These are among the important policy questions today. There is reason for optimism on both counts.

Industry was the focus of the reforms unleashed in 1991. And yet, in the last two decades, the services sector has grown faster than industry. There is a mystery within a mystery: a big chunk of services growth has come from traditional services not targeted by reforms. These account for about 60% of the services sector.

Some modern services, such as IT, communications and insurance, benefited greatly from reforms. Reforms in banking have happened in a very guarded way. Education and health care have both grown more in response to demand than as a result of sector-specific reforms. Ditto for trade,hotels and railways.

How do we explain the services sector becoming an engine of growth in India, unlike in China where growth is manufacturing-led? Barry Eichengreen and Poonam Gupta attempt an explanation in a recent Paper. (The service sector as India's road to economic growth, NBER Working Paper 16757).

They contend that much of services growth since 1990 represents a catching up with international norms for the share of services in GDP after a long period of repression. In the period 1950-90, the share of India's services sector in GDP was lower than the international norm, going by per capita income. This was because, in India's then controlled economy, a large portion of resources in the earlier part of the period had been preempted by heavy industry.

Economic reforms liberated the services sector to claim its due share. Much of the rapid growth since 1990 is from a low base. But the story does not end there. There is at least one striking departure from international experience.

Services can be disaggregated into three groups. Group I is traditional services - retail and wholesale trade, transport and storage, public administration and defense - which tend to be slow growing. Group II is a hybrid of traditional and modern services - education, health and social work, hotels and restaurants, and other community, social and personal services - whose share in GDP in economies has risen in step with per capita income.

Group III is made up of modern services - financial intermediation, computer services, business services, communications, and legal and technical services. The interesting departure is that, in India, this group has taken off at a lower per capita level than seen in OECD economies.

We cannot brush aside this group on the ground that it constitutes a small portion of GDP. The growth rates of communications, business services and financial services have been so high that they have together contributed more towards growth of GDP than manufacturing.

Some have argued that a large portion of services growth merely represents outsourcing of jobs earlier done in industry. The Paper finds that this is not true. Only about a quarter of services growth is due to outsourcing by industry. Most of the growth is on account of an increase in private final demand and exports. Tradability of many services has risen sharply in recent years thanks to developments in communications and IT. India has done a good job of riding the new wave of service exports.

The outlook for both modern and traditional services remains bright. Outsourcing by foreign companies is bound to continue because it is a business imperative. The market for IT as well as financial services within India remains under-penetrated. Education and healthcare both need to expand considerably in order to meet domestic demand. Transport, hotels and retail trade all have untapped potential.

The more critical question is whether services can absorb enough of India's burgeoning labour force. Many have argued that while services may provide growth, low-cost manufacturing alone can provide adequate employment. The vast majority of workers would not have the skills necessary for employment in services. The authors try to refute this proposition by showing that the skill content in manufacturing and services is converging.

This is not a terribly convincing argument. The convergence may have happened because manufacturing in India has become more skill-intensive. It does not prove that services are capable of absorbing large numbers of workers with relatively low skills. But we do have anecdotal evidence of this happening. Several firms have set up call centres and data entry centres in the rural areas. Financial services and communications too have shown they can generate large numbers of relatively low-skilled jobs.

It may be difficult to train large numbers of workers for highly skilled jobs in services but it should be possible to train them for lower-skilled jobs in services. Services by themselves cannot be the answer to India's employment needs. But the high growth rate of India's services does imply that we do not have to imitate the East Asian or Chinese growth model.

July 6, 2011

No, It's not a Downward Spiral

As investment and industrial output plummeted in 2011-12, last December many doomsayers were quick to forecast an even worse economic performance in 2012-13. If growth in 2011-12 will end up at 7 per cent, they said, it would be 6-6.5 per cent in 2012-13. The period of high growth rates starting in 2003-04 was over.

Just two months on, it is becoming clear that these fears were exaggerated. The PM's Economic Advisory Council (PMEAC) forecasts growth in the coming year in the range of 7.5-8 per cent. The Centre for Monitoring Indian Economy likewise sees an improvement in the growth rate to 7.7 per cent. Their optimism is well founded. Of a sudden, it is possible to spot a number of positive factors in the environment.

One big positive is the indication that the Eurozone crisis is being contained for now. Last week, Greece and its Eurozone partners agreed on a bailout package aimed at preventing a disorderly Greek default. Few believe that the bailout, which aims to reduce Greece debt to GDP ratio to 120 per cent by 2020, will work. Nevertheless, it staves off an immediate implosion within the Eurozone and the risk that the contagion will spread. In other words, it buys time for a year or two.

This development is bound to have a positive impact on investor sentiment within the country. During the sub-prime crisis, emerging markets, including India, were impacted primarily by disruption of capital flows. In 2011, any additions to capacity that were dependent on overseas financing and overseas markets looked risky. This could be one reason for investors taking fright.

Investment was also adversely impacted by higher interest rates and the persistence of a high rate of inflation. The inflation rate has shown a fall in recent months. Unless oil prices again shoot up sharply, we can expect an inflation rate of 6-7 per cent in the coming year. While this is strictly not within the RBI's comfort zone, it may just suffice for the RBI to cut its reference rate, given the clamour for monetary policy to shift in favour of growth.

Yet another positive is the revival of the stock market since the beginning of the year. The Sensex has risen by 13 per cent on the back of a revival of FII flows. The PMEAC expects portfolio flows at $ 5 bn this year. It expects flows to rise to $10 bn next year, which is of the same order as portfolio flows in 2005-07. It should suffice to keep the Sensex at a level that enthuses companies and investors.

The revival of the stock market bodes well for the government's disinvestment plans. The government has failed miserably to meet its disinvestment target of Rs 40,000 crore for the current year, thanks partly to the slump in the stock market. In the current year, it should be better placed to do so and, to that extent, contain the fiscal deficit.

Another important component of capital flows, net foreign direct investment, has been buoyant this year-it is expected to touch $21 bn. Contrary to what many pundits have been saying, neither the so-called 'policy paralysis' not the regulatory and policy uncertainties created by the 2 G Spectrum sale seem to have had any impact on FDI inflows into the country.

The nation was impacted last year not so much by 'policy paralysis' as by 'execution paralysis', that is, the inability on the part of government to take decisions, thanks to the enormous fear psychosis created by the Anna Hazare movement and the demand for an omnipotent Lokpal. With the movement running out of steam, the decision-making apparatus in government appears to be coming out of its stupor.

There is thus a range of factors that should impact positively on business sentiment this year and contribute to an improvement in the growth rate. An acceleration in growth, in turn, will have several benign consequences. One, it will make the fiscal deficit to GDP ratio look a lot better by improving both the numerator (due to higher tax revenues) and the denominator. Two, it will help dispel fears about banks being severely hit by rising NPAs following an extended slowdown. Three, it could result in better profitability for companies, including public sector enterprises.

The last is especially crucial for addressing a key structural issue, namely, the overall savings rate in the economy- from 36.8 per cent of GDP in 2007-08 to 32.3 per cent in 2010-11. As the PMEAC report points out, of this 4.5 percentage points decline in savings, 3.3 per cent is accounted for the public sector- an increase in the fiscal deficit contributed to 2.1 percentage points and the remaining 1.2 percentage points was reduced surplus in PSUs and the railways. Improving public sector performance is thus crucial to raising the savings rate.

As for household savings, there has been a shift of 1.6 percentage points away from financial to physical assets, mainly gold. The preference for gold, reflected in large gold imports, is largely on account of elevated inflation in recent years. The good news is that gold imports have shown a sharp decline in the last quarter, thanks, perhaps, to signs of a fall in inflation.

Everybody is reminding the finance minister of the need for fiscal consolidation but our compulsions are very different from those of the advanced economies. There, debt sustainability and access to external finance are the issues. Here, consolidation is more about re-directing expenditure towards more productive uses and reining in inflation. In other words, it's about growing at 9 per cent instead of at 7-8 per cent. Why such a predicament should occasion doomsaying is a mystery.

March 1, 2012

2

Reform

Practitioners of Political Economy

Not only are we seeing the beginnings of a turnaround in the fiscal but it arises from a most unexpected quarter. Eighty per cent of the increase in revenues relative to the budget estimates for 2003-04 comes from loan recoveries, the result of the debt swap between the centre and the states that Jaswant Singh announced in the last budget.

The debt swap works as follows; The states repay the principal amount on some of the loans made to them by the centre. This causes the centre's fiscal deficit to decline. The states are then allowed to borrow a corresponding amount from the market at much lower rates than the rate on central loans. The states' debt position remains unchanged because borrowings from the centre have merely been substituted by cheaper borrowings from the market.

In announcing a big push to the debt swap scheme in his last budget, Mr Singh clearly sensed that the States' incentive to repay the centre's loans had become overwhelmingly strong with the interest differential being as wide as it is. He pegged loan recoveries at a modest level in the budget but he must have known that the potential was much larger. So he could afford to take a relaxed view of fiscal consolidation in last year's budget and in the run-up to the interim budget as well. Mr Singh has thus chosen a route to fiscal consolidation that the authors of the Economic Survey had never envisaged. The politician's mind can work in very different ways, it wonders to perform.

The turnaround in the fiscal makes you wonder: whatever happened to the devastation that the Fifth Pay Commission was supposed to have wrought for all time? The Pay Commission wanted

30 per cent of government employees to be retrenched. That would have been politically explosive. The political class has tackled the problem more creatively. It has frozen or cut back on recruitment. As a result, wages of government employees as a proportion of GDP has declined over time, producing the same result that a one-off retrenchment would have. Mr Singh's move to merge 50 per cent of the DA with basic pay in for government employees is a bold one, reflecting a judgement that the centre has by now absorbed the impact of the Pay Commission.

One of the highlights of the interim budget is the decline in subsidies and in revenue expenditure relative to budget estimates. We are witnessing a similar trend in many of the states. Subsidies are being cut, user charges hiked and recruitment frozen. The higher wage bill has compelled governments to search actively for solutions to the fiscal problem. This is the politician's way of reaching an objective: create a problem and force a solution.

The supreme exemplar of this approach in recent times was Ronald Reagan. Mr Reagan came to power with two principal objectives in mind: undermining the Soviet Union and pruning welfare expenditure at home. He raised defence expenditure sharply and sent the fiscal deficit soaring. The Soviet Union was wrecked trying to catch up with American defence spending. Congress was forced to confront welfare spending. Economists worried that the huge deficits the US had run up would bring about an economic collapse. They were proved wrong just as their counterparts in India have been thus far. Mr Reagan's instinct that growth would take care of the fiscal problem was borne out in the nineties.

Nearer home, Indira Gandhi showed the same instinctual understanding of what was required in the realm of economic policy. In the late sixties, the Indian economy was stuck in a rut thanks to stagnation in industry. Then came Mrs Gandhi's nationalisation of banks. As IG Patel recounts in his memoirs, Mrs Gandhi's economic advisors did not favour the move. It was widely denounced as populist. But it turned out to be a masterstroke.

Bank nationalisation caused the savings rate to almost double in the late seventies from the level in the late sixties, thereby easing a crucial constraint on growth. It helped boost agricultural output, which relieved another constraint, the balance of payments. These two developments together set the stage for the breakthrough from the Hindu growth rate of 3.5 per cent to the growth rate of 5.5 per cent in the eighties, something the proponents of India Shining would do well to remember.

Politicians tend to be reviled rather than revered. The better lot, however, are capable of the sort of creativity that, while defying the conventional economic wisdom, produces impressive results. India's politicians have often been faulted for not pushing harder with reforms, for playing to the gallery. But it is fair to suggest that it is the moderation of economic advice through political wisdom that explains our quite exceptional record of growth with stability through more than a decade of reforms.

February 12, 2004

Growth without "Reforms"

The current debate on matters economic must strike many as extraordinary. The government was formed on the basis of a Common Minimum Programme that the Congress agreed with its allies. Yet, its greatness is sought to be measured by how much it deviates from the CMP! When the Left insists that the CMP be adhered to, it is accused of perfidy- it is being "anti-reform".

The CMP talks of a National Employment Guarantee Act that will provide at least one able-bodied person in every needy household with 100 days of employment at the minimum wage. But the government's reformist prowess will be judged by how much it whittles down this commitment. The CMP talks of a sharp increase in spending on education with a National Commission on Education that will monitor programmes. For the "reforms" brigade, this is a waste- the government should give the money to the CII instead. The CMP makes no mention of FDI in the retail sector or in banking. Yet, the government is being reformist when it seeks to push ahead with FDI in these sectors.

The meaning is clear. The CMP is not to be taken seriously, it is merely an artifice needed for political survival. The reformist finance minister may find it expedient to throw crumbs at the Left every now and then - such as a hike in the EPF rate without the funds needed to support the hike- but his mission must be to stick to the original reform agenda, not the one outlined in the CMP. To be "pro-reform" is to be anti-CMP.

In the UPA's first budget, presented in July last year, Mr Chidambaram let down both the advocates of the CMP and the "reforms" brigade, pleading that his government had had little time to prepare and that the period after the budget was too short for him to shift gears. He raised the budgetary support to the Plan by Rs 10,000 crore, a paltry sum in relation to the social expenditures envisaged in the CMP. Apart from the promise of continued tax reforms, Mr Chidambaram's only substantive reform proposal was a hike in FDI limits in telecom, civil aviation and insurance.

Those waiting for Mr Chidambaram to deliver on "reforms" in the coming budget may be in for a disappointment. The CMP repudiates at least three key tenets of liberalisation- privatisation, a hire-and-fire policy for labour and (if only by implication) dereservation for small-scale units. There is little in the government's pronouncements thus far that suggests it is in a mood to resile from the CMP's positions on these issues.

This is not just a matter of having to contend with political opposition both within and outside the government. The rather dramatic change in the outlook for growth over the past two years weakens the political case for "reforms". The economy is poised to grow at between 6.5-7 per cent this year, shrugging off soaring oil prices, a disappointing year for agriculture and the effects of the tsunami. This will be on top of the revised figure of 8.5 per cent for 2003-04. These two years of high growth have undermined one of the key tenets of reforms, namely, that the Indian economy was stuck in a new Hindu growth rate of 5.5-6 per cent from which deliverance was impossible without a whole slew of reforms.

However, the case for delivering on the social sector agenda of the CMP remains strong. The notion that the verdict of 2004 had anything to do with economic issues is fiercely contested by many. And yet, it is difficult to dismiss the idea that "India Shining" simply did not vibe with a large section of the electorate who seem to have been bypassed by the improvement in economic performance over the past decade.

It was this perception that informed the CMP and there is little sign that the government is inclined to disown it. Not just the employment guarantee programme but also education, health and food and nutrition security are all items on which we can expect to see higher levels of spending than before. The higher level of resource transfers to the states mandated by the Twelfth Finance Commission and On a strict reading of the CMP, even disinvestment is not on-the CMP only talks of public sector undertakings raising additional resources through the capital market, not the sale of government equity in PSUs.

February 24, 2005

Time to Shed "Reform" Blinkers

The Union budget is a time for clichés - and the worst time at that. For years, we had pundits telling us sagely on TV: "the reassuring message of the budget is that reforms will continue". Last year, there was widespread relief that there had been no "major rollback" of reforms. This year, expect pundits to declare that "political realities" have kept the finance minister from "going for broke".

The clichés of the past have turned out to be wide off the mark. "Reforms" haven't continued. There have been no big cuts in subsidies, no reduction in the government workforce, no "big ticket" privatisation, no labour market reforms, and no great opening up to FDI.

In the 2005-06 budget, we had no "rollback" but what the finance minister characterised as a "pause" on the fiscal deficit targets mandated under the FRBM Act. A year later, it turns out there may not have been a "pause" at all. And thereby hangs a tale-of how the Indian economy has evolved in ways that have confounded the pundits.

Under the FRBM Act, the revenue and fiscal deficits are to be brought down by a minimum of 0.5 per cent and 0.3 per cent respectively every year starting from 2004-05. As the FM did not expect these targets to be met for 2005-06 (see RD initial and FD initial). The revenue deficit was expected to stay at the same level as in 2004-05, while the fiscal deficit was to decline by 0.2 per cent and not 0.3 per cent as mandated. That is what the FM termed a "pause".

But that was a year ago. The GDP figures have since been revised and the picture changes dramatically. In his budget speech last year, the FM used the estimate of 4.8 per cent for 2003-04 as his starting point. This would have meant a reduction of 0.6 percentage points to 4.2 per cent by 2005-06. But the RBI's provisional figures show that the fiscal deficit was 4.1 per cent in 2004-05 itself, placing us well ahead of the FRBM time-table! (see FD revised).

Even if we were to take the revised figures for 2003-04 as the starting point, the FRBM targets for both the deficits will have been met for 2004-05. For 2005-06, the fiscal deficit would have to end up at 3.8 per cent and the revenue deficit at 2.1 per cent in order to comply with the FRBM Act. The coming budget will tell us what the position is.

But even if we overshoot these targets in 2005-06, that is hardly cause for alarm because the goal-posts have been moved. The actual reductions in the fiscal and revenue deficits over two years should be measured against the deficit figures posited in 2003-04 and not the revised figures. After all, the targets for reduction were specified with reference to the high deficit levels at the time.

The improvement in the fiscal at the centre is part of a larger story in which the finances of the states have improved even more. The combined fiscal deficit of the centre and the states has fallen by over 2.5 percentage points relative to the level of 10 per cent in 2001-02. This has happened not on account of "reforms". It has happened because growth has boosted tax revenues and the fall in interest rates has cut interest payments.

Thus' a crucial premise underlying the "reforms" agenda, namely, that the growth rate cannot rise above 6-6.5 per cent unless "reforms" are pushed through has been undermined. And the fiscal problem has turned out to be substantially self-correcting- no call for blood, tears, toil and sweat. The improvement in the fiscal has contributed to half of the increase in the savings rate of 5.5 percentage points since 2001-02. Higher savings create the basis for sustained growth of over 8 per cent.

So the "reforms" brigade was wrong. Yet it insists that we should push ahead with the "unfinished" agenda. Why? Because growth would rise from 8 per cent to 10 per cent - or from 10 per cent to 12 per cent. "Reforms" will add that extra to the growth rate.

India's successful record argues otherwise. First, any insistence on the politically contentious and economically dubious set of "reforms" could derail the consensus that has facilitated the acceleration in growth in the first place. Secondly, a gradual increase in the growth rate may be preferable to a sudden burst- the financial system can better digest the former than the latter. Thirdly, since the fiscal is not as worrying, we can afford to be much bolder on things needed to accelerate growth-massive investment in infrastructure, education and health and in broad-based employment.

In short, economy policy must cease to be hostage to any preconceived "reform" agenda. It is time to shed our "reform" blinkers.

February 23, 2006

Mythology of Post-Reform Growth

With each passing day, it is getting easier to believe that the acceleration in India's economic growth from around 6 per cent to 8 per cent is here to stay. The hard part is trying to explain just why this has happened. How we explain the acceleration is important because it has a bearing on future policy.

The conventional wisdom on India's growth story runs as follows. Growth accelerated to around 6 per cent in the nineties from the historical rate of 3.5 per cent because 'reforms' had unleashed the pent-up energies of Indian entrepreneurs long shackled by the socialist Raj. It slowed subsequently because 'reforms' had lost momentum. The last three years' spurt in growth is the fortuitous result of a global economic boom. Once the world economy slows down, we will be back to 6 per cent growth- unless we proceed with 'second generation reforms'.

Every one of these propositions bristles with problems. It is simply not true that economic growth accelerated to 6 per cent in the nineties. There is a significant body of research that has shown that the 'structural break' in India's economic growth occurred, not in the early nineties, but in 1980. Economic growth accelerated close to 6 per cent in the eighties. The growth rate in the first decade after reforms was not significantly different from the growth rate in the eighties.

This body of research argues that that 'reforms' in the sense of market-oriented or even pro-business policies did not commence overnight in 1991. The shift towards such policies had commenced even earlier. Economic policies in the nineties merely helped consolidate an underlying trend.

Why the slowdown in growth in 2001-03? The world economy slowed down in 2001-03 and this put the brakes on the Indian economy. Then came the crucial change, an acceleration to 8 per cent in 2004-06. This cannot be ascribed to any fresh bout of 'reforms' or even to the global boom. There have been important structural changes in the economy.

One is the rise in the savings rate from 23.5 per cent in 2000-01 to 29.1 per cent in 2004-05. Most of this increase - 4.0 per cent- has come from the turnaround in public savings. Thanks to the rise in the savings rate, the economy has moved on to an altogether higher investment rate.

The second important structural change is enhanced export competitiveness, reflected in the rising share of exports. The total exports (trade plus invisible receipts)/GDP ratio has risen sharply from 16.9 per cent in 2000-01 to 24.6 per cent in 2005-06. A third, less noticed, change in recent years is financial deepening. The bank assets/GDP ratio rose from 48 per cent in 2000-01 to 80 per cent in 2005-06 on the back of a surge in bank credit.

One factor is common to these three structural changes: lower interest rates. The decline in interest rates has helped fiscal consolidation, it has boosted firms' competitiveness and it has led to a huge increase in retail credit. Lower interest rates have been made possible by the rise in inflows on both the current and capital accounts.

The rise in inflows, in turn, reflects growing overseas confidence in India's economic potential- confidence created by two decades of economic growth of 6 per cent . The sharp depreciation in the rupee in the nineties undoubtedly helped but it is worth recalling that a trend towards rupee depreciation was under way in the eighties itself.

The state sector has played a vital role in ushering in better times. Fiscal consolidation is the result not just of lower interest rates but also of rising productivity in government (the government expenditure/GDP ratio has declined). The turnaround in firm performance has embraced the public sector as well. Financial sector deepening is the work of a banking system dominated by the public sector. With competition and changes in the governance structure, we are seeing vast improvements in public sector performance.

All this is very different from the self-serving thesis trotted out by the 'reform' ideologues: there was a burst of 'reforms' in the nineties, this caused an explosion in private entrepreneurship and - lo and behold!- our growth prospects underwent a sea-change. Entrepreneurship is, of course, a factor but it has been made possible by profound changes in the economy, some of which have been in the making over a long period.

If we go by the conventional wisdom on India's recent economic performance, it follows that we need 'second generation reforms' and a shrinking of government even in areas such as health and education. If, however, we accept that structural changes in the economy which underlie our improved fortunes- changes to which the state sector has contributed- we are likely to have a more nuanced appreciation of what the future course of economic policy might be.

November 16, 2006

Redefining the Reform Agenda

Last July, when the Left withdrew support to the UPA, many commentators were ecstatic. They forecast that the UPA would come up with a fresh burst of "reforms" in order to vow the electorate. Alas, nothing of the sort happened.

Now, the Left is not in the picture. Once again, there is a clamour from industry bodies and commentators to get on with the "reform" agenda. The Sensex zoomed after the election results were out, reflecting hopes that the Congress would now seriously pursue "reforms". Such hopes are based on a serious misreading of both the electoral verdict and the Congress' position on "reforms".

The Congress did not win the elections by being gung-ho about "reforms". Indeed, the verdict on the UPA government had been that it was a comprehensive failure when it came to "reforms". Commentators were outraged that the 'dream team' of Manmohan Singh, Chidambaram and Ahluwallia should have turned out to be such a disappointment.

We can only guess every time what considerations prompt voters to favour a particular party or alliance. The record of the party or coalition in power is not the sole determinant of the outcome of elections. The electoral arithmetic, which way the votes are split amongst the various parties or alliances, is an equally important factor.

If the Congress benefited from its record at all, it was from measures that "reformers" had relentlessly opposed: NREGA, the farm debt waiver, the Sixth Pay Commission award, an increase in subsidies and OBC quotas. There was also the impressive performance in recent years of agriculture, an area least touched by "reforms".

NREGA covered four crore families, the farm debt waiver to four crore farmers and the Sixth Pay Commission one crore employees in the central and state governments. That adds up to a significant proportion of the 75 crore electorate and the 42 crore who actually voted.

Special Economic Zones are an important item in the "reforms" agenda. The one formation that embraced this aspect of "reforms" and lost heavily was the Left in the West Bengal which went all out to usurp farm land in order to give a push to industrialisation. Paradoxical as it may seem, the Congress benefited from measures generally associated with the Left while the Left itself lost out on account of its reformist ardour.

Stock market enthusiasts who rejoice at the ouster of the Left must remember that in West Bengal, Mamata Banerjee had positioned herself to the left of the ruling coalition. The Trinamool Congress has already indicated that it will oppose disinvestment. People tend to forget that the Congress itself is Leftist in orientation and the Gandhi family's political instincts have also tended in that direction whatever the corrections made from time to time.

The outcome of the 2009 elections should moderate expectations about the future course of "reforms". It is time we stopped thinking in terms of reforms with reference to the now discredited 'Washington Consensus'. The Congress has understood the need to redefine the reform agenda and this is clearly reflected in its last manifesto. Election manifestos are not read, otherwise commentators would not be harping on 'second generation' reforms in the coming budget.

The Congress manifesto is clear that privatisation will not happen but disinvestment will. There is no mention of labour market reforms. The manifesto does mention fiscal prudence and the need to better target subsidies. But everybody knows this is quite the wrong time to seek any fiscal correction. There is little chance of returning to the path of fiscal correction until 2011- much of Europe expects to have a debt to GDP ratio of close to 100 per cent.

Again, financial sector reforms, especially banking sector reforms, are a hot potato. Until some consensus is reached worldwide on a new regulatory framework for banking, we must expect the government to tread warily on this area. Understandably, the Congress manifesto is silent on this subject.

In the familiar "reforms" agenda, the only item other than fiscal prudence that finds mention in the Congress manifesto is the move towards a goods and services tax. The thrust of the manifesto is overwhelmingly on inclusion and improved governance-extension of the NREGA, a right to food law, health security, affordable education, democratization of cooperatives, strengthening of panchayats, comprehensive social security, etc.

Now, these may not be reforms that will send the Sensex shooting up, they may not be the ones that businessmen want. Economic commentators and market enthusiasts would like to see policies that swiftly return India to the 9-10 per cent growth path. But the balance to be sought between growth and equity, the content of economic reforms, is a political decision. Some two decades after it initiated a bout of economic reforms, it appears the Congress party has made its choice.

May 28, 2009

Indira Gandhi the Reformer

Last year, both Sonia Gandhi and Pranab Mukherjee sang the virtues of bank nationalisation. They said it had helped India survive the slowdown. Many ridiculed these as political statements intended to glorify the author of bank nationaliation, Indira Gandhi.

Now comes a defence of bank nationalisation from chief economic advisor Kaushik Basu. Basu says that bank nationalisation led to a rise in savings and investment and helped push up India's growth rate. I have myself long contended that bank nationalisation contributed to the acceleration in growth in the eighties and provided the basis for improved bank performance in the nineties and thereafter.

That is not how today's liberalisers perceive bank nationalisation. They perceive it as the apogee of India's socialist past, an act that undermined the culture of bank lending and saddled us with an inefficient banking sector. In short, the very antithesis of reforms. Wherein lies the truth? The question is worth addressing because the answer may give us a more nuanced understanding of what constitutes economic reform.

In 1969, Prime Minister Indira Gandhi announced the nationalisation of 14 banks. At the time, Mrs Gandhi faced a challenge from the old guard in the Congress. She also believed that the private owners of banks were in cahoots with the Swatantra party. By nationalising banks and sacking Morarji Desai as finance minister, Mrs Gandhi felt she could upstage her opponents within and outside the Congress, bolster her slogan of 'garibi hatao' and gain the votes of the masses. She succeeded admirably.

Politicians will always have an eye on votes. The test of their actions is whether there is congruence between their pursuit of power and the larger national interest. Was there more to bank nationalisation than sheer political opportunism?

Even then, there were reasons to think so. Mrs Gandhi had advocated 'social control' of banks as early as in 1967 after the Congress debacle in the general elections. In 1969, she said nationalisation was intended to reach banking services to the weaker sections of society.

In retrospect, the economic argument for bank nationalisation becomes even clearer. I explained this in an article in *EPW* (March 11, 2007). Under government ownership, bank branches jumped from 8000 in 1969 to 32,000 in 1980 and further to 60,000 in 1990. Savings are not money under the mattress. Savings are what come into the financial system. By sweeping money from individuals into the financial system, bank branch expansion caused in an increase in the savings rate from 12 per cent in1969 to 20 per cent in 1980.

The rise in the savings rate, in turn, set the stage for the acceleration in growth from the 'Hindu' rate of 3.5 per cent to 5.5-6 per cent in the eighties. There is thus a clear link between bank nationalisation and the acceleration in India's economic growth. Growth has gained further momentum since. But the break-out in the eighties was crucial.

Critics of bank nationalisation say that it made a mess of India's banking system. They also claim that the same objectives could have been better met through regulation instead of government ownership. These points do not stand up to scrutiny.

True, profitability in banking took a beating consequent to nationalisation. But that is because for two decades thereafter, public sector banks were told to simply grow their balance sheets. They did a great job of this. Consequent to deregulation in the nineties, they were asked to focus on profitability. They have done a good job of this as well. As a result, we have today a banking system that is among the most profitable in the world.

If Indian banking is profitable and sound today, it is because one-third of deposits are low-cost deposits, thanks to the network of branches created in the nationalised era. Thus, the two phases, bank nationalisation and deregulation, are not distinct but inter-linked. It was the investment in distribution made in the first phase that made possible the improvement in performance in the second.

Private ownership and regulation could not have produced the same result. What private owner would want to invest for two decades in distribution in the hope of future gain? That is not all. The investment in branch expansion had an all-important externality: it helped boost the growth rate of the economy.

Whether Mrs Gandhi had indeed grasped the full potential of bank nationalisation we shall never know. What we do know is that she showed a decisiveness that only great leaders are capable of. I G Patel, then special secretary for economic affairs, was among those opposed to the move. Mrs Gandhi gave him 24 hours to prepare the bill for parliament, a speech and a note for the cabinet.(In 1980, Patel was to urge Mrs Gandhi to go in for another bout of bank nationalisation!).

This sort of decisiveness is born of an instinctual grasp of what will produce dramatic results and it often involves out-of-the-box thinking. History is replete with instances of the instincts of leaders getting the better of the advice of professionals- Hitler's belief in the possibilities of blitzkrieg; Truman's conviction that the siege of Berlin could be broken through airlift; Reagan's strategy of outspending the Soviet Union to ruin.

Nearer home, few economists saw India moving on to a growth rate of 8 per cent in the last decade. Jaswant Singh as finance minister did. In 2003, just ahead of the boom years, he said that the Indian economy had reached an 'inflection point'.

In the wake of the sub-prime crisis, there is better appreciation of the merits of government ownership in banking in India. We need also a better appreciation of what constitutes reform. Basu says that the government is now keen to emulate the nationalisation model of increasing savings through branch expansion and quickly raise the savings rate to 40 per cent.

Which brings us to the larger point. Reforms are not some items on a list prepared in Washington. Reforms are what reforms do. If government ownership in banking delivers higher and more stable growth, then putting that to creative use is also reformist. Judged by this yardstick, Mrs Gandhi could well qualify as the original reformer.

January 21, 2010

3

Fiscal Consolidation

No Longer a Bugbear

It's official now- and it comes from the horse's mouth. India's fiscal deficit, for long the cynosure of much economic punditry, is no longer a problem in the eyes of the World Bank. The Bank's Country Director Michael F Carter has been quoted as saying that there was no need for concern over India's fiscal deficit (Rediff.com, November 12).

Says Mr Carter, "I feel it will not be much of a problem as with growth, the fiscal def icit is expected to come down in the long run. Though the consolidated fiscal deficit of the centre and the states is above 10 per cent, the Indian economy has higher underlying growth potential. India can live with higher fiscal deficit."

These comments should cause many in this country to sit up and take note. No macroeconomic indicator has attracted as much attention in the post-reform period as much as the fiscal deficit. The balance of payments and foreign exchange reserves may have been the focus of attention in the initial years after reform. From the second half of the nineties, however, this problem began to diminish in intensity, giving way eventually to a problem of abundance. But the fiscal deficit continues to be viewed as the one problem the reformers have been unable to grapple with successfully.

However, lately there has been a shift in perceptions of the fiscal deficit as well. In the early years of reform, the issue was one of sustainability of public debt in the face of high levels of fiscal deficit. The conventional wisdom was that if the fiscal deficit remained high, it would soon push both domestic and external debt to a level at which investors would no longer be willing to hold Indian debt.

But this rests on the premise that interest rates would rise and the exchange rate would appreciate in response to a high fiscal deficit. In fact, interest rates have declined consequent to financial deregulation and the exchange rate depreciated until recently, so the Indian experience has not conformed to the text-book model of the effects of a high fiscal deficit.

In the text-book model, net exports fall consequent to high levels of fiscal deficit because the exchange rate appreciates. In India, the steep depreciation in the exchange rate has, in fact, triggered a boom in export earnings through software and also led to phenomenal inflows through remittances. As a result, high levels of fiscal deficit have not brought on the problem of high external debt.

More recently, the fiscal deficit has been viewed primarily as inhibiting the economy's growth potential through the "crowding out" of private investment. This effect again operates through a rise in the interest rate. As mentioned, interest rates have declined even in the second half of the nineties in the face of a rising debt to GDP ratio. You could argue that interest rates might have declined even more but for the persistence of the fiscal deficit level but this misses the point.

High lending rates to industry today, which is what impacts on investment, have a great deal less to do with the fiscal deficit level than with incentives to lend in the banking sector today. In fact, there is a school of thought that contends that the investment famine that we are seeing in industry is very substantially the result of denial of credit to small and medium enterprises.

Even where the text-book model operates, the impact on growth of a high fiscal deficit can be overblown. One study looked at how badly the US economy might have been impacted by high fiscal deficits over a long period. It estimated that fiscal deficits would have set the US back by about three years, meaning the US would have achieved in 1995 a level of GNP that it would have achieved in 1992 sans the fiscal deficits. This hardly qualified as a disaster compared to, say, the impact of the decline in productivity growth in the same period. (What do budget deficits do? Laurence Ball and N Gregory Mankiw, NBER Working Paper 5263).

In the current fiscal, India is poised to attain growth of around 7% in the face of one of the highest levels of fiscal deficit projected in recent years- 5.9% of GDP. There is every possibility that, as a result of high growth, the total debt to GDP ratio will decline for the first time since 1997-98.

Finance minister Jaswant Singh should have come in for brickbats for fiscal irresponsibility. Instead, he will be receiving bouquets for presiding over an economic revival. The only debate on now is whether the sustainable growth is 7 per cent plus or closer to 6 per cent. At either of these growth rates, the fiscal deficit ceases to be a bugbear. Politicians like Jaswant Singh seem to have sensed this in a way that eluded the tribe of economists.

November 20, 2003

States Lose as Centre Gains

Part of the India Shining story is that the centre's fiscal problem is at last showing signs of tractability. It is the states' fiscal problem that promises to be obdurate. While the latter is commonly ascribed to states' profligacy, a good chunk of the blame must rest with the centre.

Last year (2003-04) could be the first since 1997-98 when the centre's debt to GDP ratio showed a decline. With a little luck, this could continue in 2004-05 and thereafter as well. Viewing the problem in terms of the fiscal deficit to GDP ratio, there have been improvements in both the numerator and the denominator. The numerator shows improvement thanks to the decline in interest rates, reining in of expenditure growth and an increase in revenues on the back of a booming economy. Again, growth has caused the denominator to improve.

Why would states not benefit similarly? Surely economic growth should surely help the states' fisc as well? And haven't the states too doing their bit to curb expenditure growth? True enough. Yet, the states differ from the centre in two key respects. A high proportion of their revenues is accounted for by transfers from the centre. Thanks to fiscal adjustments at the centre, growth of such transfers has decelerated - from 14.6 per cent in the eighties to 11 per cent in the nineties.

Secondly, interest rates are virtually exogenous to the states. The centre could, perhaps, plead helplessness in respect of the trend in transfers. Not so in respect of states' crippling interest burden. The centre (along with the RBI) first sets stringent limits on market borrowings by the states. Then, on loans the centre makes to the states, it charges interest rates way above market rates. The states lose, the centre gains in this arrangement.

The centre determines not only the total loans a state can raise in a year but also the composition of loans. Open Market Borrowings, which constitute potentially the cheapest source of funds for states, are subject to stringent limits. Today, such borrowings account for just 12 per cent of total outstanding liabilities of the states. In 2002-03, total state borrowings were limited to Rs 13,000 crore while the centre borrowed Rs 113,000 crore. Nobody would quarrel with the notion that there must be limits on states' borrowings. However, it is necessary to be clear about the basis for such limits so that these can be revisited when economic circumstances change.

As market borrowings are limited, central loans to states form a big chunk of states' borrowings. On these, the centre charges a significant spread not only over its own market borrowing rate but over that of the state in question as well. According to calculations made by the Maharashtra government in its memorandum to the Twelfth Finance Commission, the average interest rate on central loans to states worked out to 13 per cent in 2002-03.

There has been some attempt to ameliorate this burden through the debt swap scheme formulated by Jaswant Singh but the relief to the states on this account is as yet quite small. This is partly because high cost central debt is swapped, for the most part, not with market borrowings but with costlier funds from the National Small Savings Fund.

States' borrowings against Small Savings collections too are subject to anomalies. In transferring these funds to the states, the centre not only charges a spread over its cost of borrowings but ensures that the spread is charged for the entire tenor of the loan, not just for the period of the original liability. Thus, while the savings instruments may be for seven years, the centre locks in its spread over the entire tenor of its loan to the states, which could be 30 years! Loans from financial institutions also carry high spreads over market rates.

External loans for state projects, made available to the centre at soft rates, are transferred to states at what can only be regarded as extortionate rates of interest in today's context. High spreads may have been justified earlier on account of exchange rate risk but this certainly does not hold today. Even more questionable is the practice of splitting external grants into loan and grant components while making these available to the states.

The present treatment of states' borrowings amounts to dressing up the centre's finances at the expense of the states. The Twelfth Finance Commission must address this issue in right earnest. Restructuring states' existing debt is an immediate solution. The longer-term solution must be to put in place a clear basis for determining both the level of states' market borrowings and interest rates on various central loans to the states.

April 22, 2004

Time to Revisit the FRBM Act

Now that we have the FRBM Act, keeping the fiscal deficit within the limits prescribed has become sacrosanct for the finance minister. In the current economic situation, however, it is the attempt to adhere to the FRBM limits, rather than the breach of these, that poses the greater danger.

In 2004-05, Mr Chidambaram managed to contain the fiscal deficit at 4.5 per cent but only by pruning Plan expenditure by over Rs 8000 crore. For 2005-06, the fiscal deficit is estimated at 4.3 per cent . The finance minister has partially met the expectations of the Left on what he calls the "flagship programmes" of the CMP by raising the allocations on these by Rs 25,000 crore.

But this comes at a heavy cost- central assistance to state plans will be cut by nearly Rs 21,000 crore. The expenditure budget shows total Plan expenditure at Rs 172,500 crore. The expenditure summary, however, gives the more accurate figure- Rs 143,487 crore, or a mere 4.3 per cent over the figure for revised estimates for 2004-05. The difference of about Rs 29,000 crore between the two figures is to be raised by the states from the market.

As the states too are expected to subject themselves to fiscal rules, there is every prospect that this expenditure will turn out to be notional. Both physical and social infrastructure in states, already reeling under years of neglect, will be adversely impacted in consequence. As it is at the state level that governance issues are experienced on a day to day basis, this could turn out to be bad politics for the UPA government.

The FRBM Act, it is said, leaves the finance minister with little choice. But this begs the question: how valid today are the objectives and rules enshrined in the FRBM Act? It is necessary to raise this question because none of the malign effects ascribed to the fiscal deficit-low growth, high interest rates, a balance of payments problem, an internal debt crisis-has materialised to date.

Once India's economic growth moved to the 5.5-6 per cent trajectory, the conviction grew among policy-makers that the combined fiscal deficit of the centre and the states of around 10 per cent of GDP constituted an insurmountable obstacle to higher growth. Savings and investment were stuck at around 23 per cent. Cut the fiscal deficit to 3 per cent, the objective laid down in the FRBM Act, and savings and investment would rise to 30 per cent-just what was required to raise growth to 7-8 per cent.

Well, there has been little change in the fiscal deficit ratio but-lo and behold!- the Economic Survey finds that the economy has moved closer to a sustainable growth rate of 7 per cent. Savings have bounded up to 28 per cent and the investment rate has risen to 26 per cent. Interest rates were expected to shoot up and cripple investment. They had stayed low, we were told, only for want of investment demand. Investment is said to have risen over the period 2001-02 to 2002-04 and yet we have seen only a modest firming up of interest rates.

This is because the surge in liquidity caused by forex inflows has exceeded all expectations. What started as a turnaround on the external front is now impacting on the domestic economy as well. One thing is fairly clear now: you do not need the fiscal deficit to come down to 3 per cent in order to raise growth to 6.5-7 per cent.

But do we need to lower the fiscal deficit to 3 per cent in order to ward off an internal debt crisis? Well, foreigner investors certainly are not behaving as though one is imminent. Leaving that aside, the good news is that the centre's debt to GDP ratio has begun to decline after having risen for five years in succession.

The Economic Survey (2004-05) shows that it declined from its peak of 63.3 per cent in 2002-03 to 62.5 per cent in 2003-04 and further to 62 per cent in 2004-05 (if we exclude borrowings on account of the market stabilisation fund, which is not really a function of government finances). Even as the growth rate accelerates, the debt problem shows every sign of coming under control.

How sustainable the debt problem is depends partly on how you define debt. The Kelkar Task Force on the FRBM act placed the centre's debt at 68 per cent of GDP. The RBI estimates it at 63 per cent. In a forthcoming paper (*EPW*, March 5), the writer and two of his colleagues contend that the ratio is even lower- 57 per cent.

In government, policies follow problems with a huge lag. By the time the policies are in place, often the problem has changed character. The FRBM Act was conditioned on the outlook for growth and interest rates of five or even ten years ago. The outlook has changed dramatically since. So we need to revisit the fiscal deficit objective as well as the yearly targets enshrined in the rules framed under the FRBM Act. Not to do so is to restrict the room for government spending in ways that could hinder both growth and equity.

March 10, 2005

More Transparency, Please

Budget fatigue sets in within 48 hours of the presentation of the budget. This year, the slide in global stock markets has given the media added cause to switch off. The media's short attention span renders difficult any close examination of the budget. As a result, it is the instant judgement, made on budget day, that matters to government. This does put a huge premium on appearances. Forget the substance, how the budget is dressed up is everything.

We all know what the judgement was this time. The finance minister (FM) had failed to push reforms. He had chosen to focus instead on *aam admi*. He had done so primarily by stepping up expenditure on the social sectors in a big way. A survey carried out by *ET* showed that 86% of respondents had a positive view of the budget. Whatever the reforms brigade might say, the wider public seemed to think the budget was redeemed by what it had done for *aam admi*. The FM had won the battle for perceptions. Cheers!

Just what any budget does for the social sectors is not easy to determine. Finance ministers have developed a technique for showing how much their hearts bleed for *aam admi*. They will launch into a lengthy recital of various schemes- Bharat Nirman, Sarva Shiksha Abhiyan, Mid-day Meal etc.

Then, they will inundate you with detail. Sample Mr Chitambaram's speech. Additional irrigation potential of 2,400,000 hectares.....Drinking water .... to 55,512 habitations... 12,198 kilometres of rural roads... Since the figures are in thousands, we are supposed to be bowled over.

Details of allocation are given selectively. Mr Chidambaram's speech mentions a 31.6% increase in allocation for Bharat Nirman. For most of the other flagship schemes, the FM mentions the allocations but is silent on the increase over last year. Mr Chidambaram mentions the increases in allocation for the education and health sectors but not those for rural development and agriculture.

The intent is clear. Highlight changes where it suits you and leave these out where it doesn't. It is up to us to delve into the budget papers and fish out figures left unmentioned in the budget speech. Since this is not easy to do on budget day, FMs can get away with obfuscation.

The accompanying table provides comparisons for some ministries. For HRD, the increase in allocation this year is actually lower than the increase last year. The allocation is higher this year for the Mid-day Meal scheme but lower for Sarva Shiksha Abhiyan. At least on the HRD front, Mr Chidambaram has exerted himself less for *aam admi* than he did last year. The FM scores on health and, to a lesser extent, on rural development. But certainly not on agriculture.

Overall, the notion that this is a budget where Mr Chidambaram has spent liberally for *aam admi* or otherwise is hard to sustain. The increases in both Plan expenditure and total expenditure are lower than last year. On Plan capital expenditure, the budget is a disaster. But all this hardly matters. From the UPA's point of view, what matters is that the public seems to have bought the government's line: this budget is all about spending in a big way for *aam admi.*

Intense media scrutiny of budgets will not go away. And judgements made on budget day will continue to matter most. Parliament and the public must, therefore, ask that the budget speech carry a summary table. For all heads of expenditure as well as schemes highlighted in the speech, the table should have figures for three years and year on year changes. Similarly, for major revenue items, changes must be shown broken up into the volume effect and the price (tax rate) effect.

The budget process is transparent. But not transparent enough to facilitate the sort of quick judgement that determines popular perception. Providing a table as suggested will demystify the budget and enable better judgements to be made on budget day. Bad, perhaps, for obfuscating FMs and media pundits who revel in piercing the fog. But good certainly for *aam admi*.

March 8, 2007

We Withdrew Stimulus Last Year!

Many commentators complained that the budget for 2010-11 lacked a big headline. There is one but it was missed. The much-awaited withdrawal of the fiscal stimulus happened in 2009-10 itself. Moreover, the withdrawal in 2009-10 was larger than the one planned for 2010-11.

In 2008-09, the fiscal deficit increased from 2.7 per cent to 6.2 per cent of GDP. In the budget for 2009-10, the fiscal deficit was set at 6.8 per cent , higher than the revised estimate of 6 per cent for 2008-09. Time to withdraw, economists said in the run-up to this year's budget, but do so gradually. When the budget for 2010-11 showed a sharp decline in the fiscal deficit, economists were gratified.

Look more closely at the budgetary numbers and you find a different story. The fiscal deficit, correctly estimated after taking into account off-budget items, was 7.8 per cent in 2008-09 and it declined to 6.9 per cent in 2009-10. If the size of the fiscal deficit is a measure of stimulus, India commenced the withdrawal of stimulus last year, long before the thought had even crossed the minds of economists!

This is really the headline story to this year's budget. The story does not end there. There is reason to believe that the withdrawal of stimulus was greater in 2009-10 than in 2010-11. Here is why.

The fiscal deficit to GDP ratio or a change in this ratio is an inaccurate measure of stimulus. What underlies the change in the fiscal deficit also matters. Only changes in government expenditure or in tax revenues can be said to contribute to a fiscal stimulus, not changes in non-tax receipts.

In 2010-11, the fiscal deficit declines by 1.4 per cent of GDP but a big chunk of this decline (0.8 per cent) is expected on account of disinvestment and sale of spectrum, both non-tax receipts. So, the decline in the fiscal deficit exaggerates the withdrawal of stimulus.

One way of measuring the stimulus would be to look at the

change in government expenditure net of change in tax revenues as a proportion of GDP. This is shown in the table. The figure turns out to be 4.6 per cent in 2008-09, 0.5 per cent in 2009-10 and 0.1 per cent in 2010-11. It is evident that the big withdrawal in stimulus occurs in 2009-10 and not in 2010-11.

Thus, not only did the withdrawal of stimulus start in 2009-10 but the withdrawal was greater than is projected for 2010-11. The exhortations of economists to commence a gradual withdrawal of stimulus in this year's budget have thus been irrelevant to the proceedings. We have had withdrawal by stealth.

Analysts missed this story and focused on another, namely, the finance minister showing resolve on fiscal consolidation. For 2010-11, the FM has set the fiscal deficit target lower than recommended by the Thirteenth Finance Commission (TFC). For the next two years, his targets accord with those prescribed by the TFC.

The applause on this account is somewhat misplaced. Any improvement in the fiscal brought about by one-off measures such as sale of spectrum is deceptive. So is an improvement through disinvestment. Sale of government equity in PSUs amounts to forgoing the future stream of dividends. Thus, disinvestment trades off current improvement in the fisc against a future worsening.

A structural improvement in the fisc happens when the tax/GDP ratio goes up. On this parameter, there has been a serious slippage in recent years. The tax/GDP ratio improved from 9.4 per cent of GDP in 2004-05 to 12 per cent in 2007-08. Lower growth in the subsequent two years and the tax cuts of 2008-09 caused the ratio to decline to 10.1 per cent in 2009-10. On current projections, we have to wait until 2012-13 before the ratio gets back to the level of 12 per cent. So, jubilation over the improvement in the fisc is premature.

However, on a long view, we have reason to be optimistic about the fiscal outlook. Fiscal consolidation in 2004-08 happened because of an increase in revenues. It did not happen because of the expenditure compression advocated by economists. As India heads back towards growth of 9 per cent, we can expect the story to be repeated. The introduction of the goods and services tax and the direct taxes code and a widening of the service tax net will all be bonuses.

The concern must be that we will cut back on badly needed expenditure on the social sector and on public investment because of short-term concerns about fiscal consolidation. Here, the targets set under the FRBM Act present a problem. The TFC has added another target, namely, a reduction in total debt to GDP ratio to 68 per cent by 2014-15.

The debt to GDP target should be one that the economy tends towards over a very long period. A medium-term target is uncalled for and may become a needless constraint on essential expenditure. Fiscal consolidation is desirable but fiscal fundamentalism must be eschewed. Pranab Mukherjee must rethink his commitment to target an explicit reduction in the debt to GDP ratio in the medium term.

March 4, 2010

UPA Defines a New Trade-Off

Tomorrow's budget, more than most budgets in the past, will be judged by the FM's efforts at reversing the deterioration in the government's finances. Many analysts view the coming budget as a make-or-break one: either the government effects a drastic correction or we are condemned to low growth and high inflation in the near future.

It would be unwise to take such an absolutist position. It is best to recognise that, given the government's orientation towards social spending, correction can happen only over an extended period. It is the broad direction rather than the magnitude of correction that should be the yardstick for judging the budget.

The fiscal position is challenging but it is useful to note a couple of positives in the situation. One is that sustainability of debt is not the issue. The Thirteenth Finance Commission (TFC) had set a target for total debt to GDP ratio (of the centre and the states) of 68 per cent by 2014-15, with the centre's share coming down to 44.8 per cent. The budget for 2011-12 had forecast a ratio of 44.2 per cent for the centre. This will not happen because borrowings will exceed the budget forecast but the ratio will still be within 45-46 per cent.

Some commentators say that the centre's fiscal deficit this year is almost the same as it was at the start of reforms. True, but the centre's debt to GDP ratio at the time was 56 per cent. India's debt position looks far more sustainable today than it did then. It also looks a lot better than that of many of the advanced economies where the ratio has crossed 100 per cent of GDP.

Secondly, state finances are in better shape. As the finance ministry's Mid-Year Review notes, prior to the global crisis in 2007-

08, the states' fiscal deficit was just 1.5 per cent of GDP and they had a revenue surplus of 0.9 per cent of GDP. According to the latest review of the PM's Economic Advisory Council, the fiscal deficit of the states today adds up to 2.1 per cent of GDP which is well within the limit of 3 per cent set by the TFC.

The Mid-Year Review notes that the combined fiscal deficit of the centre and the states, which ballooned to 9.3 per cent in 2009-10, declined to 7.7 per cent in 2010-11. It should end up at around 7.5 per cent for 2011-12. Thus, fiscal consolidation for the economy on the whole remains on track even though it will not be true for the centre's finances in 2011-12.

How do we carry forward the process of consolidation? Thus, far, growth and tax reform rather than expenditure cuts have been responsible for fiscal correction. In this respect, India's experience has differed from that of other countries where fiscal correction has taken place primarily through expenditure correction.

In respect of tax reform, two important proposals are on the table: the Direct Tax Code and the Goods and Services Tax. The latter will involve more discussions between the centre and the states but the first should go through soon. In addition, there is scope for extending the service tax to all services except for a small negative list.

These reforms should help lift the centre's tax to GDP ratio from the current level of around 10 per cent to the 2007-08 level of 12 per cent and, perhaps, even higher. Along with growth, tax reforms should help bring about approximately 3 percentage points of adjustment in the fiscal deficit. Disinvestment and other one-off sources of revenue could contribute 0.5-1 per cent . Put together, these should help lower the centre's fiscal deficit below the target of 3 per cent set in the FRBM Act.

If the combination of growth and tax reform will not suffice now, it is because expenditure is poised to rise on three major counts: food security, education and healthcare. The PMEAC review believes that containing the total fiscal deficit of the centre and the states at 5.4 per cent of GDP by 2014-15 and making provisions for additional expenditure on these counts will require an adjustment of 5-6 percentage points of GDP in the next three years.

That would mean that, on top of the 4 percentage points of adjustment postulated above, an adjustment of around 1-2 per cent of GDP will have to be covered by subsidies and transfers. A correction of this order cannot happen in one budget, it has to be spread over several years. Since the government is to come out with a new FRBM Act based on the recommendations of the TFC, the time frame for meeting the targets needs to be suitably extended. That would ensure that investment expenditure does not suffer and it would also give time for the GST to come into effect.

It should be clear that those expecting a major cut in subsidies or a drastic fiscal correction in this year's budget are likely to be disappointed. They need to understand that any failure to do so will have arisen from a decision on the part of the government to push ahead with spending on social sector schemes. In other words, the UPA government is defining a new trade-off between growth and equity, one that, possibly, involves growing at 8% rather than 9% in the medium-term. Whether such a trade-off is right or desirable is ultimately for the electorate to judge.

March 15, 2012

4

Disinvestment

Myths that Lead a Charmed Life

The success of Maruti's IPO has demolished at least one myth about disinvestment, namely, that there is no appetite among investors for large public offerings of government equity. The government now feels emboldened to use this route for other public sector companies, such as the Shipping Corporation of India (SCI), in whose cases strategic sale has faced opposition.

So far so good but other myths continue to lead a charmed life. Swaminathan Aiyar contends that the Maruti IPO succeeded only because control had already passed to a private party, Suzuki, and this is what stoked the public's appetite for the sale of the government's remaining shares in the company. (Swaminomics, *Times of India,* July 13).

SCI was listed many years ago and its share price, Mr Aiyar avers, shot up on expectation that it would be sold to a private buyer. To attempt sale of shares to the public while the government retains control would cause the share price of SCI to drop and lead to a loss of revenue for the government. As this argument is routinely trotted out in favour of strategic sale, let us examine it carefully.

SCI's price has risen from Rs 14 in March 2000 to Rs 51 in March 2003. The price rise, is on account of two factors-a sharp increase in profit (reflected in the earnings per share) and a rise in the price-earnings multiple.

The company's EPS has risen from Rs 5.7 to Rs 9.7- and this accounts for about 40% of the rise in the share price. The multiple has gone up from 2.5 to 5.2. It could be contended that the increase in the multiple, which accounts for the remaining 60% of the increase in the share price, reflects the "privatisation effect",

But there is no means of being certain about this because the re-rating of the stock could just as well be on account of improved profitability. When a firm's underlying earnings potential is perceived to have increased, there is every chance of its multiple going up. Most likely, the re-rating of the stock reflects the influence of both the factors, improved profitability even under government ownership and the prospect of strategic sale. But the myth endures- stock prices of PSUs have shot up only because strategic sale has seemed imminent.

It could be argued that even if the prospect of strategic sale accounts for only a portion of the increase in stock price, it would still justify strategic sale. Wouldn't the government lose to that extent if it went down the public offer route? Indeed, this is seen as the clinching argument for strategic sale. Whenever a strategic sale is announced, the increase in share price is more than when disinvestment under government ownership is proposed.

Plausible as the argument sounds, this is a false comparison to make. In a strategic sale, a big chunk, 26 per cent or more, of the government's equity is sold at one go. In public offers, a small stake is offered initially followed by further tranches. IPOs tend to be under-priced in order to entice investors into the firm. As information about the firm is disseminated over time, share prices will rise and subsequent tranches can be priced at higher levels.

In other words, the value of the firm in public offers is realised over several tranches, starting off with calculated under-pricing at the start. Hence it is incorrect to compare the price of an offer of a 26 per cent stake in a strategic sale with the price of, say, an offer of 10 per cent in an IPO. We need to know the average price realisation over the cumulative sale of 26 per cent or more through successive rounds of public offers in order to make a meaningful comparison. So much for the argument that the superior impact on stock price of a strategic sale announcement is reason for preferring strategic sale to a public offer.

One other myth needs to be debunked. This is that strategic sale alone is in some sense 'genuine' privatisation, not disinvestment where the government retains majority control. There is so much disinformation on the subject that it is worth proclaiming the salient facts from the roof-tops.

First, two-thirds of all privatisation sales worldwide have involved disinvestment, not strategic sale. Secondly, strategic sale is overwhelmingly a Latin American phenomenon, not the preferred mode in most other continents. Thirdly, the well-known empirical studies that document improvement in performance consequent to privatisation relate to disinvestment where governments typically sold only a third of their equity and did not shed majority control at one shot.

To persist with the myths about privatisation that abound in the country is to betray ignorance of the literature on privatisation.

July 17, 2003

Divest Shourie of his Portfolio

He who lives by the Sensex must perish by the Sensex. On September 16, when the Supreme Court ruled that the privatisation of BPCL and HPCL would require parliamentary approval, the Sensex stood at 4275. Some three weeks later, the Sensex has surged past 4600.

The writer is not among those who read meaning into every movement of the Sensex. However, advocates of privatisation, who invariably invoke such movements in support of their contentions, should acknowledge that their prophecies of doom have been proved wrong. The heavens have not fallen in the wake of the Supreme Court verdict.

This is no surprise. It is absurd to suggest that the fate of the Indian economy hangs by a slender thread called 'privatisation' and that investors will take fright every time a privatisation move is stalled. Yet that is precisely what the minister for disinvestment, Arun Shourie, would have us believe.

Saner heads in government have ensured that a legal challenge to the Supreme Court verdict, which would have set the executive on a collision course with the judiciary, will not be mounted. Shockingly, however, Mr Shourie seems to have persuaded the Cabinet committee on Disinvestment (CCD) to give him the go-ahead to put IOC on the block. Like a petulant child, Mr Shourie insists that if he cannot have his ice-cream in the form of BPCL and HPCL, he must at least have his chocolate in the shape of IOC- and the CCD has obliged.

The CCD decision not only reverses the earlier one that considered IOC off-bounds for privatisation along with ONGC and GAIL, it does so in a manner that shows scant regard for the interests of IOC. Everybody knows that if a big chunk of IOC's retail outlets is sold to a private party, today's thriving oil giant will slowly bleed to death.

If the privatisation of IOC was to be considered by the CCD, then it was incumbent on the ministry for disinvestment to have first worked out a scheme in consultation with the petroleum ministry - this would be elementary government procedure. Instead, the parent ministry has now been presented with a fait accompli: it must present a report on the divestiture of retail outlets in three months' time.

Going by the experience with NALCO, BPCL and HPCL, the odds are against Mr Shourie's being able to make much headway with IOC. The snowballing political opposition to his plans as much as the imminence of state elections will stymie Mr Shourie's ill-considered proposal. The only outcome would be that the credibility of government once again takes a beating as it finds its self unable to deliver on what it has promised and the process of disinvestment facs yet another setback.

This may seem ironical given Mr Shourie's fierce commitment to disinvestment but it is inevitable given the path of confrontation that Mr Shourie has chosen. Out of the 230 or so firms in the public sector, only a handful cannot be disinvested without parliamentary approval. Yet, it is these few high-profile, well-performing firms that Mr Shourie has chosen to focus his energies on to the neglect of others that cry out for immediate attention. Mr Shourie has erred not merely in his choice of firms but in his insistence on a particular method, strategic sale, as the norm for disinvestment.

It should be clear to the Prime Minister and his senior colleagues in government that disinvestment cannot proceed smoothly or expeditiously on this basis. Disinvestment needs to be part of a broader objective of securing better returns from the entire portfolio of 230 firms at the centre. The former chairman of the Disinvestment Commission, G V Ramakrishna, has argued that this objective would be best met if a single minister were to be placed in charge of disinvestment as well as the Department of Public Enterprises (DPE).

Mr Shourie himself is unsuited for this role given his antipathy to the very concept of PSUs. Finance minister Jaswant Singh, with his statesman like grasp of the art of the possible, would be admirably suited but he is much too valuable in his present capacity. Another worthy candidate is George Fernandes, a man who today can be counted upon to combine an awareness of the importance of the public sector with a sensitivity to the need for reforms, including privatisation.

Prime Minister Vajpayee's biggest asset as the leader of the ruling coalition is his unerring sense of what would be politically acceptable without compromising unduly on performance or results. Mr Shourie may be the darling of the media but his approach to disinvestment is not winning the BJP any friends. Mr Vajpayee must act boldly to replace Mr Shourie so that disinvestment can proceed with vigour.

October 9, 2003

Clearly Wrong on this one

Economic experts will find it easy to find fault with the UPA government's performance in its first year. The government has passed a Fiscal Responsibility Act but its two budgets have not delivered on deficit reduction. It has nothing to show on privatisation or disinvestment. It has not ushered in labour reforms. It has not been able to push through FDI in the financial sector in a big way. In short, it has not heeded expert advice on reforms.

The disregard for expert wisdom on reforms is by no means unique to the present government. In the NDA regime, Yashwant Sinha did show some reformist ardour - remember the budget that was given a perfect score of 10 by industry? He ended up creating a pervasive sullenness, not least because his reforms coincided with an adverse international environment. With elections on the horizon, he was eased out in favour of Jaswant Singh. It was left to Singh to rouse animal spirits in the economy, a task that he proceeded to accomplish with aplomb by opting, in his first budget, for one of the highest fiscal deficit to GDP ratios in the post-reform era.

So, after the initial burst of reforms, we notice an interesting phenomenon: expert wisdom does not find takers in the political class. Politicians, responding to popular sentiments in a democracy, think it necessary to soft-pedal reforms. The experts chide them for doing so. So who has got it wrong: the political class or the experts?

We can say now with a measure of confidence that in at least one respect, privatisation, the experts were off the mark. The expert believed that privatisation was central to an acceleration of the growth rate of the economy. They also saw it as part of the cure for the fiscal deficit. Because the private sector was more efficient than the public sector, handing over public sector enterprises (PSEs) to the private sector would lead to higher growth. The sooner PSEs were sold to private buyers, the better because, with each passing day, the values of deteriorating PSEs were sure to decline.

We know better now. There has been a convergence in performance between the public and private sectors in the post-reform period. This is most dramatically illustrated in the case of public sector banks (PSBs). From being outcastes in the stock market, these banks have gone on to become the darlings of investors on the back of huge improvements in performance. When exposed to competition, listed on the exchanges and given a clear message to go for profit, many PSEs have shown they can deliver commercial performance.

The contention that outright sale was better than gradual disinvestment would fetch the government more revenues has also turned out to be wrong. Had the PSBs been sold to private buyers at the commencement of financial sector reform, the government would have earned very little for the PSBs as a group were loss-making. Today, the government is sitting on a gold mine. Or, to put it more accurately, it always was sitting on a gold mine, only it did not seem to know it.

Whether in banks or in other PSEs, it would have been unwise to let government ownership decline below 51% too quickly because we are still far removed from a culture of managers being accountable to large institutional owners. Take away monitoring by government- however inefficient, however prone to abuse- and you have a monitoring vacuum. Privatisation in India necessarily means phased disinvestment- and indeed this has been the norm in most of the world, with the possible exception of Latin America.

The strategic sale route itself bristled with dangers, some of which are becoming apparent from the controversy of the sale of the Centaur hotels. Without competitive bidding, assets could be sold on the cheap. This would, of course, result in windfall profits from private owners colluding with politicians and would create a new version of crony capitalism. But, more importantly, the prospect of easy pickings would diminish the new owners' motivation to improve efficiency of the enterprises sold to them, supposedly the rationale for privatisation.

Whether the objective was to maximise revenue for government or to improve efficiency, gradual disinvestment was the way to go. Yet, the experts, with rare exceptions, rooted for strategic sale as the only 'genuine' form of privatisation. The electorate did not seem to buy this and the political class, sensing the popular mood, chose not to go down the privatisation path, preferring disinvestment instead. Politicians were acutely resistant to this one 'reform'- and they were right. That does raise the tantalising question: might the experts be wrong on other things as well?

May 19, 2005

A Framework for Disinvestment

The NDA government was fond of claiming that there was a 'consensus' in favour of privatisation, the outright sale of public sector undertakings (PSUs) to private parties. The BHEL episode shows that we do not have a consensus even on disinvestment, the sale of minority stakes to retail and institutional shareholders. That is because the case for disinvestment has not been properly made and a policy framework that would inspire confidence all round is missing.

Both privatisation and disinvestment have two objectives: raising resources for government and improving efficiency of PSUs. Why disinvestment and not privatisation? Disinvestment yields revenues for the government through successive sales of small tranches; privatisation through the sale of a large, controlling stake. There is no reason to suppose, *a priori*, that one method will produce more revenues than the other.

As for the impact on efficiency, neither the literature on privatisation nor the experience with disinvestment in India supports the premise that privatisation alone can deliver superior performance. One of the most cited studies on the impact of privatisation on efficiency, that of William Megginson and others (1994), related to samples of both partially privatised firms and fully privatised ones. Both samples showed strong performance improvement.

Another study (also involving Megginson) showed that disinvestment, not strategic sale, is the norm worldwide, with the former accounting for more than 60 per cent of the total proceeds from the two forms of privatisation. In India itself, as the writer's recently published book points out, there is a clear trend towards convergence in performance of PSUs and private sector firms in the post-reform period. (*Privatisation in India: Challenging economic orthodoxy,* Routledge)

Disinvestment thus has much to commend itself. It fosters the objective of improving firm performance. It helps raise resources that could be usefully invested in physical and social infrastructure and for turning around sick PSUs. It enhances PSUs' brand equity among the public at large. Over time, it would help move listed PSUs towards the Anglo-Saxon model of professional managers accountable to institutional and retail shareholders. As the Indian private sector itself is dominated by family-owned enterprises, listed PSUs stand a better chance of approximating this model than the private sector.

How do we make disinvestment acceptable to those who today oppose it? First, the government must address the suspicion that disinvestment is "creeping privatisation", that once the government shareholding moves close to 51 per cent, it may become easier for some future government to privatise these.

Last February, this column had proposed that the government identify potentially competitive PSUs and introduce legislation seeking parliamentary approval for any dilution in government holding in these below 51 per cent. A better alternative, perhaps, is to cover designated PSUs by an Act, similar to that for nationalised banks, that ensures that the "public sector character" of these PSUs would be retained, irrespective of government's shareholding in these.

Another concern is raised by the finance minister's reported statement that only the returns on the National Investment Fund, to which the proceeds of disinvestment would be credited, would be available for designated purposes, not the corpus itself. This means that even if the government were to raise Rs 100,000 crore over the next few years through disinvestment, only about Rs 10,000 crore would be available for social and other sectors. If that is so, where is the urgency to disinvest?

No, the government must ensure that the entire proceeds of

disinvestment are available for designated purposes. Moreover, any social sector expenditure made possible by the NIF must be over and above normal levels of expenditure in the central government's budget. Disinvestment must not be viewed as a substitute for resource mobilisation through the budget.

Thirdly, the government must seek a higher quota for retail investors where it is disinvesting its holdings in PSUs. This will ensure that the benefits of disinvestment accrue substantially to the Indian public, not to foreign institutional investors.

Disinvestment must not become a ruse for the eventual objective of handing over well-run PSUs to industrial houses. It must conduce to the goals of creating a vibrant, competitive public sector and providing resources for worthy purposes. That is best achieved through commitment to the framework we have outlined.

August 11, 2005

Wrong, Messrs Shourie and Sinha

By ruling out strategic sales or privatisation of profitable public sector undertakings (PSUs), finance minister P Chidambaram has created the right climate for disinvestment to continue. His statement in itself may not suffice to undo the damage created by the NDA government's espousal of strategic sales. Nevertheless, by stating that the strategic sale route is deficient in many ways, Mr Chidambaram has restored perspective to the debate on disinvestment.

For the first few years after it was initiated in 1992, disinvestment went off smoothly. Governments were clear that disinvestment was an instrument for public sector reform. This was also the philosophy of the Disinvestment Commission set up by the United Front government in 1996. There would be disinvestment and there would be strategic sales. But in not a single Navratna enterprise did the Commission recommend strategic sale.

The NDA government sought to overturn this philosophy. The objective now was to dismantle the public sector. Strategic sale or privatisation, not disinvestment, would be the norm. Having disposed of a clutch of hotels, Arun Shourie sought to take the axe to the petroleum companies. He failed only because he was pulled up short by the Supreme Court. All that Mr Shourie succeeded in achieving was discredit the process of disinvestment itself. That is why we are seeing such a fierce backlash now.

The arguments put forward to justify strategic sales are spurious. Strategic sales, it is said, give the government better realisations than disinvestment. Yashwant Sinha contends that price-earnings multiples were higher in the strategic sales route relative to multiples earned when minority stakes were sold. This argument is flawed on several counts:

- The initial round of disinvestment did not involve public offers to domestic and international investors. Shares were disinvested by being sold in "bundles" to government-owned financial institutions.
- It is inappropriate to compare price-earnings multiples for a company at two different points in time. The comparison must be adjusted for any change in the Sensex multiple over the period.
- The two methods are not directly comparable. In strategic sales, a large chunk is sold at one go. In disinvestment, shares are sold in several tranches. The price-earnings multiple in strategic sales must be compared with the average price-earnings multiple over all the tranches, not with the first tranche alone.

Strategic sales are not always efficient in the sense of maximising the seller's revenues. They are efficient only when a number of conditions are satisfied, a key condition being that there are a large number of bidders. Yet, Mr Shourie pushed or tried to push strategic sales through even when there was only one bidder. Mr Shourie says the process was "transparent". Maybe, but because a process is transparent, it does not follow it is efficient: the process can be transparently inefficient.

In general, strategic sales will give better realisations only on the assumption that there will be no improvement in firm performance over time under government ownership. Advocates of strategic sale in India have argued this is indeed true. Yet, the world over, it is disinvestment, not strategic sale, that has been the preferred mode of sale and it has been accompanied by improvement in performance.

In India, listed PSUs have shown significant improvement in performance consequent to disinvestment. In the period 1997-2005, the market capitalisation of 25 listed PSUs virtually doubled. In the nineties, those who favoured strategic sale were telling the government, "Please get rid of your equity while the going is good, otherwise you will lose value". Had the government done so, there is no way it would have obtained a premium that reflected the appreciation that has taken place.

There are many reasons why disinvestment works. Once a PSU is listed and there is an observable share price that reflects performance, management tends to focus better on commercial objectives. The fact that there are retail and institutional shareholders out there, whose interests cannot be disregarded, gives listed PSUs a measure of protection from unhealthy government interference. The presence of independent directors also contributes towards commercial orientation and autonomy.

Critics of the government say that in turning its back on strategic sale, the UPA government is giving in to the Left's ideological attachment to the public sector. They are wrong. It is their preference for strategic sale over disinvestment that is ideological in nature.

August 25, 2005

Booming Sensex, Smiling GOI

The government of India is a big gainer from the surge in the Sensex. The gains are sufficiently large to take care of the potential impact on the exchequer of the recommendations of the Sixth Pay Commission. In conceptual, if not in practical terms, the government is sitting pretty.

The market capitalisation of 29 listed PSUs has soared from Rs 2,34,000 crore on June 1, 2004, shortly after the UPA government took over, to Rs 10,90,000 crore on October 24, 2007. The current value of the government's shareholding in these PSUs works out to a colossal Rs 8,80,000 crore- enough to wipe out a quarter of the total public debt.

A mere 10% sale of its portfolio would fetch the government over Rs 88,000 crore. That is around 2% of GDP, more than adequate to cover the immediate impact of the Sixth Pay Commission award, which is expected to be of the order of 1% of GDP. It is the impact of any wage award in the initial two or three years that is lethal. Over time, as nominal GDP rises at around 13-14 per cent annually, the impact declines progressively as a proportion of GDP.

The government has stakes in banks as well. The market capitalisation of public sector banks (PSBs) has shot up in the same period from Rs 69,000 crore to Rs 232,000 crore. Government shareholding in these PSBs is today worth Rs 145,000 crore. (Some of the PSBs have been listed post 2004, hence do not figure in the comparison in market capitalisation between 2004 and 2007).

The fiscal deficit of both the centre and the states has been showing a downward trend. Total public debt too has begun to decline. These declines understate the extent of the improvement. If the fiscal deficit is interpreted as a change in net worth of government, the rise in the value of government shareholding in public sector companies also implies a decline in the fiscal deficit. Take this into account and the Sixth Pay Commission loses much of its terrors.

Some will say that this is all notional. The Left will not allow disinvestment in PSUs to proceed. The government cannot, under the present statutes, sell its equity in PSBs. Maybe there is an improvement in conceptual terms but this will not be reflected in cash flows.

First, let us acknowledge that there is something to thank the Left for. When the Left announced its opposition to disinvestment after the UPA government came to power, the Sensex tanked. Critics of the Left yelled highway murder. This is the end of the rise in the Sensex, they said. We know now it was only the beginning. The Sensex has risen nearly 300 per cent since June 1, 2004. PSU stocks have outperformed the Sensex, rising by 366 per cent in the same period. The market did not suffer because of the Left's opposition to disinvestment and the government itself has gained hugely.

Secondly, if the government is still around when the Pay Commission recommendations arrive, it can work out a deal with the unions and the Left: let us go with a generous award by all means but please allow disinvestment to proceed at least in PSUs where the government's shareholding is well above 51 per cent.

The government could present the unions with two versions of a wage increase, one without disinvestment and an improved one, subject to disinvestment. Further, it could allay fears of any decline in government shareholding below 51 per cent by offering to enact legislation that will not permit any such decline without approval by a parliamentary majority.

There is a lesson in humility for firebrand reformers in the phenomenal increase in the market capitalisation of PSUs and PSBs. The reforms brigade could not have imagined that disinvestment, the gradual sale of government equity, could produce such results. They believed that disinvestment was a disaster as the value of PSUs and PSBs would only erode with time. The best way for government to maximise its revenues was to go for strategic sale, the transfer of a controlling stake to private companies.

These assertions have turned out to be completely wrong. The writer was almost alone in arguing that disinvestment, far from being a political compromise in India, had, in fact, been the dominant mode of privatisation worldwide and that it had produced splendid results. Strategic sale was rarer and happened more in economies with underdeveloped capital markets.

On a broader note, the evolution of the Indian economy has shown that there is little room for certitudes of any kind and that a scrupulous regard for the democratic process and respect for minority viewpoints on contentious issues are in order. In the case of disinvestment, what was interpreted as cussedness on the part of the Left has worked to the benefit of government. A point worth remembering in the heated debate on the Indo-US nuclear deal.

November 1, 2007

Why Air India is in Trouble

Air India, the brand that today encompasses both the erstwhile Air India and Indian Airlines, is in serious trouble. The National Aviation Company of India (NACIL), formed by the merger of the two airlines, ran up losses of Rs 2200 crore in 2007-08. Losses for 2008-09 estimated at over Rs 5000 crore. In 2009-10, losses could exceed Rs 12,000 crore. How did the airline get into such a mess?

Parliament's *Committee on Public Undertakings* (COPU) has come up with a report that seeks to identify the underlying causes. The report does not put its finger on why Air India has run up huge losses. But it has posed the right questions and provides information that helps zero in on the causes of the problems at Air India today.

It is useful to begin by listing some perceived causes of Air India's losses and examining how far these are valid:

1. **Public ownership is the problem:** Governments just can't run commercial enterprises. There is no way that Air India and Indian Airlines could have survived in the face of greater competition.

There is a problem with this story. Several public sector enterprises (PSEs) have successfully weathered greater competition post-liberalisation and are doing better than before. In the period since 2001, Air India made a profit every year until 2006-07. Indian Airlines made a profit in three out of those six years.

Losses in aviation are not unique to the Indian public sector. Private airlines in India too have been in the red. The airline industry is notoriously prone to losses. Worldwide, the International Air Transport Association estimated losses at $17 bn in 2008, $11 bn in 2009 and $ 3bn in 2010.

2. **Air India suffers from a bloated work force typical of the public sector:** Air India performs in-house a wide range of functions that other airlines outsource. Still, Air India's workforce per aircraft of 214 compares favourably with that of several other airlines: Malaysian Airlines (230), Virgin Atlantic (282), KLM (220), etc. Wages account for just 16% of total costs, so the scope for reducing losses through wage or employee reductions is quite small.
3. **The failed merger is responsible for non-performance and losses:** There is little doubt that the merger of the two airlines, done in 2006-07, has turned out to be a nightmare. But it is hard to ascribe the mounting losses to the merger per se. The synergies expected from the merger were fairly modest in the first place: around Rs 900 crore. Of these, Rs 500 crore was realised in the first year itself. The failure of the merger cannot explain losses of over Rs 5000 crore in 2008-09 and the even higher losses projected for 2009-10. Merger makes it more difficult for Air India to respond to the situation it is in, it is not the cause of the situation.

Thus, none of the perceived causes can explain the mess Air India is in today. The report provides useful clues. Air India's problems, it turns out, arise from two errors, one strategic and the other structural.

In 2007-08, one-third of the increase in losses was on account of increased interest and depreciation charges. Increase in wage costs contributed a little less than a third. In 2008-09, estimates indicate that half the increase in losses will be on account of increase in interest and depreciation.

It is clear that the root cause of the present situation is the massive fleet expansion plan initiated by the two airlines prior to merger. Was such an expansion necessary? Officials have justified it on two grounds. Both the airlines needed to replace their aged fleet. They also needed to augment their fleet in order to maintain market share given that the market was expected to grow faster than in the past.

The market has not grown as fast as expected. As a result, NACIL is stuck with planes with low utilisation and is having to lease out aircraft. In the case of Air India, 46% of addition to fleet was towards augmenting capacity; at Indian Airlines, the figure was 30%. (The rest was towards creating new capacity).

At least, this component was avoidable. In a market that is expected to grow faster than in the past, it is not necessary to maintain market share. Several PSEs have lost market share over the past decade but profit growth has been better than ever thanks to an exploding market. The focus on market share is often a source of value destruction. In the case of Air India, it appears to have been a major strategic error.

The second cause of Air India's problems is structural. The airline industry is inherently problem-ridden because it combines high capital intensity with volatility in revenues. Leverage in this business is bound to be high but it must be kept within reasonable limits. Air India embarked on a fleet acquisition plan costing Rs 44,000 crore on a paid up capital of Rs 145 crore. This was a recipe for disaster.

Additions to fleet should have been more gradual and should have been governed by the need to keep leverage within limits. There is a tested formula that the government has followed in exposing PSEs to greater competition: recapitalise and restructure; go public and list; revamp governance. Regrettably, this sequence was not followed in the case of Air India and Indian Airlines. The government should have strengthened their equity base even as it deregulated the airline sector.

But that is in the past. What is to be done now? The government has reconstituted the board. It has brought in a foreigner as chief operating officer. Neither will dissolve the structural problem. The government will have to infuse substantial equity. It may try to induct a strategic partner into some of Air India's subsidiaries and sell some property. Leasing out excess capacity can, perhaps, be expedited under an empowered committee of the Board.

Pushing ahead with the merger will only further sap the energies of the company. It is best to put the merger on hold and settle for a virtual merger for now. As the report suggests, NACIL may be made a holding company with Air India and Indian Airlines operating separately under its aegis.

April 15, 2010

PART-II

INDIAN BANKING

5

Banking Sector Reforms

Is it Time to Open up to Foreign Banks?

In 2005, the RBI announced a roadmap for the presence of foreign banks in India. The policy stated that foreign bank expansion in India would proceed in two phases. In Phase I, the RBI promised to go beyond the existing commitment of 12 new branches for foreign banks in a year. This wasn't giving away a great deal in light of the pace of expansion of branches of the new private banks.

In Phase I acquisition of private banks would be permitted only in private sector banks identified for restructuring and that too in a phased manner. In general, the RBI has not favoured a foreign bank having a stake of more than 5 per cent in a private bank, although there are exceptions such as Ing Vysya Bank.

In Phase II, which was to commence in April 2009, foreign banks could contemplate mergers and acquisitions with private banks subject to a ceiling of 74 per cent. Foreign banks subsidiaries that had completed a prescribed minimum period of operation would be allowed to list and dilute their stakes so that at least 26 per cent of the equity was held by resident Indians. But, these actions in Phase II would happen after "reviewing the experience with Phase I"- in other words, the RBI stopped short of making explicit commitments about Phase II.

India has been under pressure from the advanced economies to speed up the opening of its financial sector for quite some time now. The RBI policy had the effect of putting the brakes on their ambitions at the very least until 2009. The RBI's intention was to give time for Indian banks, especially public sector banks, to get their acts together before exposing them to the full blast of foreign competition. Well, 2009 isn't far away. So, it is fair to ask: is it time now to open up to foreign banks?

This question can be broken up into two parts. One, is a larger foreign bank presence in the country desirable or, to put it differently, what are the benefits and costs that go with such a presence? Two, assuming that we do not want foreign banks to overrun the sector and that some Indian ownership is desirable, how well prepared are Indian banks to cope with foreign competition? In this article, I will confine myself to the first question; the second I will reserve for a later column.

The World Bank's Global Development Finance (GDF, 2008) has a chapter that summarises some of the work on the role of international banks. The first thing to note is that, among developing economies, India falls in the category of economies in which the share of banking assets held by foreign banks with majority ownership is on the lower side- under 10% in 2006. India has for company China, Vietnam, South Africa, Thailand, Philippines and even Turkey, among others.

A possible inference is that there is considerable scope for an increase in foreign bank presence in India. However, India's experience in the recent past and the experiences of China and Vietnam do suggest that a high foreign bank presence is by no means a pre-condition for rapid economic growth.

Secondly, as the GDF report notes, a higher foreign bank presence is more common in Central Asia, sub-Saharan Africa and Latin America than in East Asia, South Asia, the Middle East and North Africa. Elsewhere, the report indicates why this is so.

In many of the countries that have a high foreign bank presence, this was a sequel to a banking crisis. Banks were often nationalized after a crisis, then privatised through sale to foreign banks as neither the state nor the domestic private sector had the capital to sustain these banks. Even in East Asia, which still has a lower foreign bank presence than other regions, it was only after the 1997 crisis and its devastating impact on the banking sector that foreign banks enhanced their presence.

Elsewhere, one finds other contextual reasons for foreign bank entry. In Central and Eastern Europe, an opening up to foreign banks has been related to accession of these economies to the

European Union. Where, one wonders, are the economies with relatively stable banking systems that have permitted large foreign bank ownership without duress of some sort?

A third fact, one that is omitted in the report, is that foreign bank ownership in the higher income countries is surprisingly low-it did not amount to more than 10 per cent of assets according to the World Bank's earlier comprehensive work on banking sector liberalisation, Finance and Growth.

Taking all these facts into account, it makes little sense to compare foreign bank presence in India with that in other economies and argue that we need to catch up with others. We have not had the kind of banking instability that others have gone through, we have seen an improvement in efficiency on a variety of parameters and our banking system does not lack access to capital required for further expansion.

Those who argue in favour of a faster opening up to foreign banks must show that such an opening up better conduces to national objectives-financial deepening, improved efficiency, financial inclusion and the pursuit of larger national objectives such as promoting agriculture as well as SMEs.

The GDF report contends that indeed many of these benefits are there. It highlights three principal benefits: improved access to financial services; improved efficiency of domestic financial systems; and easing of domestic credit constraints on manufacturing firms. However, these benefits are specific to certain contexts. One needs to evaluate whether in the Indian context, these benefits will apply and the contentions made in the GDF report will hold.

Take the first claimed benefit, improved access to financial services. The report cites several examples. In the Czech Republic, foreign banks were the first to offer ATM and remote banking facilities. In other economies, they have offered sophisticated products such as derivatives. Elsewhere, they have stimulated the development of bond markets.

Are these priorities at all in the Indian market? We have not only a good network of ATMs but one of the largest network of branches. When we talk of access to financial services, we mean plain vanilla deposits and loans, not sophisticated products. One has no difficulty accepting that foreign banks will spur access to derivatives.

Will they be as enthusiastic about offering basic banking services to large numbers of people? It does appear that what the GDF report has in mind when it talks of "access" is not quite what we mean when we talk of "financial inclusion".

Turn now to the second claimed benefit, improved efficiency. The theoretical argument is straightforward: foreign banks bring in serious competition for domestic players, they bring with them superior risk management practices and deeper pockets and all this should result in higher efficiency in the banking system.

Take a closer look at the efficiency argument, however, and you begin to spot a number of holes. For one thing, the improvement in efficiency seen in many economies consequent to the entry of foreign banks may merely reflect the fact that the banking system was in the throes of a crisis before they came in. The improvement may be ascribed largely to the injection of capital into moribund banking systems.

We need evidence that in a system that has attained a reasonable level of efficiency and stability, such as the Indian banking system, ceding a large presence to foreign banks will confer large benefits. This sort of evidence is hard to come by if only because, as mentioned earlier, an enlarged foreign bank presence is a sequel to inefficiency and failure in a banking system.

Whatever limited evidence we have is to the contrary. Where banking systems are strong and stable, as in Chile prior to foreign banks' entry, the contribution of foreign banks to efficiency tends to be small. This is also true of systems where financial liberalisation has ushered in competition and spreads have declined.

We also need to distinguish between improvement in efficiency at the firm level and improvement at the sectoral level. Can foreign banks improve return on assets at a given public sector bank? Most certainly. It's not hard to see what this will take: eliminate unprofitable branches that exist mainly for reasons of inclusion; downsize staff; exit a number of small, relatively unprofitable relationships at the retail as well as corporate level; focus on wealth management products; and make the most of advantages in cross-border transactions.

This will produce a more profitable bank. Will it produce a more efficient banking sector, assuming again that we would want a mix of foreign and domestic banks? This is the issue. The danger is that foreign banks will "cherry-pick" the best relationships in the system leaving the domestic banks enfeebled. We may end up having successful foreign banks and a vulnerable banking sector.

There may also be different effects on efficiency in the banking sector depending on whether foreign banks are entering through the greenfield route- and thus enhancing competition- or whether they are entering by acquiring large banks, which could have the effect of reducing competition.

Lastly, ever increasing levels of efficiency cannot be the sole objective for the banking sector. We need a level of efficiency that is consistent with other objectives- financial inclusion, development of agriculture and, not least, financial stability. Is it conceivable that we could have achieved the 150 per cent increase in agricultural credit that we have witnessed in 2004-07 with a foreign bank-dominated system? As for financial stability, we have seen how the relentless pursuit of so-called efficiency has led to grave crises in international markets of the sort we are witnessing now.

Finally, the third significant benefit claimed for foreign banks, greater access to credit for domestic firms. Presumably, this happens for two reasons: a superior ability to assess risk; and foreign banks' ability to access funds outside the domestic market. Granting the first advantage, the second is relevant only where domestic savings are inadequate in relation to credit requirements.

This is not so in India where investment is overwhelmingly financed by domestic savings. For a variety of reasons, the commercial credit/GDP ratio in India was low by international standards- until a few years ago, it hovered around 30 per cent . But the rapid rate of credit growth has pushed the ratio to a more respectable level-over 50 per cent of GDP. Commercial credit has grown at over 30 per cent in recent years, so it cannot be contended that, at the aggregate level, there is a credit constraint although particular firms, such as SMEs, may still have problems accessing adequate credit. In such a situation, again the case for a rapid opening up to foreign banks is rendered weak.

We must also reckon with the downside to foreign banks entering in a big way. One, as the GDF report points out, a larger foreign bank presence could lead to more rapid transmission of shocks from the international financial system, such as the ones we have seen in the sub-prime crisis in the US.

Foreign banks may react to erosion of capital in their parent economies by cutting down on balance sheet size. They may face liquidity pressures because of adverse conditions in inter-bank markets. They may also tighten credit standards in the face of a global economic slowdown. All these could impact adversely on the host country. Foreign banks' response to domestic crises could also present problems- in the Argentine crisis of 2001, as many as 10 foreign banks chose to exit the country.

A second problem is that a large foreign bank presence may weaken monetary policy transmission because foreign banks have access to a large pool of funds beyond the control of the monetary authority. The GDF report cites evidence that a higher foreign bank presence reduces the pass-through from money-market rates to lending rates.

Thirdly, foreign banks pose significant challenges to regulation. There is an asymmetry that lies at the heart of foreign bank operations in a host country: many of the crucial economy-related and risk-related decisions are taken abroad while the consequences are felt by the host country. There are also problems in monitoring the parent institution located abroad and that is operating a branch or a subsidiary in a host country. The pace of foreign bank expansion in a country has to be consistent with regulatory capacity.

Where does all this leave us in respect of policy post-2009? Foreign banks bring with them innovation, they raise the level of competition and they provide access to cross-border services of a scope and quality that Indian banks cannot match. These are welcome. But these can be available to the Indian banking system without a dominant foreign bank presence.

The literature suggests that the contribution of foreign banks to systemic efficiency and stability in a context such as ours cannot be as high as in systems that had been devastated by bank failures. We must also accept that the level of preparedness of Indian banks is not of the order that was expected when the RBI unveiled its roadmap in 2005. It follows that the calibrated approach to foreign bank expansion that has served us well thus far must continue post 2009.

July 12, 2008 (EPW)

Reforming the Banking Sector

Introduction

The Committee on Mumbai as International Financial Centre submitted its report last year. The committee had been given a fairly limited remit, namely, the development of bond, currency and derivatives markets. It proceeded instead to enlarge the scope of its work to a point where virtually no important aspect of the economy was left untouched. The outcome is that, in attempting to implement its recommendations, policy-makers would not know where to begin.

It is to the credit of the Raghuram Rajan Committee that it is more focused in its approach. It also shows a keen awareness in various places of what is feasible in political and even economic terms. But it is in the nature of any Committee tasked with reviewing a system to propose sweeping changes; not to do so would give the impression that the Committee was bereft of ideas or did not take its job seriously.

The Rajan Committee is no exception. One cannot resist the feeling that many of its proposals have been made because they are theoretically appealing. One lacks the conviction that the facts on the ground warrant such proposals. This article will confine itself to proposals related to banking sector reform and contained in the chapter titled, "Leveling the playing field". It does not address issues related to the regulatory architecture, the regulatory environment and the conduct and performance of the regulator, which are addressed in separate chapters.

State of the banking sector

It is best to begin with the observed facts about the Indian banking system. What prescription is required depends on the condition of the patient. If there is a trend towards improvement, we are doing something right. If there is worsening, we must be doing something wrong and we need to drastically change the medicine.

The committee notes that growth in Indian banking has come without "significant instability". This is an understatement in respect of the post-reform period- one has to only look at well documented studies on economies that have gone through bank deregulation. If we are an outlier when it comes to the degree of government ownership in banking, as the committee notes elsewhere, we are also an outlier when it comes to banking stability. The committee also notes that in terms of return on assets, the Indian banking system is among the better performers in the world.

What are some of the committee's concerns and how valid are these? One, India's banking system is relatively underdeveloped going by the ratio of commercial loans to GDP. This ratio is over 50 per cent at the moment. It is true the ratio is lower than some other developing countries (although it is higher than that of Brazil with which India is often grouped). The key question is: what is the present trend? The ratio has been rising rapidly thanks to loan growth of 30 per cent in recent years and it will continue to do given projected loan growth of 20-25 per cent. It is only a matter of time before we catch up.

Two, Indian banks are small relative to some banks in other economies- China, for example. So what? China's banks do not compare with ours in profitability. As the committee itself notes, the size of banks is not disproportionate to those of Indian companies. As the Indian economy grows and as corporates grow, so will Indian banks. Some will try to leapfrog the process through mergers.

True, to the extent that banks lack scale, they will miss out on some large loan requirements of the top corporates. But, in general, banks must accept that the top corporates will not need them as they can access capital markets. Isn't that what disintermediation is all about? Banks must reinvent themselves so that they can make a viable market out of the middle and low corporates. Viewed thus, the issue for Indian banks is not so much scale as the ability to judge and price credit risk.

Three, India's banking market is extremely competitive if we look at the share of the top three banks in total assets. The committee, however, says that if we view public sector banks (PSBs) as one group, then one type of owner has 70 per cent of all assets. If the suggestion is that there is lack of competition, that is incorrect. PSBs are competing with each other, they do not behave as they are all part of one happy family.

Four, the report states that India's intermediation costs are high going by the spread- the difference between lending and borrowing rates of bank- of over 5 per cent. This spread, the report notes, are offset by priority sector and SLR requirements. It could also be that the spread is warranted by the riskiness of certain types of credit. It could be warranted by higher intermediation costs arising from the huge network of branches and the numbers of people involved.

The committee believes that the burden of a high spread in banking falls on the Indian saver. The presumption here is that if some of the social obligations were to be removed, the benefits would accrue to savers and not to shareholders. This may not be true. In the post-reform period, yields on loans have fallen but yields on deposits have fallen even more, resulting in a net benefit to bank shareholders, not to savers.

An important reason for the banking system's enjoying a high spread is the overwhelming preference among savers for bank deposits. It is only when there is a big flight of savings to other savings instruments that banks will start offering higher returns to savers. So, merely removing social obligations for banks may not help savers- it could simply mean fatter profits for banks on top of the very high returns they enjoy today.

Five, the committee points to the low usage of technology to reduce transaction costs in India- for instance, ATMs per million of population is lower in India than elsewhere. But this overlooks two aspects of the use of such technologies. First, banks elsewhere and also the newer banks in India have opted for such technologies as a way to avoid the bigger investment in branches. However, where a huge branch network has been created at historical cost, as in India, the compulsion to reach out through ATMs and other technologies is commensurately lower. In branch coverage, India ranks at the top along with the US.

Secondly, there has been a sea-change in banks' own perception of the importance of these technologies. Whereas some years ago, ATMs or online banking were seen as a substitute for branches, today they are seen as complements to brick and mortar. Branches are essential for customer acquisition; ATMs and the rest are essential for customer retention. Coverage of ATMs and other channels in India is increasing. But the low coverage of new technologies is not a weakness because the Indian banking system has inherent strengths in the branch network created after bank nationalization.

Six, the committee makes too much of PSBs' decline in market from over 80 per cent to 72 per cent of assets and the smaller rate of growth of their balance sheets relative to private banks. Partly this reflects the lower base from which private banks started off. The critical variables are growth in commercial credit and in profits or earnings. In respect of these variables, PSBs never had it so good.

It is also not appropriate to compare PSBs with other groups on profit per employee, as the committee has done. These figures will necessarily be lower for PSBs because they use a people-intensive business model. Private banks may incur huge costs on other elements crucial to their business model. It is the overall cost to income ratio and total factor productivity that must be compared if we are to arrive at meaningful conclusions.

Lastly, the report points out how the comparable levels of profitability of PSBs and new private banks mask fundamental differences about the sources of profit. The latter have superior organisational capabilities (one is not as sure about sales and distribution channels or risk management, dimensions on which the committee rates them superior) and are better placed to tap the affluent segments. This is indeed true.

PSBs lag behind new private banks and foreign banks in wealth management and fee income generally. Private banks do a much better job of catering to affluent customers than PSBs. These differences show up in higher market valuations for new private banks. (It is worth pointing out, however, that SBI does not suffer much in comparison.)

But how big a problem is this? It could well be that, over time, we see a clear segmentation among banks- PSBs do "mass banking" while private banks cater to a more select clientele. Each could be viable in itself. For PSBs, the challenge may well be to make a commercial success of the mass market instead of trying to mimic their counterparts in the private sector.

The report highlights how PSBs are big losers from the 'grand bargain' inflicted on them, having to incur various social obligations in exchange for certain benefits that go with public ownership. Doing away with these would impose a cost, namely, higher rates on savings deposits due to deregulation. There would be benefits if SLR and priority sector obligations were dispensed with. The report cites a McKinsey estimate of the net benefit- about 20-30% of net operating profit- or, say, 15-20% of net profit.

The computation deserves careful scrutiny. It is well known that not all of the priority sector requirement constitutes a burden. Some of it, such as housing loans up to a certain value and vehicle loans in rural areas, are indeed commercially attractive and have been included in the priority sector computation only to make it easier for banks to meet the 40 per cent target. (This may explain why private banks have of late exceeded the overall priority target while falling short in respect of agriculture and having low exposure to SSIs). So, if the benefit to banks is computed on the assumption that all of the 40 per cent is at present at non-commercial rates, we would have an over-estimate.

On SLR too, it must not be presumed that all of the mandated 25 per cent is a burden. There have been periods when banks have, on their own, invested way beyond the 25 per cent limit- at one point, such investment was over 40 per cent. In light of the sub-prime crisis, Indian banks' holding a reasonably high proportion of liquid, government securities does appear as a strength, just as the low levels of such securities with banks abroad comes as something of a shock.

If we accept that an SLR requirement is not such a bad thing- and that it is bound to go down over time- the presumed benefits of liberating banks from this requirement would not be large. In other words, the addition to net profit of releasing PSBs from the 'grand bargain', correctly computed, could be more of the order of 5-10 per cent. Given their current profitability, this is not such a big deal. Or, to put it differently, social obligations may not constitute such a crushing burden.

Proposals for Reform

The intention in making this dissection of the analysis of the Indian banking sector leading up to the committee's prescriptions for leveling the playing field is to show that the concerns that underlie the committee's reform proposals are neither as material nor as urgent as the report makes them out to be.

Sure, there are umpteen things we could do by way of improving the Indian banking system. But both the nature of the improvements and the pace of change will be governed by our assessment of where things stand today. The committee looks at the glass and finds it half empty; some of us prefer to think it is half full.

Let us now turn to the committee's proposals for reform of

PSBs. The committee considered and rejected the option of privatisation although the majority on the committee saw little reason for continued government ownership of banks. Privatisation of all of the PSBs was not favoured because it was not considered a realistic option in the present environment.

However, the committee favours selling some of the smaller, underperforming PSBs and seeing the results. This sounds like a pragmatic compromise. But the present statutes do not permit sale of government's equity in PSBs, so these would have to be amended. An amendment would, however, open up the possibility of such a sale in PSBs across the board and would, therefore, be stoutly opposed by unions as well as some political parties. It does appear that selective privatisation may be difficult.

The committee is right in saying that whole-hogging privatisation poses a host of problems, quite apart from not being favoured by public sentiment. Selling large PSBs to private banks would raise issues of concentration. Selling them to large industrial houses would revive the ghost of related-party transactions. Selling to foreign banks is politically unacceptable, as the committee points out, but there are regulatory concerns as well. PSBs could be sold through a public offer as in the case of British privatisation but this requires a greater degree of confidence in corporate governance than obtains at present.

The practical course, then, is to effect improvements in governance in PSBs. The committee makes a number of proposals. Let us take up the key proposals.

Strengthening of Bank Boards

The committee points to dissatisfaction about government nominees who often lack knowledge of business or banking. It would like all directors to be appointed by an independent Selection Board. It is hard to see how any government will forgo the right to appoint its nominees- in private companies, all 'independent' directors are selected by the promoters or management. The best we can do is ensure a minimum of competence in government nominees as well. We can do this by having the regulator prescribe 'fit and proper' criteria for all directors on a board, be they government nominees or independent directors.

There is already an Appointments Committee, headed by the RBI Governor, which selects top management of banks. Its scope could be extended to include appointment of independent directors. A suitable composition for the Appointments Committee can also be prescribed. It could include, say, a nominee of the Chief Justice of India, a distinguished public figure and so on. There could be 'fit and proper' criteria for the non-official members of the Appointments Committee as well.

The committee would like to see representatives of non-government shareholders as well on bank boards. There is already a provision for such nominees but, as the committee notes, this only leads to directors proposed by management being voted in by shareholders. Widely dispersed ordinary shareholders, perhaps, cannot be expected to organize themselves to select their nominees. A better alternative would be for financial institutions, domestic and foreign, to take the lead in proposing non-government nominees. In all listed companies, public sector or private sector, we need to get financial institutions to bring in their nominees.

The committee echoes the familiar clamour for 'autonomy' of PSU boards, chiefly in relation to appointment and termination of CEOs. Since this has been demanded and not conceded for at least two decades now, it is hard to see the situation changing. It cannot be that government is ultimately responsible for a PSU but does not have the right to appoint top management.

We do not yet have a culture of governance strong enough to ensure accountability of professionally-managed firms - and the experience with some of the best known financial institutions in the sub-prime crisis does little to enhance confidence. The best we can ask for, under the circumstances, is that top management appointments not be influenced by political considerations. The strengthening of the Appointments Committee along the lines suggested above is all we can hope for.

Delinking Banks from Government

The proposal to delink PSBs from government and from oversight by the CVC, parliament also does not appear realistic. Having government indirectly own PSBs through holding companies or through other government-owned financial institutions or reducing government stake to below 50% to exempt them from PSU norms will not take us far either. Government is unlikely in any of these situations to cede full authority to an independent board.

The problem with PSBs is not so much that government appoints top management. PSBs are different from other PSUs in that the appointment of top management has been reduced to a game of musical chairs with managers jumping from one bank to another at the ED and CMD levels. This has made nonsense of top management accountability and succession planning. We do not have this syndrome in oil, power or insurance companies- somebody from within the organisation has a reasonable chance of getting the top job. It is for the Appointments Committee to rectify this anomaly which is peculiar to the banking sector.

HRD should be the number one priority for PSBs today and compensation, to which the report draws attention, is one of many HRD issues that must be tackled. There is no question that pay in the public sector needs to be improved. Whether this can include a large variable component, as the committee recommends, is doubtful. In the very nature of things, large disparities and performance-linked pay can prove disruptive of the public sector culture.

Bank Consolidation

On consolidation, the report recognises the constraints, mentioned earlier, on privatisation of PSBs and it also wisely counsels against forced mergers amongst PSBs. The suggestion that the focus of consolidation must be on small, regional, unprofitable banks is appropriate as also the suggestion that this process may have to be prodded along by the authorities.

Reducing Barriers to Competition

The committee makes a number of proposals on reducing barriers to competition. It wants abolition of branch and ATM licensing. It argues that licensing is primarily an instrument for forcing banks into under-banked areas and that this can be easily dealt with by instituting a service norm- say, for every x branches opened in urban areas, y branches must be opened in semi-urban or rural areas. These service obligations could even become tradeable like priority sector norms.

There is room for disagreement on these proposals. Getting banks into under-banked areas is an important objective in bank licensing but it is not the only objective. The RBI uses the power to license banks as a means of disciplining banks and securing compliance on various counts. The annual financial inspection report and the CAMELS rating have a bearing on the RBI's decision on granting branch licenses. Take away this power and you weaken the RBI's ability to discipline- everybody knows financial penalties meaning little.

Secondly, what happens if service provisions are not complied with? Should the banks in question be asked to close down some of their urban branches? What if banks favour only certain under-banked areas and ignore others? Again, trading of service provisions presumes that there is an excess supply of these on account of the efforts of certain financial institutions. But, if the system collectively undershoots in relation to a desired target, trading of service provisions will not contribute to enhancement of the quantum of services; it will only lead to appropriate subsidies for those who over-perform.

The proposal to license small banks by reducing the present entry capital requirement of Rs 300 crore is also not persuasive. It is all very well to say that alternative stringent criteria, such as promoters' backgrounds can be looked at but the supervisory headaches at the licensing as well as monitoring stages will simply multiply.

We already have several small players that are not viable, that collectively pose systemic risk and for which consolidation is required. Finally, the idea of holding company structures for banks is unexceptionable and the report makes several useful suggestions in respect of operationalising this concept.

Conclusion

What do the concerns of the Rajan committee and its proposals add up to? The committee highlights several concerns - about financial deepening, inadequate competition, lack of scale, high spreads in Indian banking, the low usage of new technologies, the decline in market share of PSBs and the inability of PSBs to make the most of fee income opportunities. These concerns, we have seen, are either valid only up to a point or are misplaced when viewed against the totality of the Indian banking situation.

The committee sees banks, especially, PSBs, as hobbled by the 'grand bargain' that involves getting some privileges in return for bearing certain social obligations and would like to see this bargain unraveled. However, this bargain need not be such a big deal as SLR requirements are lowered over time and as the priority sector, correctly defined, comes to constitute a low proportion of assets.

The committee also sees the absence of a level playing field as a big issue. A level playing field can mean different things. One, ensuring that financial institutions must be placed on the same footing. There are limits to this, as the committee itself acknowledges. Banks will necessarily be treated differently in some crucial respects from other financial institutions.

Two, it can mean that institutions must be "ownership neutral". This, in effect, means only private players should exist and that is the committee's preference. This is a moot point. The Indian experience suggests that there is merit in ownership diversity because this makes for heterogeneity in business models. Three, a level playing field could mean that regulation should be "ownership neutral". This is appropriate at least where PSBs and private banks are concerned and on this count, the Indian system measures up well.

Whatever its preferences on "ownership neutrality", the committee accepts a large public sector presence in the near future as a given and it rightly points that the focuses must be on improved governance at PSBs. This is in line with current thinking in government and the RBI.

The committee believes that better governance requires that government not appoint its directors on PSB boards and that PSBs be delinked from government. Neither appears feasible and they may not even be desirable. We argue that the preferable course is to lay down "fit and proper" criteria for all directors, be they independent directors or government appointees. Further, governance at PSBs must focus on HRD, including the issue of succession planning and bringing new skills into these banks.

The committee wants greater freedom for private banks. This is happening but abolition of branch and ATM licensing does not seem a realistic option. We also need greater freedom for foreign banks but here the pace of liberalisation must necessarily be governed by considerations of regulatory capacity, reciprocity and the stability of the banking sector.

In sum, Indian banking is evolving in the right direction. There is much to be done but there is a strong case for proceeding through incremental, not sweeping, changes.

Aug 9, 2008 (EPW)

New Private Banks: Don't Say 'Yes' if You Want to Say 'no'

In August 2010, the RBI issued a discussion paper on licensing of new private banks. It released its draft guidelines on the subject last month. This does not mean that a fresh set of entrants is around the corner.

The RBI will accept comments and suggestions on the draft guidelines until October 31, 2011. It will issue the final guidelines only after certain "vital amendments" to the Banking Regulation Act are carried out. These are: removal of restriction of voting rights and concurrently empowering RBI to approve acquisition of shares and/ or voting rights of 5% or more in a bank to persons who are 'fit and proper'; empowering RBI to supersede the Board of Directors of a bank so as to protect depositors' interest; and facilitating consolidated supervision. How long these amendments will take to be passed by parliament is anybody's guess.

Once the amendments are passed and the RBI issues its final guidelines, it will be open to applications. The applications will be scrutinised by a High Level Advisory Committee to be constituted for the purpose. The Committee will comprise eminent personalities with experience in banking, financial sector and other relevant areas. The Committee will be free to devise its own procedures for processing applications and will make recommendations on applications to the RBI. However, the decision on granting a license will be the RBI's.

It does appear that the grant of licenses to new private players is at least two to three years away from now. The RBI is in no hurry. It could well be that the issue of draft guidelines is a concession to those seeking a fresh burst of "reforms" and is intended to show that the finance minister's promise of new licenses, made in his budget speech in February 2010, is being met.

The RBI's reluctance to rush into new private licenses is entirely understandable, given that the global economic environment has turned turbulent and is unlikely to return to normal in the near future. Stability in banking has proved a bulwark against any undue contamination of the Indian economy on account of the global economic crisis of 2007; it would be unwise to do anything to disrupt this stability.

In devising guidelines, it would have been advisable for the RBI to spell out the principal objective in licensing a new set of private banks. (It is also not clear why only private players should be licensed, that is, potential public sector entrants such as LIC or the Rural Electrification Corporation should be kept out). Once that is done, key elements of the policy for licensing will automatically fall into place. Is the principal objective greater competition or is it financial inclusion? If the former, then it would be alright to subject new banks to the same branch licensing norms as the existing ones; if the latter, then the new banks must be told to focus to a greater extent on unbanked centres.

Unfortunately, the RBI has not thought it necessary to make the case for new entrants. The RBI's draft guidelines quote the finance minister on the subject:

We need to ensure that the banking system grows in size and sophistication to meet the needs of a modern economy. Besides, there is a need to extend the geographic coverage of banks and improve access to banking services.

The above paragraph doesn't tell us much. Growth in size and sophistication can happen with the existing players, as it has over the past decade or so. If, however, the intention is to extend geographic coverage of and improve access to banking, that is, financial inclusion, then the guidelines for new banks should have fully reflected this priority.

The guidelines do not indicate the latter. They state that the newly licensed banks "shall open at least 25 per cent of its branches in unbanked rural centres (population up to 9,999 as per 2001 census) to avoid over concentration of their branches in metropolitan areas and cities which are already having adequate banking presence." Since existing banks are also subject to this stipulation, the new licenses will not impose any special requirement of inclusion on the banks concerned.

If financial inclusion were indeed the priority and if we were looking for new banks to provide a technological breakthrough in the area of inclusion, then it would have been appropriate to mandate stiffer requirements of inclusion. The RBI has chosen not to go down this route. One must infer that the RBI believes that greater competition even in urban and semi-urban areas is the need of the hour. If that is indeed what the RBI believes, it should have argued its position by providing the appropriate measures of competition in Indian banking and comparisons with other banking systems.

One of the important questions in the issue of new licenses is whether corporate houses should be allowed into banking. A close reading of the draft guidelines shows that the RBI has given itself enough room to keep corporates out altogether without saying so explicitly. It lays down stringent criteria that have to be met, with enormous scope for interpreting each of these criteria in any way that suits the RBI.

Thus, promoters must have "diversified" ownership (what this means is not spelt out) and a track record for at least 10 years of running their businesses. The RBI may seek feedback from regulators and enforcement agencies. Moreover, companies or industrial groups that have more than 10% of their income or assets from or in broking and real estate activities will be barred from consideration. The RBI believes the culture of such businesses does not conduce to that required in banking. The RBI cites the recent initiatives elsewhere to bar banks from proprietary trading.

However, banks in India are not barred from proprietary trading nor are they prevented from having interests in broking or investment banking, so there does appear to be a contradiction here. It could well be that the RBI identified some corporates that would have otherwise qualified and decided to introduce these criteria to keep them out. On top of it all, the RBI reserves the right to withhold licenses even from those who meet all the eligibility criteria listed in its guidelines!

Some commentators have observed that it is hard to see many industrial houses meeting this entire set of criteria; the end result may well be that no industrial house qualifies. But if that is the outcome the RBI desires, it is better for it to say so explicitly. To formulate guidelines that create the theoretical possibility of some corporate houses getting in is for the RBI to expose itself to charges of arbitrariness or inconsistency in the application of criteria.

Besides, it is not beyond the ingenuity of corporate houses to structure their operations in ways that allow them to meet criteria for diversified ownership, limits for income from broking and real estate and, having received a license, criteria for inter-connected lending as well. It would always be open to future top management at RBI to interpret provisions in ways that favour entry of corporate houses.

On the other hand, if the intention is to let in corporate houses, then the RBI might do better than laying down stiff eligibility criteria. I had argued in these columns that corporate houses should be asked to operate only in unbanked centres for an initial period. (Private bank licensing: very few will qualify, *EPW*, October 9, 2010). This would also give the RBI an opportunity to finesse its surveillance of corporates that enter banking. Once corporates demonstrate that they can contribute to financial inclusion and the RBI develops a certain level of comfort in regulating them, we could think of letting them into other geographical areas.

The capital requirements and governance standards for the new banks are proposed to be stiffer than the ones we have for existing banks. Minimum paid-up capital required is Rs 500 crore with a minimum capital adequacy ratio of 12% for the first three years. These are not as onerous as they seem. First, the average capital adequacy of the Indian banking system today is 13.8%. New banks will have to operate at this level or an even higher level if they are to be taken seriously.

Secondly, newly licensed banks need to be listed within two years of licensing of the banks. To do so, they need to be sufficiently profitable. The minimum equity capital and capital adequacy requirements together would translate into a balance sheet size of around Rs 8- 10, 000 crore, which would hardly suffice for the purpose of profitability- it's hard to see banks making a reasonable profit at a size of less than Rs 20,000 crore. In all probability, therefore, newly licensed banks will soon require equity capital much greater than the regulatory requirement.

In terms of governance, a few requirements stand out. One, promoters will be required to create a 100% owned non-operating holding company (NOHC) which will hold the bank as well as other financial services companies. Only non-financial entities and individuals in the promoter group would be allowed to own shares in the NOHC; financial services companies in the promoter group would not be allowed any shareholding in the NOHFC. The idea is to ring-fence the banking and financial activities of the group from its other activities. This is a salutary requirement.

Two, the NOHC will have to own 40 per cent of the capital in the bank (and no more) in the first five years; the NOHC holding must drop to 20 per cent within ten years, and 15 per cent within 12 years. Thus, the RBI appears to be signalling that it is okay with promoter shareholding of 15 per cent in a bank, up from the present level of 10 per cent. (It is not clear whether this will apply to existing private banks). Three, foreign shareholding in new private banks to be capped at 49 per cent in the first years. The RBI clearly has concerns about the lack of transparency in what passes for FDI.

Four, 50 per cent of the directors of the NOHC shall be independent directors. (Since the bank is to be listed, presumably its board will be governed by listing requirements). If the RBI believes that this requirement (or the presence of independent directors on banks' boards) provides safeguards against the promoters controlling the bank, it is sadly mistaken. The so-called independent directors, whether on the NOHC or on the banks, will be chosen by the promoters and hence there will always be a question mark over the degree of independence they will exercise. It will be possible for promoters to decide the composition of the boards even where their shareholding is a mere 15 per cent.

As I have argued earlier, it would be better if the RBI were to limit the proportion of independent directors that the promoters can appoint and insist that a certain proportion be appointed by institutional and retail shareholders. The same principle should apply to banks' boards as well. But this will require the RBI to make the post of independent directors at banks a little more attractive than it is today. Directors at private banks are limited to a sitting fee of Rs 20,000; at public sector banks, the fee is a pathetic Rs 5000. We need some liberalisation of these norms if we are aiming at an improvement in governance (which is not to say that the matter of directors' compensation should be left entirely to bank promoters or management).

In order to prevent conflicts of interest, the RBI stipulates exposure limits of 10 per cent and 20 per cent of the paid-up capital and reserves of the bank to any entity within the promoter group and the entire group respectively. This is fine but conflicts of interest do not arise only on the asset side of the banks' balance sheet. There are conflicts on the liabilities side as well, for instance, when a bank has salary accounts or corporate deposits from entities within the promoter book. This may not be in the best interests of the companies in question. Besides, easy access to bulk deposits of group companies could render the bank vulnerable to problems in the group at large. It will be necessary to frame guidelines with respect to such issues on the liabilities side as well.

It does appear, as has been generally noted, that it is NBFCs with an interest in setting up banks that appear to be best placed to secure licenses under the new guidelines. The RBI is likely to take its time in dealing with applications from corporate houses. The entry of corporate houses is an issue that is fraught with serious implications for the banking sector and it is not something that will resolve itself with the passage of time. Even the actual processing of applications from corporate houses may not help the RBI to make up its mind on this vexed issue. Some aspects will become clear only after corporate houses begin running banks. One can only hope fervently that it is not too late then.

Sept 10, 2011(EPW)

6

Policies and Prospects

Tread Warily on Bank Mergers

Somebody, somewhere in the higher echelons of power has pulled a rabbit out of his or her hat. It goes by the name of consolidation among public sector banks (PSBs). The IBA has reportedly set up a committee to examine the legal and regulatory hurdles to bank mergers. It would be better off examining the commercial argument for mergers among PSBs first. When do you merge? And what are the dangers, if any, of not merging?

You merge when you have exhausted possibilities of organic growth or if you find that organic growth could be too slow in coming. In the deregulated environment, we are talking of growth in earnings and market capitalisation. Mere balance sheet growth is passé.

Applying this criterion to the PSBs, what do we find? In 1998-99, the ratio of net profit to total assets at PSBs was 0.42. In 2002-03, it had risen to 0.96. The RBI's Report on Trend and Progress in Banking (2002-03) has a table showing that, in 2002, the Indian banking system, dominated by the PSBs, was the second most profitable in the world after the US. Read my lips: the- second- most-profitable. Between 2000 and 2004, the market capitalisation of nine listed PSBs has soared from Rs 156 bn to Rs 447 bn. It is hard to argue against organic growth of this order.

True, trading profits have been a big chunk of the profits but even at their peak in 2002-03, these accounted for about a third of the operating profit. Profit has gone up on other counts as well. Moreover, it is not as if there is no scope for growth in profit through loans- banks have simply not had the incentive to exploit the potential for loans. As the opportunities for windfall gains from treasury diminish, banks will be constrained to focus on growing their loan portfolios faster than in the recent past.

The case for PSB mergers rests mainly on cost savings to be had from eliminating overlapping branches among PSBs. But these savings could be overwhelmed by problems arising from people issues and incompatible systems and work cultures. Besides, today PSBs do not need to merge in order to effect cost savings. There is ample scope for cost reduction even on the existing basis.

Turn now to the supposed dangers of not merging. It used to be said that you needed scale in order to take advantage of technology. But this argument has been weakened by changes in technology that make for scalability. It is possible now to make incremental additions instead of going for large scale at one go. Secondly, there has been a sea-change in perceptions regarding technologies such as online banking, ATMs and the like. These are now perceived as supplementing, not supplanting, brick-and-mortar branches. It is the newcomers who are sweating in their bid to catch up on branches even as PSBs slowly close the technology gap.

The other danger is said to be competition from global majors. Forget about taking on global majors in the international arena-no amount of merger is going to give PSBs the necessary clout. In the Indian market, however, PSBs have shown they have little to fear. Foreign banks compete with the new private banks rather than with PSBs.

The challenge from global majors will come not from their size but from their ability, under Basel II, to lower their requirements of regulatory capital by using sophisticated risk management practices. To face this challenge, PSBs need to focus on systems and re-skilling people. Mergers, far from facilitating this, could be a hindrance because of the difficulties inherent in managing systems on a larger scale.

Those urging consolidation among PSBs need to confront a striking fact: to this day, SBI has not thought it necessary or prudent to merge with its own subsidiaries. Why?

Partly because many of its subsidiaries are faring better than the parent itself. But, also, because of the perception that a State

Bank of Patiala or a State Bank of Indore brings to its region distinctive competencies that might get eroded if it gets absorbed by the parent. The experience elsewhere has raised serious concerns about the adverse impact of mergers on consumer service and small business and local lending. The supposed efficiency benefits of mergers must always be weighed against the benefits of competition.

If at all any consolidation is required in the Indian banking system, it is among old private sector banks and cooperative banks. It is these banks that today pose a systemic risk. With mergers, at least some of them can emerge as viable regional players and lower the risk to the system. They need to be goaded into thinking along these lines. To ignore these banks and instead to talk of consolidation among PSBs is to get our priorities hopelessly wrong.

September 23, 2004

Indian Banks' 'Possible Trinity'

State Bank of India's decision to raise deposit rates is seen as signalling in decisive terms the turn of the interest rate cycle. Interest rates on government securities had risen much earlier but banks had avoided following suit. SBI's move has raised concerns about the outlook for bank profitability and credit growth in the coming year. Economy watchers need not lose sleep: the outlook remains reassuring.

SBI's move may have been prompted by the recent retirement of the Indian Millenium Deposit Bonds but an increase in deposit rates was inevitable given that banks' deposit growth had not been keeping pace with the explosive growth in credit in 2004-05. Deposits grew by 15.4% in 2004-05 compared with credit growth of 26%.

Banks face acute competition for deposits from postal savings and other investment products. Last year, they managed, nevertheless, to sustain credit growth through greater resort to borrowings and equity. There is only so much scope for raising more capital and greater reliance on borrowings can put pressure on banks' spread, the difference between the cost of funds and the return on funds. Banks have to step up deposit growth.

Higher deposit rates need not, however, tell on bank profitability. As the RBI's Report on Trend and Progress in Banking

(2004-05) notes (hereafter Report), there is an asymmetry in the movement of banks' lending rates. When market rates decline, banks are slow to lower their lending rates. However, when market rates move up, banks are quick to raise their lending rates. In the period 1996-2005, there was a decline in eight percentage points in bank deposit rates while lending rates declined by seven percentage points. Thus, banks' spread increased by one percentage point in the period.

Banks will probably hang on to this bonanza for some time by raising lending rates in tandem with the increase in deposit rates. As the lending rate will rise from an all-time low- 60 per cent of all lending is at below the base PLR-the impact on credit growth will be minimal. Rates for prime borrowers will now rise, making some dent into firms' profitability, but banks' own profitability will not be immediately impacted.

Banks' profitability over the past year has defied the prognostications of many pundits. When interest rates on government securities began to rise, we were warned that losses on government securities would deal a major setback to banks' profitability. The impact has been modest: the net profit to total asset ratio for all banks declined from 1.1 per cent in 2003-04 to 0.9 per cent in 2004-05. This is because Indian banks enjoy today what might be regarded as an 'impossible trinity' in banking: high credit growth, high spread and high asset quality.

The net interest margin to asset ratio, a measure of spread, was 2.9 per cent in 2004-05, which is higher than in most parts of the world. High asset quality co-exists with high asset growth for many reasons: the revival in economic growth, improved risk management at banks and the shift towards retail assets. Housing loans grew by 45 per cent in 2004-05 on top of growth of 42 per cent in 2003-04; non-priority sector personal loans by 67 per cent and 26 per cent in the two years. On retail loans, NPAs are just 2 per cent. Since the growth is on a low base, there is still considerable scope for growth in retail assets without compromising quality.

The Report has a table (III.21, page 83) that shows new private banks as having a lower cost of deposits than PSBs. This flies in the face of the belief that PSBs enjoy a funding advantage because of their ability to garner low-cost savings accounts through their branch network. Why would new private banks then be investing in expansion of their retail network? The same table shows the return on advances for PSBs as 7%. This seems odd considering that the weighted average lending rate following successive years of decline was 13% in 2004. The Statics need explaining.

At the start of reforms, many perceived banking as a zero-sum game in which PSBs would lose out heavily to private and foreign players. It hasn't quite turned out that way. The share in total assets of private and foreign banks, which was under 10% at the advent of reforms, has indeed risen to 25%. However, as the asset cake itself has expanded, most PSBs have been able to sustain deposit growth and increase credit growth.

In this respect, banking is similar to some other sectors- insurance, telecom, automobiles- where the entry of new players has opened up the market. With the ratio of loans to GDP in India at a mere 40%, financial deepening still has a long way to go. The cake will continue to expand. Indian banks' 'possible trinity' translates into win-win, not zero sum.

January 12, 2006

Beware of Bank Autonomy

Bank autonomy seems almost impossible to quarrel with. Who wouldn't want management of public sector banks (PSBs) to have more operational freedom?

So when the finance ministry directs PSBs to put on hold their schemes for performance-based incentives, the cry goes up: autonomy under threat.

Yet, it is not obvious that variable pay is the way to go for PSBs or public sector enterprises (PSEs). The public sector needs to think through the incentives it needs, not play catch up with the private sector.

In general, variable pay works where effort or performance is readily measurable. Individual effort is seldom readily observable. Individual performance is hard to measure because results flow from the performance of groups and often from factors extraneous to the firm itself. Hence devising performance measures that align individual incentives with firm performance is difficult in any situation. At PSBs, the problem can be compounded for three reasons.

First, measures of revenue or profit, commonly used in industrial firms, are inappropriate in banking because they do not capture the risks that go with various activities. A bank manager may show high revenue or profit in a given year by pushing loan growth but the related non-performing assets may show up a few years later. The right measure to use would be return on risk-adjusted capital. But using this measure requires information systems that PSBs lack today. Variable pay with unsatisfactory measures of performance will not only fail to meet the objective of improving firm performance, it risks disrupting industrial relations.

Secondly, PSB employees enjoy job security. Having a variable pay scheme at PSBs implies that an employee is rewarded if he does well but will not be penalised if he does badly. This is hardly a satisfactory state of affairs especially at senior levels where rewards can be high.

Thirdly, a commonly used measure of performance of top management, stock price, bristles with problems in banking. We know that the presence of debt can cause managers to take hugely risky decisions. If the gambles work out, there are big payoffs to managers. If they don't, the costs of failure are substantially borne by debt holders. Thus, debt creates "risk-shifting incentives" for managers. This problem is exacerbated at banks because banks happen to be highly leveraged institutions. At PSBs, fixed tenure for CEOs makes the problem even worse.

How, then, do we address incentives at PSBs? Banks need to move away from industry-wide settlements. PSBs that can pay better should do so. But this does not mean that PSBs match private sector salaries.

PSBs- and PSEs in general- must accept that their business model is different from that of the private sector. The private sector provides a high-risk, high return environment. The public sector offers job security and lower compensation. The public sector must compete for talent on the strength of a variety of non-pecuniary incentives: the challenges that go with the bigger size of operations at many PSEs, job rotation, the ability to encash the experience in the private sector at some point, deputations to overseas branches and subsidiaries and housing, medical and other benefits. PSEs must be seen to offer a different "lifestyle" altogether.

PSEs must also use as selling points their culture of professional management and their superior governance practices including adherence to the law. As Stanford professor John Roberts observes in his classic work, *The Modern Firm,* there is more to motivation than contractual rewards. All aspects of the organisation can be used to motivate: vision, culture, structure, strategy and processes.

Autonomy at PSEs has improved considerably in recent years and so has performance. There may be room for more autonomy but it is important to be clear as to what autonomy means and what it does not mean. It means that political considerations will not be brought to bear on commercial decisions. It does not mean that PSEs are to be freed from government direction or government monitoring.

Autonomy is often interpreted to mean that all matters must be left to the board. This overlooks the fact that the board is but an agent of shareholders. And we know that the board is most effective where the dominant shareholders are active. At PSEs, the board is accountable wholly or principally to government and it must be subject, therefore, to direction by government. Not to accept this and to invoke autonomy in support of dubious schemes such as variable pay is to create a dangerous lack of accountability that could ultimately destroy the ethos of PSEs.

January 26, 2006

Mr Chidambaram has a Point

The finance ministry asks public sector banks (PSBs) to get their boards to take a view on lending rates. The move evokes a storm of criticism. The government, critics say, is trying to impose its views on banks in disregard of the interests of minority shareholders. It wants to scuttle the RBI's efforts to nudge interest rate upwards. The government's attempts at preventing banks from raising interest rates will damage the banks' financials.

The chorus of denunciation is astonishing because none of these propositions stands up to critical scrutiny. To start with the first proposition, proper pricing of loans is indeed an issue at PSBs. It is entirely appropriate that boards should be asked to apply their minds to this issue instead of leaving it to asset liability management committees.

It is not true that the government can easily impose its views on bank boards. PSB boards today include representatives of workers, officers and the RBI as well as independent directors. Bank management can be suborned by the government's representative but not everybody else. This is borne out by the fact that several boards that had been asked to review their decision to raise interest rates have stuck to it.

Many have sought to portray the episode as yet another in the feud between the finance ministry and the RBI. Even as the RBI is trying to nudge interest rates up and slow down credit, the ministry wants otherwise. This again is a caricature of the situation. Every bank does not have to match every rate hike announced by the RBI. Banks that had raised rates earlier may deem it appropriate not to do so after the last round. Others may choose to raise rates. A given rate hike on the part of the RBI will thus evoke a differentiated response across the banking sector.

However, over several rounds of rate hikes announced by the RBI, we do expect to see a secular rise in interest rates amongst banks- and indeed this has happened. The rise should help slow down credit although not as much as the RBI would like. But that is because the demand for credit depends not just on interest rates but also on income.

There are other nuances that should not be overlooked. Sometimes, the central bank changes short-term interest rates in response to conditions in the financial markets. These may not require a response from banks. Rates for certain products are not linked to the PLR. Banks can revise these without revising the PLR.

Besides, the yield on the loan portfolio can be increased without changing the PLR. For instance, banks may reduce the band for sub-PLR rates (as some have done now), which would translate into an increase in yield. This has the merit of raising interest rates for corporates without imposing a burden on the SME sector for which the lending rate is linked to the PLR. Thus, the presumption that banks must leap to revise their PLRs in response to a signal from the central bank has little basis.

It is also not obvious that not raising lending rates would damage every bank's financials. As three of the banks in question have increased their net interest margin in the first quarter of this year relative to last year. They need to make a business decision: do we raise interest rates or do we hold rates and try to grab market share? Their boards are entitled to take a view on this question.

The increase in net interest margin is no mean achievement in a rising interest rate regime. It could point to deft management of the maturity structure of assets and liabilities. Equally, it could point to pricing power and the absence of adequate competition. The latter again would justify the government's wanting to be heard on bank boards- after all, the RBI has used moral suasion when it comes to setting the price band over the PLR.

The brouhaha over the ministry's directive has to do with the belief that anything that emanates from government must be evil and that professional managers are lily-white angels of purity. The reality, alas, is rather more complex than that. Managers need to be monitored. And the best kinds of monitoring are provided by dominant shareholders. To say, "Leave it to the boards", means precious little.

Autonomy at government-owned institutions does not mean that the dominant shareholder cannot express its views. It only means that government must not influence commercial decisions in ways that undermine performance. If that is the point finance minister P Chidambaram has sought to make, the controversy that has followed is an overreaction.

August 10, 2006

A Fair Deal for Bank Customers

This should have been a golden era for bank customers in India. We have more banks than ever before. Private banks have gained market share. Banks have placed the most modern technologies at the service of customers. Yet, customer dissatisfaction on some counts is pervasive. It has been loud enough to catch the attention of the regulator and the government. If banks don't watch out, they could be in for some tough regulation and even tougher laws.

Three areas of concern have come to the fore in recent weeks. One, the use of strong-arm methods by recovery agents. Two, usurious rates on loans, lack of transparency in pricing and hidden charges. Three, different lending rates for old and new borrowers.

The Delhi Consumer Commission recently fined ICICI Bank Rs 5.5 million for using goons to recover an asset. The RBI has warned banks that it will bar them from using recovery agents if their actions attract court strictures. Bankers grumble that the RBI's injunctions will only encourage borrower indiscipline. But problems in recovery often arise on account of flawed lending decisions.

In lending, the dividing line between aggression and imprudence can be pretty thin. Banks want to grab market share, so they offer lower rates than their competitors and go all-out to push loans on to customers. Upper limits for loans dictated by internal norms are relaxed. Variable rate loans may be getting sanctioned without factoring in the borrower's ability to repay when lending rates go up. Lack of prudence in lending rests on the premise that when the borrower is squeezed hard enough by goons, he will find ways to repay.

There are problems with documentation as well. In home loans, an "aggressive" bank will promise sanction of loan within, say, four days. This is possible only when the bank fails to create equitable mortgage which ensures that the borrower has clear title to property. Given the ways of our builders, there is always a chance that the purchaser does not have clear title. When the borrower defaults, the bank does not have recourse to the underlying property, so it goes after the borrower instead. Again, problems in recovery have their origin in faulty lending practices.

Customers are also at the receiving end of usurious lending rates, lack of transparency in pricing (for instance, customers are not told that "fixed rates" on loans are fixed only for two or three years) and hidden charges. However, complaints about differences in lending rates for old and new retail borrowers may not have much substance. Lower rates for new borrowers may reflect a decline in marginal cost of funds. They may also be intended to gain volumes so as to meet targets. It may not be feasible for a bank to extend the lower rate to old borrowers. Besides, borrowers may be able to transfer a loan to a bank that offers a lower rate.

Banks that practice fairness and transparency can use these to gain competitive advantage. But competition cannot in itself address deficiencies in customer service. In banking, there are formidable "switching costs". It is not easy to close and open accounts or to change mandates for electronic payments into or out of bank accounts. A better bank may not be close to home. A bank that promises a better deal may prove as devilish once the customer has walked into its lair.

There is talk of lender liability legislation. Banks have also been warned that laws related to usury may be extended to cover banks. But legislation cannot be the answer in a country where the judicial system is already overwhelmed by numbers. We have to rely on tighter regulation.

This requires, first, use of disclosure. The RBI must ask banks to have a separate link at their websites on customer service. This link must contain data on customer complaints for the past three years, including critical complaints referred to bank boards and ombudsman and court judgements that have gone against the bank. The RBI must also have a link at its own website where comparative data on customer complaints is provided.

Secondly, the RBI must include customer service in the parameters it uses for rating banks. Thirdly, the RBI must use customer service as a criterion for awarding branch licenses and other approvals- court strictures in loan recovery cases must invite severe penalties. Banks denied approvals must be told that they have lost out on the customer service dimension.

Lastly, the RBI must ask banks to establish a clear chain of responsibility for customer service starting from the loan officer or branch manager right up to the CEO. Boards must be asked to ensure staff accountability for serious lapses in customer service as in the case of NPAs. The RBI should make clear that, if things get out of hand, the CEO or executive directors may be asked to step down. The prospect of hanging, you can be pretty sure, will wonderfully concentrate bankers' minds on customer service.

Nov 15, 2007

We're all for Public Ownership now

This is a time for rescues of financial systems everywhere. Britain's plan is considered especially bold. Under the plan, the UK government will inject up to £50 bn in capital into eight of Britain's largest banks and building societies.

In the first step, the UK has injected £37 bn into three banks. This will give it a 60% stake in one bank and a 40% stake in two banks that are undergoing a merger. The UK government plans to have its directors on the boards of these banks- just when the Raghuram Rajan committee wants the Indian government to exit its own.

There appears to be no escape from public ownership of banks in the US as well as Europe. Nothing else will restore confidence in the banking system. Most people accept this. But they also say that public ownership should be a temporary affair.

Why so? Because, it is said, public ownership of banks makes them prone to failure. Governments will feel obliged to save them and the costs are borne by the exchequer. This is an astonishing statement to make- and not just because of private bank failures in the present crisis.

Economies worldwide have gone through the same thing over the past several decades. Private banks fail, the government recapitalises them, later restores them to private ownership. Banking failures are costly. They impose recapitalisation costs in the range of 5-45% of GDP. And yet there is a presumption that public ownership alone imposes fiscal costs.

There is one distinguished exception to the story of banking failures in recent decades: the Indian banking system. In 1992-93, India opted to retain public sector dominance in banking. The government provided public sector banks (PSBs) with $5 bn in capital- a pittance compared to the sums being talked about now.

These two decisions have contributed to stability in Indian banking. Public sector dominance is not the only factor: sound macroeconomic management and strong regulation have helped. But it is certainly a key factor. Seeing the plight today of the nation's largest private bank, one shudders to think of what might have been had public ownership been absent.

Critics say this may be true but we have paid a heavy price for stability. The banking system is hugely inefficient. The RBI Report on Currency and Finance (2006-08), which focuses on the Indian banking sector, squarely addresses this criticism. This is a monumental study, bringing to bear on the entire gamut of policy issues a vast body of research. Let me highlight its key findings on ownership and efficiency in Indian banking.

One, efficiency in Indian banking has improved, especially since 2001-02, going by several accounting measures. Two, the Indian banking sector compares favourably with banks in both developed and emerging markets on most performance indicators. Three, using economic measures of efficiency, "ownership has no definite relationship with efficiency".

How is it that the Indian experience defies the conventional wisdom that private ownership is superior? There are good reasons.

Typically, state-owned enterprises (SOEs) run out of steam because the state's finances are in a mess and the state is unable to provide capital. These firms are then sold to private (often foreign) owners who bring in capital.

Academics compare the performance of firms in years when they were starved of capital under government ownership with performance following the infusion of capital. They find an improvement in performance. They conclude it is privatisation that made the difference.

Not many economies have experimented with serious public sector reform: allowing SOEs to raise capital by going public; ushering in improvements in governance; and allowing SOEs to compete with private firms. India has done all of these. The improvements are there for all to see. India's somewhat unique approach to the issue of public ownership has paid off richly.

Enterprise reform has been complemented by strong regulation. Former RBI governor Y V Reddy has received well-deserved plaudits for his management of monetary policy and exchange rates in the face of a surge in foreign inflows. His contributions towards bank regulation were as substantial. Their value is beginning to be grasped in today's turbulent conditions. During Dr Reddy's tenure, the RBI unveiled separate roadmaps for private ownership of banks and for foreign banks in India. These served to ensure that neither private bank nor foreign bank expansion happens in ways that undermine stability in Indian banking.

Dr Reddy was roundly criticised for over-protecting the public sector. The Percy Mistry report of 2007 asked that all PSBs be privatised. The Rajan committee wants selective privatisation of PSBs. How ironical that close on the heels of these reports, we should be seeing a world-wide embrace of public ownership in banking even if under duress!

Oct 16,2008

A New Paradigm for Lending Rates

You expect banks to price their loans correctly. They can't afford to under-price their loans because then they are not covering their risks. They can't over-price their loans either because, in a competitive market, they would lose customers. Yet, the astonishing truth is that banks don't get the pricing of their credit products right. That, after all, is one of the important issues thrown up by the sub-prime crisis.

There are good reasons for regulators to lay down guidelines for loan pricing. First, banking has an anti-competitive character to it because entry into banking is not free. Secondly, customers cannot easily switch from one bank to another- as they can with, say, soap or biscuit - because there are "switching costs". Thirdly, bank management has incentives to price loans incorrectly in the short-run because the costs of failure only show up over a long period.

In India, the RBI, which has shown itself ahead of the regulatory curve in many ways, has long had guidelines for loan pricing in place. Since April 2003, banks in India have been required to compute a benchmark prime lending rate (BPLR) and indicate the minimum and maximum lending rates.

The BPLR is the rate offered to the best borrower, so one would not expect any loans to be made below the BPLR. It is a floating rate, so it should respond to changes in the RBI's policy rates. Neither expectation has been met for several years now. Sub-BPLR lending has become the norm- nearly 70% of all loans are today below the BPLR. Lending rates don't fall when the RBI cuts policy rates.

There are other problems. Banks would rather adjust discounts to the BPLR than change the BPLR itself. As a result, borrowers think lending rates aren't transparent enough. It is difficult for the RBI to get a clear picture of trends in lending rates by looking at BPLRs. The range of banks' BPLRs is pretty wide.

Clearly, we need a system that is more transparent, more responsive to monetary policy and that ensures that lending rates of banks adequately cover costs. Last June, the RBI constituted a Working Group on BPLR. The Group submitted its report on October 20. I was a member.

We were quick to realise that many of the problems with the existing system are built into the very formula for BPLR. The BPLR today is based on the actual cost of funds, operating costs and a margin to cover provisioning and profit. The actual cost of funds is the weighted average of all historical costs.

When the policy rate declines, only incremental costs change significantly and the actual cost of funds changes very slightly.

Banks cannot afford to lower their BPLR as that would translate into lower rates on the entire loan portfolio. Rates can fall only on incremental loans.

Many banks fixed their BPLR at a time when the cost of funds was high. Thereafter, as incremental costs fell, banks kept the BPLR unchanged and passed on the benefit to incremental borrowers through sub-BPLR rates. The present situation, where 70% of loans are below BPLR, is the logical culmination of this process.

Clearly, sub-BPLR lending cannot end as long as lending rates are based on historical costs. They need to be forward-looking. Since most of the loans today are for one year or more, the one-year deposit rate is the appropriate choice for a forward-looking cost.

Would a PLR that is linked to the one-year deposit rate address the sub-BPLR problem? Not quite. We have to reckon with another element in the pricing formula, operating costs. The operating cost used in the PLR formula is an average. For some products, such as housing loans, the operating costs are much lower than the average. The lending rates for such products would, therefore, end up lower than the PLR and, again, we would have sub-BPLR lending.

Having two BPLRs, one for wholesale and another for retail, does not solve the problem either. Within wholesale, there is a big difference in operating costs for large corporates and for small enterprises. In retail, a chasm separates housing from credit cards. The answer would be to have a BPLR for each business segment. But, then, we would end up creating a clutter in the name of transparency.

The Group concluded, therefore, that we need to move away from the very concept of BPLR. Instead, it opted for a reference rate called the Base Rate, which could serve as the basis for loan pricing. The Base Rate is arrived at after taking into account the one-year card rate for retail deposits (adjusted for current and savings accounts and costs of statutory requirements), the unallocatable operating costs and return on net worth.

Why not include all operating costs in the Base Rate? If we did, we might end up with a large dispersion in the Base Rate, given the differences in operating costs between banks. The market would perceive banks at the upper end of the range as hugely inefficient and this could undermine confidence in them. In the scheme proposed, the dispersion would be narrower.

Banks can now arrive at the lending rate by adding to the Base Rate other elements: credit and tenor risks and product-specific operating costs. As the Base Rate represents the minimum rate, the question of sub-Base lending should not arise. However, the Group recognised that there could be short-term opportunities for lending below the Base Rate. So, loans of less than one year are not subject to the Base Rate.

At the same time, we thought it appropriate to limit such lending to 15% of incremental loans in any year. This need not be seen as regulatory overkill. It is elementary risk management for banks to have a ceiling on sub-Base lending. The ceiling also ensures that banks don't set their Base Rate unduly high by manipulating cost elements.

The Group recommended doing away with administered rates on small loans. Banks have stopped lending to this category. If they can charge appropriate interest rates, they would be more inclined to lend. A modest degree of regulation remains for two important categories: exports and education loans.

The switch from BPLR to a Base Rate should make lending rates more transparent and more responsive to monetary policy. Hopefully, it should also cause lending rates to settle at lower levels than today.

October 29, 2009

A Crisis-Proof Banking Sector

The sub-prime crisis peaked in September 2008 following the collapse of Lehman Brothers. Many forecast that 2009-10 would be the year of reckoning for the Indian economy and for Indian banking, both of which had successfully weathered the crisis until then. I disagreed. I said that banking would be a bright spot in the economy given the strengths inherent in the sector.

The pessimists have been proved wrong about the Indian economy- the economy is projected to grow at more than 7 per cent in 2009-10. They are going to be proved even more wrong about the banking sector. The Bankex has outperformed the Sensex in the period April-December 2009. It rose by 123 per cent while the Sensex rose by 73 per cent . In 2008-09, the Bankex had declined by 40 per cent, a little more than the decline of 37 per cent in the Sensex.

We have to await the details of financial performance for 2009-10 but the RBI's Report on Trend and Progress in Banking (2008-09) tells us what happened last year and gives us clues to what we might expect this year. It is indeed a revelation. In the midst of the worst financial crisis of the century and when banks in the industrial world were falling apart, the Indian banking sector fared as well as in the boom years.

Banks managed a return on assets of 1 per cent in both 2007-08 and 2008-09, slightly higher than the 0.9 per cent return of 2006-07. That should place the Indian banking sector amongst the most profitable in the world today. Banks elsewhere saw their capital eroded and required infusions of capital from governments. In India, capital adequacy actually improved in 2008-09. What better indicators of banking soundness do you need than world-class profitability and improved capital in the midst of devastation in the banking sector worldwide?

After the Lehman collapse, pundits forecast that the moment of reckoning for Indian banks had arrived following years of commercial credit growth of around 30 per cent. They said banks would face a mountain of non-performing assets (NPAs) as Indian companies and the housing sector felt the impact of the global crisis. There are models that predict that a sustained credit boom leads to bank failures and even a banking crisis. This did not happen in 2008-09 and is unlikely to happen in 2009-10 either.

Bad times for the economy spell lower credit growth. In 2007-08, commercial credit growth slowed to 22 per cent. It slowed further to 18 per cent in 2008-09. But banks maintained their return on assets in 2008-09 at the same level as in the preceding boom years of 2004-08. This is truly astonishing. It suggests that no matter what the ups and downs of the economy, the Indian banking sector can deliver a return of 1 per cent on assets, a benchmark of good performance in banking. India today seems to have a crisis-proof banking sector.

What explains this phenomenon? One, banks' ability to sustain spreads (return on advances minus cost of funds) at all times. Volume growth slowed down in the last two years. But the spread on loans actually increased in 2008-09. A key factor driving large spreads in Indian banking is the high proportion of current and savings account (Casa) deposits. These account for a third of all deposits in Indian banking. Banks pay zero interest on current accounts and 3.5 per cent on savings accounts.

Secondly, banks have woken up to the potential for fee income. Apart from conventional products that generate fees such as letters of credit, guarantees and mortgage products, banks now generate fee income from sale of mutual fund and insurance products.

Thirdly, falling interest rates in a slowdown lead to a surge in treasury profits on banks' investment in government securities. By the same token, rising interest rates in boom periods should cause these profits to decline. They do but there have been other offsetting factors: gains on equities and forex products.

Fourthly, the slowdown that we have seen in the past two years has not caused any increase in provisions on account of rising NPAs. That is because a deceleration from 9 per cent to 7 per cent may mean lower growth in earnings but it hardly spells disaster for companies. Besides, companies entered the crisis with sound balance sheets after five boom years. There was a large increase in housing prices before the slowdown but this does not appear to be a bubble. It is based on genuine demand and increased affordability.

Experts told us that India's antiquated banking sector was constraining growth. "Reforms" in the financial sector would deliver another 2 percentage points of growth. We have since found that the banking sector can support economic growth of 9 per cent.

Banks, of course, need to do more. We need more sophisticated products. There is the challenge of financial inclusion. But those who urge banking sector "reforms" need to tell us what exactly needs fixing in a system that ain't broke.

January 7, 2010

Let Foreign Banks into Rural Areas

Pranab Mukherjee's mention of additional banking licenses to private players in his recent budget created a buzz. It is hard to understand why. There is a policy for private bank licensing in place and anybody is free to apply.

Perhaps the expectation was that the policy would be diluted. The RBI has been quick to clarify that governance norms would not be diluted in awarding bank licenses. At the same time, it has indicated that a committee would be appointed to look into international practices for licensing of private players, including corporate houses.

The message is clear. The RBI will proceed cautiously, as always, but is open to new ideas. The time is indeed ripe for considering new ideas. The Indian banking system has fared well over the past decade and in the recent financial crisis. It is among the best capitalised and profitable in the world today. We can make changes in policy in the confidence that we operate from a position of strength.

The challenge in bank regulation, underlined by the financial crisis, is to strike a balance between stability and innovation. It is a balance that can and must change over time. We have mastered a trick or two when it comes to financial stability. We can now attempt some tinkering at the margin aimed at fostering innovation.

But we must be clear as to what innovation must achieve. It cannot be innovation for innovation's sake - complex financial products that serve no loftier social purpose than to produce bonuses for bankers. The only worthwhile financial innovation in recent years, Paul Volcker has remarked acerbically, is the ATM. Financial innovation must be dovetailed to the needs of the economy.

We know what our economy needs. It needs financial deepening and financial inclusion. It is possible to have financial deepening, a bigger banking system, without inclusion. That is not what we want. We want deepening that is married to inclusion. It follows that changes in bank licensing policy must focus on innovation that can meet the overriding objective of financial inclusion.

The existing players are in no position to come up with new business models for greater inclusion. Public sector banks (PSBs) were responsible for the expansion in geographical coverage that happened after nationalisation. But that effort has run out of steam long since.

Through most of the nineties and the early nineties, the focus on commercial performance meant that PSBs cut back on their initiatives in rural areas. In recent years, they have succeeded in pushing more credit into agriculture but much of this is indirect lending.

PSBs today lack the human resource capability to innovate. Many of them will see a decimation of top management in the next two or three years. Large numbers of staff are being recruited at the lower levels and it will take a while to bring them up to speed. PSBs have their work cut out for them simply in managing what they have on their plate. Regional rural banks (RRBs) and cooperatives are in disarray.

Private banks lack the incentives to venture forth- there is so much opportunity in the areas in which they operate currently. They may go into tier 2 cities but the small depositor and small borrower in lower tiers do not make commercial sense to them.

We need a fresh set of players who can design business models for financial inclusion. There are two sets of players who are, in principle, capable of this feat: foreign banks and a new crop of private banks.

Concerns about foreign bank entry relate to regulation and reciprocity. There is a way to address both these concerns: licensing foreign banks exclusively for rural areas.

The entry of foreign banks into rural areas would not undermine PSBs and domestic private banks as the latter are not big players in those areas. Cross-border exposure would not be an issue or can be prohibited. Foreign banks should be permitted into rural areas only through well-capitalised subsidiaries. Thus, important regulatory concerns can be taken care of. Reciprocity would not be such a big concern because we would not be opening up the bigger portion of our market to foreign banks.

The market itself is poised to become a lot more attractive. Commercial banks have stayed away from small loans (loans up to Rs 2 lakh) thanks to regulated lending rates for these. Under the new Base Rate regime proposed by RBI, small loan rates will be deregulated. This changes the nature of the game. There is an opportunity for those who can manage the risks that go with small loans.

We could add some incentives. In phase I, entry into rural areas. In phase II, acquisitions of regional rural banks. In phase III, access to the main market.

Will foreign banks be interested? Well, they are certainly keen to enter the Indian market. We would be saying to them: why don't you enter where you could make a difference? (We could say the same to existing foreign banks keen to expand). The onus would be on foreign banks to innovate in the rural market. It will require them to combine local talent and IT in creative ways. It is a serious bottom-of-the pyramid challenge. If it works, it can translate into enormous payoffs worldwide- and in India itself. Aren't foreign firms in manufacturing attempting precisely that?

It was foreign banks who showed the way in retail credit and cash management services many years ago. Domestic private banks learnt from them and then PSBs. If this story were repeated in financial inclusion, it would be a huge achievement.

What about new domestic players? Corporate houses may not be interested if the cap of 10 per cent on private ownership in a bank stays. We could consider raising the cap to 15-20 per cent for strictly rural banks. But we may need more stringent governance norms, say, a minimum number of directors to be appointed by shareholders other than the promoter.

Differentiated bank licenses- licenses for specific activities-obtain elsewhere and the RBI had mooted this idea in 2007. Licensing foreign banks and domestic banks exclusively for rural areas could be the spark that India's somewhat stodgy banking system needs today. It could ignite just the sort of financial innovation we need-innovation aimed at achieving financial inclusion.

March 18, 2010

Tread Warily on New Private Banks

Is it time to let industrial houses into banking? This is by far the most important question raised in the RBI discussion paper on entry of new banks in the private sector. Industrial houses will not be interested unless they can hold a substantial portion of equity. So the RBI must first address another issue flagged in the paper, namely, the limits on promoter holding of equity in a bank.

Under the present norms, promoters are required to hold 40 per cent of paid up capital at the time of issue of a bank license with a lock-in period of five years. Thereafter, promoters are required to dilute their holding to 10 per cent over a suitable time frame. Promoters may be permitted to hold up to 30 per cent of a bank's equity subject to their meeting 'fit and proper' criteria. In practice, not many promoters have qualified.

Some relaxation in these norms is required if industrial houses are to be attracted into banking. Most industrial houses like to own at least 30-40% of equity in their enterprises. Even non-industrial promoters with deep pockets will not find the present dispensation attractive. They are expected to bear a big chunk of the risk at the start-up stage. When the bank has grown bigger, they are expected to reduce their stake to 10%. What serious promoter would be interested? Only promoters with shallow pockets, such as professionals, would. As the RBI paper underlines, the record of professionals who set up banks is uninspiring.

An increase in promoter holding to 20 per cent is one of the options proposed in the paper. This appears reasonable. It is large enough to sustain the promoter's interest without leading to concentration of shareholding in a bank. It may also be large enough to interest industrial houses.

The intention in keeping promoter stake in a bank down to 10 per cent is to ensure that the promoter does not exercise control. But stringent limits on the promoter's share of equity may not be the best means of restricting control. In the non-financial sectors in India, we have promoters controlling enterprises with an equity stake of less than 10 per cent. Restrictions on control are better exercised by managing the composition of the board.

Promoters or management should not be allowed to choose more than 50 per cent of independent directors. The rest of the independent directors should be nominees of institutional investors, minority shareholders and employees. Then we will have a truly broad-based board, one where at least some 'independent' directors are truly independent of management. The entire corporate world badly needs this piece of reform because directors cannot be independent as long as they are beholden to promoters or management. The RBI has an opportunity to strike a decisive blow for governance by introducing this reform in private sector banks.

Suppose we settle for a promoter shareholding of 20 per cent. Should we take the next step and let in industrial houses? In 2006, the second Tarapore committee favoured letting in industrial houses but this was meant to create strong Indian entities in banking before foreign banks were allowed to enter in a bigger way in 2009.

This particular argument does not hold as we have not seen any liberalisation of policy towards foreign banks and are unlikely to see one in the near future. In 2008, the Raghuram Rajan committee opined that it was "premature" to allow industrial houses to own banks and it cited the prohibition on the "banking and commerce" combine that still obtains in the US.

The RBI paper cites a number of concerns on the subject: intra-group lending and other conflicts of interest; difficulties in supervising and monitoring such entities; the undermining of confidence in a bank should something go wrong anywhere in the industrial house, etc.

It proposes several safeguards to address downside risks but these may not work. Industrial houses could be asked to obtain clearances from various investigative agencies (alas, not too difficult to manage in our political system). Whether ownership is separated from management could be verified (rare in Indian industrial houses). Industrial houses could be barred from using their brand name or logo (but this could defeat the very purpose of letting them in).

The RBI proposes that industrial houses make a start by taking over regional rural banks. Given the state of the RRBs, industrial houses may not find the prospect appetising. A better idea would be to let them set up new banks exclusively in rural areas. This would help address the primary objective of licensing new private banks, namely, greater inclusion.

The banks would not be very large given that the big deposits are in the urban areas, hence systemic risk would be manageable. The industrial houses' capacity for innovation and staying power would be tested. The regulator would have a chance to monitor governance and put in place mechanisms for supervision. We need new private banks alright but caution must be the watchword in licensing these.

August 19, 2010

HRD in Banks is more than Just Pay

At a recent conference on banking, I was asked what the three priorities for public sector banks (PSBs) should be. My impulse was to say that they should simply focus on HRD. But, then, I happen to be at a business school. I had to sound like a management guru. I found myself saying with a flourish, "Public sector banks should have three priorities: HRD, HRD, HRD."

I wasn't being facetious at all. The HRD challenges at PSBs are daunting. A combination of favourable factors-rapid economic growth, sound regulation and supervision, the inherent strengths of the old guard at the banks, the absence of full-blooded foreign competition-has masked their weaknesses and sustained them thus far. But banks must not count on a continuous run of good luck. They need people of good quality at all levels to be able to cope with challenging times.

Last October, the government constituted a committee to go into the HR issues at PSBs. It was headed by A K Khandelwal, former chairman of Bank of Baroda. The committee submitted its report in June this year. I received a copy last week.

The report has some very good ideas but also some flawed ones. The good ideas are about the nuts and bolts of HRD- recruitment, training, career planning, etc. The flawed ideas are about incentives. Let me focus on the latter because these have the potential to cause harm, if accepted.

The committee wants PSBs to introduce performance-linked incentives. Total incentives should not exceed 2% of average net profit over the past two years and it should be limited to the 25% top performers. The incentive amounts would vary from 30% of annual basic pay at the junior level to 70% at the top executive level. The Chairman of SBI should be given an incentive payment of Rs 35 lakh. CMDs of other PSBs would get incentives in the range of Rs 18-25 lakh; executive directors Rs 10-15 lakh. Stock options should be given to the top 15% performers.

The committee's focus on variable pay is dead wrong. Pay in the public sector certainly needs to be improved. But the way to do this is not to introduce variable pay. It is to improve the basic pay.

PSBs are unable to do this because the basic pay of CMDs cannot exceed that of the highest official in government. They are unwilling to do it because they think it would mean a substantial increase in pay across the board, which could be unaffordable. So, today we have a modest 'incentive' system for CMDs and EDs (of up to Rs 10 lakh or so), which is just a covert means of improving their pay.

Variable pay is not the answer to this problem. The problem must be tackled head-on. The government must relax its insistence on parity in fixed pay between government and public sector companies. Salaries of CMDs can be pegged in the range of, say, Rs 30-50 lakh. An improvement in wages at the non-executive levels can also be negotiated subject to the officer-to- clerk ratio going up. But the unions must accept a higher disparity in wages between the executive and non-executive levels. Executive pay at PSBs is out of sync with the market whereas non-executive pay is not.

Why would a higher fixed pay be better than a variable pay scheme? Because the measurement of performance, difficult even in the private sector, can be a nightmare in the public sector. Banks operate across widely differing geographies, executives often have to pursue non-commercial objectives. PSBs do not have in place systems that can accurate capture all costs at the branch or product level. They cannot track a manager's contribution to return on risk-adjusted capital, which is the only meaningful measure on which incentives can be based.

Performance in a bank can be measured only over a long period. Hence the best way to reward performance is not through annual cash incentives but through periodic promotion. How, then, do PSBs distinguish between performers and non-performers? There are a number of carrots other than performance-linked pay that can be deployed- accelerated promotion, foreign postings, deputation to subsidiaries (for which period the higher pay at subsidiaries can be made applicable), assignment to a high-quality training programmes, a paid holiday with family, etc.

There is one thing the public sector must never do in its bid to attract and retain talent and that is ape the private sector. Performance-linked pay will destroy the ethos of the public sector. Limiting cash incentives every year to a select few will create demoralisation in the work force. Top management will be swamped with complaints and petitions. It is a prescription for paralysis.

The public sector must compete by offering a different model, a different lifestyle, one that combines job security, dignity, challenge and pension. PSBs can also introduce generous post-retirement medical benefits as a tool for retaining talent, as some public enterprises already do.

Will these suffice? Can PSBs attract talent? Well, the question has already been answered in a way over nearly two decades of deregulation. PSBs have hugely improved performance. Attrition is lower than in the private sector. If pay were such a big factor, the PSBs should have been wrecks by now.

HRD is more than just pay. PSBs are what they are because of the tradition of hiring probationary officers and creating career paths for them. This tradition, which was interrupted by a freeze on recruitment through the nineties, must be restored. The report highlights several other areas that cry out for improvement. Focusing on these can make a bigger difference than variable pay.

PSBs badly need succession planning at the top. The game of musical chairs for the chairman's post must end. Today, executive directors bide their time in the hope of vaulting on to a CMD's job in another bank. CMDs hop from a small bank to a bigger bank. Loyalty, continuity in management and an understanding of culture are all disregarded. There must be scope for people within a bank to rise to the top.

It is easy to over-emphasise pay in HRD. That is an affliction of the private sector. The public sector must not fall prey to it. In this respect as in others, the public sector must compete by being itself, not by becoming a pathetic clone of the private sector.

September 30, 2010

RBI Mustn't Dictate Bank Margins

The net interest margin (NIM) - the difference between interest income and income expense as a proportion of assets- is a key driver of bank profitability. The RBI thinks it is too high in India and has been trying hard to talk it down. Is the RBI right to be worried about the NIM? If yes, what is the appropriate response to high margins?

Let us begin by looking at the trend in NIM of Indian banks as a whole and of public sector banks (PSBs). Two facts are clear from. One, the NIM remained steady for a long period after deregulation. Two, it fell to a lower level in 2007-08 and 2008-09. The decline in NIM for banks as a whole was the result of a decline in margins at PSBs which account for 70% of assets in the Indian banking system.

One would expect deregulation to result in a decline in bank margins. This has happened in other banking systems but not in India until recently. Why? Deregulation leads to greater competition amongst banks. It is also accompanied by disintermediation, that is, deposits and loans move out of the banking sector and into financial markets. As competition hots up, deposit rates rise and loan rates decline. Banks' NIMs get squeezed.

India does not conform to this trend because, at the time of deregulation, we had a low level of bank penetration. In 1991-95, the credit to GDP ratio averaged 29 per cent. The ratio has since risen to 60 per cent but remains below that in many emerging markets. We are still an under-banked economy. Any economic system needs a minimum level of banking services. Only thereafter will savers and borrowers migrate in a big way to the financial markets. It will be a while before banks feel the full blast of disintermediation.

The decline in NIM in the recent past is good news for borrowers. However, it is not as if banks need to start worrying. Despite a decline in NIM in 2007-08 and 2008-09, PSBs' return on assets was around 1 per cent in both the years. This was higher than in many of the previous years. PSBs seem to have made up for the decline in margin by an increase in fee income.

This highlights a second factor underlying the level of bank margins, namely, the proportion of fee income in relation to interest income. Banks with a high proportion of fees can afford a lower NIM; those with a lower proportion will need a higher NIM. A third factor driving the NIM is the bank's business model. In a branch-intensive model, such as India's, operational costs will be high. The NIM needs to be commensurately higher.

The composition of loans and the risk profile of borrowers is another important factor determining the NIM. A bank that has a higher proportion of SMEs in its portfolio will require a higher NIM in order to offset risk. So will banks with more of certain retail loans, such as consumer loans, credit cards, two-wheeler and three-wheeler loans. Mandating a lower NIM across the board does not make sense.

We want banks to practise financial inclusion. That means investing in distribution, higher operational costs on low ticket loans and deposits and lending to riskier borrowers. All this will be reflected in higher lending rates and a higher NIM. If we want banks to be serious about financial inclusion, we must be willing to tolerate higher NIMs on that portion of their portfolio.

Comparing NIMs across countries is not meaningful either because the factors listed above will vary from one country to another. The NIM for US banks in 2008 was just under 3.8 per cent; at its peak in 1993, it was close to 5 per cent. In the period 1994-01, banks in Western Europe had an average margin of 2.7 per cent, higher than what Indian banks enjoy today; the margin in banks in Eastern Europe in that period was twice that in Western Europe. No worthwhile conclusions can be drawn from cross-country comparisons.

How do we respond to a situation where NIMs do not decline appreciably with deregulation? The regulator's job is to ensure adequate competition-and leave it at that. One way to measure competition is to look at the market share of the top five banks. The figure of 38 per cent for India looks right; it places India somewhere in the middle of a range of developed and emerging markets.

The RBI is welcome to usher in greater competition by licensing new banks. However, in the present situation, a policy bias towards higher NIMs would be appropriate. Under Basel 3, capital requirements for banks will go up and banks' return on equity will come under pressure. Indian banks will need capital from abroad in order to finance an economy growing at the present rate. Higher NIMs will enable Indian banks to maintain their return on equity and attract capital.

For all these reasons, talking down NIMs is not correct policy. It is a matter of concern on another account. Since April 2009, the policy rate has gone up by 250 basis points. However, the prime lending rate of PSBs remained unchanged. The base rate, which came into effect from July 1, 2010, has increased only by 75-100 bps at PSBs.

It does appear that moral suasion on the part of the central bank has kept PSBs from increasing their lending rates. As a result, the pass-through of policy rates to borrowers has not happened. It cannot be that the RBI professes to be tough on inflation but does not allow the logic of its policy to work through the banking system.

June 6, 2011

7

Strategy

The Shape of things to come

Slowly but surely, India's financial sector is seeing a change in ownership patterns. The process has been on for a while now but it has gathered pace with the growing global integration of the Indian economy. It is most visible in areas directly linked to the capital market- brokerage and investment banking- but others such as asset management, insurance and banking are not entirely immune.

Foreign firms are moving into brokerage and investment banking in a big way. The writing was on the wall when Goldman Sachs broke off its collaboration with Kotak, Merrill Lynch gained control over its joint venture with DSP and Morgan Stanley parted ways with J M Financial. Several foreign firms have made their moves into the retail space: Citibank (Sharekhan), Merrill Lynch (India Infoline), BNP Paribas (Geojit Securities), Standard Chartered Bank (UTI Securities).

When foreign firms came in several years ago, the broking market was smaller, the investment banking opportunities mostly related to the domestic capital market and the local firms had all the relationships. The volumes just did not justify the investment in distribution or the demands on top management time.

Over the past four years, the situation has changed dramatically. Trading volumes, both institutional and retail, have risen sharply. Mergers and acquisitions of Indian firms and by Indian firms have shot up. So has international fund-raising by Indian firms. Private equity investment is growing rapidly. Investment banking revenues have soared as a result.

Paradoxical as it may seem, the very success of India's corporates and their growing integration with the global economy poses a threat to India's financial firms. The rising share of broking and investment banking income related to cross-border activity means that foreign firms can go it alone on the strength of such activity alone.

They do not need to worry about revenues related to the domestic capital market. This means they do not have to invest for now in domestic distribution. One office in Mumbai is all they need. At the same time, they can sense the potential for growth in retail brokerage and wealth management. So they are taking equity positions in the leading Indian retail players.

Is this finis for Indian investment banks and brokers? Not really. Foreign firms will focus on the investment banking needs of top corporates and on institutional brokerage. Nevertheless, investment banking opportunities in small and mid-sized companies will still be available to Indian players.

Brokerages run by first-generation professionals will see merit in selling out to foreign players. But family-run brokerages, with their long-standing relationships, will stay. Indeed, some of them are strengthening their presence in the retail market by buying up small brokers. By combining retail brokerage with wealth management they can remain viable.

In asset management, the top five includes one public sector firm (UTI), one domestic firm (Reliance) and three joint ventures (HDFC, ICICI and Birla). There is no particular advantage that foreign firms enjoy at the moment. This could change when Indian investors seek exposure to international capital markets in a big way but that is some distance away yet.

In insurance, LIC, with a market share of 80%, remains the leader by a wide margin. Moreover, the entry of new firms has opened up the market in a big way, so loss of market share has not come in the way of healthy growth in premiums at LIC. In insurance too, it is the domestic market that counts and there is little product differentiation, so foreign firms lack a decisive advantage.

In banking, the situation is closer to that in investment banking. Cross-border business is fast becoming a big source of fee income. Foreign banks have shown a huge increase in profit over the past year on the strength of their global network. This is a material change in the competitive situation. With their entrenched advantages in distribution, public sector banks can hang on to the lower tiers of the domestic business but they need desperately to upgrade their human resources.

Wherever regulatory barriers have been dismantled, the international financial giants have come marching in and domestic players have fallen by the wayside. Will this story be replicated here? It is possible but it is not inevitable. India's geographical size and lack of financial penetration hold out the possibility that, despite the entry of foreign firms, there is space for Indian firms. But for this to happen, we require a combination of skilful regulation and nimbleness on the part of Indian firms.

July 12, 2007

PSBs Must Get Cracking on HRD

India's public sector banks (PSBs) have emerged financially stronger after a decade and a half of reforms. The boom in the economy has helped but improved operations and governance too have contributed.

Credit appraisal is sounder today. Management of NPAs is a lot better. Intermediation costs have fallen. Overall, the return of assets for PSBs of 0.82 % in 2006 does not compare unfavourably with that of the better performing banking systems in the world.

So far, so good. But is it good enough? Are PSBs equipped for a greater opening up of the banking sector post 2009? The wisdom in vogue today is that they do not have the necessary size and must consolidate in order to cope with competition from foreign banks. Consolidation, it is said, will confer scale economies and the ability to cater to large corporates.

But this line of thinking overlooks a crucial truth: merger is the appropriate growth strategy where the scope for organic growth is limited. This is not true of PSBs. Opportunities are there in abundance. PSBs are unable to grasp these because they lack the leadership and depth of management to do so. The priority must, therefore, be a focus on human resource development (HRD), not consolidation. Indeed, consolidation can only sap the energies of PSBs by creating fresh HRD problems on top of the unresolved ones.

Mention HRD in the public sector and people will quickly think compensation. PSBs, they will say, cannot retain or attract talent because they cannot pay well enough. Compensation in the public sector certainly needs to be addressed but it is not the sole HRD issue.

Several public sector firms have shown managerial drive and have done a better job than PSBs of building and motivating people. LIC has shown unsuspected aggression. BHEL is going strong. NTPC's technical prowess is undiminished. There are other success stories. All face the same constraints when it comes to compensation. Yet, managerial quality is high. How come?

PSBs are worse off because there has been a complete neglect of the basics of HRD. The biggest failure is lack of succession planning and continuity in management. Bank chairmen last for two years or so. A chairman does well at a small bank and oversees a successful IPO. In the course of the issue, he unveils a glorious vision to prospective investors.

The issue done, the chairman moves on to a larger bank where he makes a new set of rosy promises- and duly retires. At both the banks, the humdrum task of making the promises happen is left to his successor. Executive directors who do well are similarly rewarded- by being moved to the top job at another bank, not the one that they have got to understand well.

This is not management, it is a charade and a disgrace. It happens only in the banking sector because the finance ministry, in its wisdom, has thought fit to reduce top management at PSBs to a game of musical chairs. This game must end forthwith if at all PSBs are to have any hope of coping with competition.

In almost any organisation, talent is available and waiting to be tapped. The first HRD challenge for PSBs is to identify such talent and systematically groom people for top positions. At the highest levels, people must be given five years to deliver. If they fail, it should be possible to cut short their tenure.

The second challenge is to hire fresh recruits, something that had virtually stopped at PSBs for years. This does not mean going to the top b-schools and offering large salaries. The lower tier schools will do. But it does mean career planning for new recruits with job rotation and periodic training.

The third challenge is bringing in people for specialised roles. This can be done through contractual or advisory appointments. A fourth challenge is to develop a marketing orientation throughout the organisation. This again requires training as well as the induction of young people to leverage the banks' customer relationships for wealth management and other products. One could go on.

None of this is novel nor does it require fancy footwork. But it is hard work and it requires systematic thinking through at the highest levels of the ministry as well as banks. The ministry should constitute a Working Group on HRD for PSBs that will identify the HRD priorities, get banks to formulate a long-range plan for meeting these objectives and monitor implementation.

This is a task that brooks no delay. The RBI has been careful in letting in foreign competition but pressures to open up further cannot be resisted for long. If the government and the banks cannot get their acts together, they risk destroying the value laboriously created in the post-reform period.

July 26, 2007

Beware of Bank Consolidation

One outcome of the present global crisis is that large banking monsters have come to be feared. That is why the recent death anniversary of Lehman Brothers drew a barrage of comments. And Lehman wasn't even a bank, it was an investment bank. We worry now not just about large banks but about 'systemically large' financial institutions.

Economist Joseph Stiglitz and many others want banks to be limited either in size or in scope. Stiglitz wrote recently, "We need to break up the too-big-to-fail banks; there is no evidence that these behemoths deliver societal benefits that are commensurate with the costs they have imposed on others."

Stiglitz's views are echoed by several others, including Henry Kaufmann, a much respected figure on Wall Street. It's a different matter that Mr Kaufmann has woken up to the dangers of bigness rather late in the day: he happened to be on the board of Lehman Brothers.

In contrast, here in India, there is a revival of the clamour for bank consolidation. The chairman of SBI, Mr O P Bhatt, wants Indian banks to grow bigger. Mr Bhatt has been quoted as saying, "The size of Indian banks is not good enough, we need to consolidate.....Even SBI is not large enough to serve Indian corporates". Mr Bhatt thinks there should be at least two to three banks bigger than SBI and half a dozen banks the size of SBI in the country.

Can Indian banks get a lot bigger quickly? Should they do so? Do we need bigger banks at a time when others want their banks to shrink?

In the first place, Mr Bhatt's suggestions do not appear feasible, given the present sizes of Indian banks. Yes, we can have banks bigger than SBI by merging SBI with its subsidiaries or with other banks.

But having two or three banks bigger than SBI or half a dozen banks the size of SBI is almost impossible. To get just one more bank the size of SBI, we would have to merge the four biggest public sector banks (PSBs) after SBI. Mergers of private banks with PSBs are difficult to contemplate and even these will not produce banks bigger than SBI.

That apart, the arguments typically made for bank consolidation in India lack substance:

- **India banks are much smaller than global giants:** True. In 2007, SBI was not even one-tenth the size of the tenth largest bank in the world. But this also means that no amount of consolidation will give Indian banks a global size in the foreseeable future.
- **Bigger size is needed for scale economies:** Yes, scale economies are useful. But beyond a certain size, the benefits of scale taper off and tend to be offset by growing complexity. Internationally, studies have shown that a size of around $20 bn is optimal. India's top ten banks meet this size requirement.
- **Our banks need to be bigger in order to meet the needs of large corporates:** Why should one bank meet the needs of any large corporate on its own? From the point of view of risk management, consortium financing is preferable. Some large requirements of corporates, such as overseas finance, cannot be met by Indian banks, however large they may become.
- **There is too much competition in the Indian market:** Concentration in the banking market works to the detriment of customers. Fragmentation is bad for banks. You need to strike

a balance. A good way to see where a banking system stands is to compare the share of the top five banks in assets. In India, the figure is 44 per cent, which comes somewhere in between the 60 per cent for France and 30 per cent for the US.

Not only are the arguments for bank consolidation not persuasive, there are a number of compelling arguments against bank consolidation.

First, large banks are harder to manage and create greater disruption when they fail. That Indian banks are smaller in absolute terms than global giants is no comfort. When it comes to systemic risk, the relevant measure is balance sheet size relative to GDP.

Secondly, merger is required where the potential for profit growth is limited. This is emphatically not true of the Indian market. In a normal year, one can expect commercial credit to grow at 20-25 per cent, with a net interest margin of around 2.5 per cent. Not many markets in the world can boast of a similar potential.

Thirdly, mergers make huge demands on HRD capabilities. This is precisely the weak spot for PSBs. Most PSBs face a decimation of their top management in the next three to five years. So this would be quite the wrong time to attempt consolidation. Instead, PSBs should concentrate on delivering better performance at their present sizes. If you cannot get the most out of assets of Rs 250,000 crore, you are unlikely to do better with Rs 500,000 crore of assets.

As India returns to a growth rate of 8 per cent and sustains it over a decade, our banks will attain a globally respectable size. There is no need to leapfrog the process through consolidation. The motto for Indian banks should be one that applies universally: don't grow too big for your boots.

September 17, 2009

Grow But Don't Try to Rule the World

Emerging markets have come out of the sub-prime crisis better than the advanced economies. Banks are a play on the economy, so this is reflected in the condition of banks in advanced and emerging economies. In 2009, banks in the US, UK and elsewhere reported their lowest return on assets in years, if not decades.

Profitability of banks in India and China, two leading emerging markets, was not only high but higher than in pre-crisis years! The average return on assets in both India and China in 2007-09 was 1%. In the period 2004-06, the figures for India and China had been 0.8 % and 0.7% respectively (Source: IMF's Global Financial Stability Report, April 2010). Banks in other emerging markets, such as Brazil and Russia, have also remained profitable although profitability declined during the crisis years.

At the turn of the century, most people thought it was only a matter of time before puny domestic banks in emerging markets were overrun by foreign giants as the markets opened up to competition. As a comprehensive survey of banks in emerging markets in the *Economist* (May 15-2) points out, this does not seem likely anymore.

On the contrary, emerging market banks could soon reach a size (measured by market capitalisation) comparable to that of their counterparts in advanced markets. Some are already there. China has three banks in the top 10 in the world. Brazil and Russia have one each. India's SBI is in the top 50. The question for emerging market banks is not whether they can grow. It is how fast they should grow; and whether a large overseas presence should be part of the growth strategy.

In the advanced markets, banks are still going through a process of de-leveraging consequent to the financial crisis. This is causing balance sheets to shrink. Credit growth, even when it resumes, will be slow. Emerging markets, in contrast, face the prospect of credit growth of 20-30%. Many emerging markets, notably India, experienced this sort of growth during the boom years. It now looks set to continue given that the bank loan to GDP ratio is way below that in advanced markets.

Banks first need to judge whether it is prudent at all to grow the loan book at such a pace for years together. Rapid loan growth in a system is known to be one of the surer signs of an impending crisis. All too often, such growth is based on lax lending standards and it tends to fuel asset bubbles that collapse one day.

Credit quality is not the only issue. Operational risks mount when banks expand at a heady pace. Loan growth of 20-30% requires expansion in branches, hiring of large numbers of people. There are bankers who will say that it is wise to forgo some opportunities and to ensure that growth is well managed.

On this point, one cannot generalise across emerging markets. In India, there are mitigating factors to the risks of rapid growth. High loan growth in recent years is partly on account of an under-tapped retail market. Nearly 50% of retail loans are home loans and these are among the safest loans to make.

Besides, rapid expansion in branches has mainly taken place amongst private banks. Public sector banks, whose share of the market is 75%, already have in place the branch network they need. Unlike in China, loan growth in India is not driven by lending to government institutions. Commercial loans are made mostly to a vibrant private sector. Finally, there are strong regulatory checks on exposure to risky sectors- real estate, the stock market, commodities.

The second strategic issue for the stronger emerging market banks is whether they should seize the opportunity to venture into advanced economies now that banks in those economies are in disarray. Should emerging markets banks be making big acquisitions abroad?

The arguments against going global are compelling. One is the experience of advanced market banks. A telling example is HSBC whose acquisition in 2002 of the US consumer finance company, Household, proved a disaster. ABN Amro also came a cropper trying to become a global bank.

The only banks with a global presence that are making money are ones that have been long entrenched in foreign markets, such as HSBC, Standard Chartered and Citibank. Emerging market banks thinking of making foreign acquisitions need to worry about their lack of knowledge of overseas markets and the difficulties in managing foreign staff.

Then, there is the experience of emerging market banks themselves. Some Indian banks have had overseas branches for decades. Very few make profit. The contribution to total profit is negligible. Simply catering to the diaspora is not a viable proposition.

Some Indian banks talk of catering to Indian corporates that have ventured abroad. As Aditya Puri of HDFC Bank points out, the number is not large enough to justify a presence in foreign markets. Nor do Indian banks have the strengths to address the local market overseas.

A third reason against venturing abroad is that the regulatory climate has undergone a sea-change after the recent crisis. India is not alone in being wary about letting in foreign banks in a big way. Other emerging markets feel the same way. The old argument that emerging market banks need to venture abroad so that they can better deal with foreign competition at home has lost its edge.

There is also greater appreciation in emerging market of the role of state-owned banks. The Indian model of having a mix of state, domestic private and foreign banks, with state-owned banks having a significant share, is widely seen as one that works. Even private bankers concede that state-owned banks have played in a role in anti-cyclical policies in the crisis. Emerging markets are unlikely to open up to foreign banks in a big way in the near future.

Emerging market banks will thus have the home market pretty much to themselves. They can hope to quickly attain world scale on the back of strong domestic market growth and restricted foreign competition. But world scale is not world class. Emerging market banks will still lack the repertoire of skills necessary to make an impact overseas. International exposure, not international domination, is what they should aspire for. Grow but don't try to rule the world.

June 10, 2010

Stormy Tide Favours Indian Banks

These are not great times for banks. Banks in the west, which are market leaders for the most part, face low growth, an erosion in capital due to sovereign debt exposures and stiffer regulation. They have to reckon with a permanent decline in their returns on equity thanks to enhanced capital requirements under Basel 3.

In contrast, Indian banks- and those in other emerging markets such as China and Brazil- are well-placed to maintain their returns on capital consequent to Basel 3. It does appear that Basel 3 will hasten in banking the shift in power towards emerging markets that we are seeing in the broader economic landscape.

Basel 3, devised consequent to the financial crisis of 2007, lays down revised rules for capital requirements for banks. Banks will have to hold more equity than before. The minimum equity requirement or tier 1 capital (including a conservation buffer) will now be 7%, a steep increase from the present level of 2%.

Total capital requirement (including tier 2 capital) will increase from 8% to 10.5%. In addition, there will be a 'counter-cyclical' buffer and additional requirements of equity for systemically large institutions. We should expect banks to operate with capital of at least 15-17% in the coming years. Leading banks in Europe and US already have capital adequacy of more than 15%.

Banks everywhere will need to raise capital to meet Basel 3 requirements. In December 2010, the Bank for International Settlements estimated the requirement for 91 large banks at •477 bn. In complying with Basel 3, western banks face several challenges. First, the estimate was made before the enormity of the Eurozone crisis became known. Once losses on account of restructuring of Eurozone debt are factored in, the capital requirements will go up even more.

Secondly, an important reason for western banks' improved capital position today is reduction in balance sheet size. Thus, the obverse side of an improvement in capital adequacy is tardy lending. As the financial crisis stretches out, credit growth will continue to be slow and this will constrain banks' profitability.

A third challenge for banks is regulatory limits on their activities. The Dodd-Frank Act in the US proposes to keep American banks out of proprietary trading and hedge funds, both lucrative areas for banks. In the UK, the Vickers Commission wants banks' retail activities to be ring-fenced from other activities through provision of higher capital for retail activities- this will add to costs in retail banking.

Western banks now face a permanent decline in their return on equity. Banks will be lucky hereafter to generate a return on equity of 10-15%, way below the 20% they were earning before the crisis. They will have to raise enormous amounts of capital precisely when their return on equity is declining.

Investors are bound to balk at putting their money in western banks. Banks can argue that investors should settle for lower returns because the new regulatory norms are intended to make banks safer. But investors are not going to accept claims of greater safety in a hurry.

Observers point out that India's own banks are in for stressful times in the short term. Some of the recent increase in interest rates will have to be absorbed by the banks and this will cause the net interest margin (NIM) to decline. Credit growth has slowed down.

Non-performing assets are rising. Banks are beginning to feel the pressure of stricter norms for lending to priority sector and the weaker sections.

So, yes, return on assets or equity could decline somewhat in the short-term. Take a longer view, however, and India's banks appear distinctly well placed to ride out the storm in international banking. The big plus is that, unlike their counterparts in the west, Indian banks have the opportunity to maintain their return on equity in the face of rising regulatory requirements of capital. For three reasons:

First, India;s public sector banks have woken up to the potential of fee income. NIM in the Indian banking system has declined in the last two years but this has been offset by rising fee income. As a result, return on assets remains close to 1% (Remember, Indian banks maintained a return of 1% on assets at the peak of the financial crisis).

Secondly, financial inclusion provides an opportunity to improve yields and even NIMs. Thirdly, on the retail side, two high-yielding products, credit cards and personal loans, have gone through a phase of cleaning out (the number of credit cards in circulation has fallen) and now look promising.

The contrast between our situation and those of banks in the west could not be starker. Banks in the west are desperately looking to cut costs (HSBC and BoA have both announced job cuts of 30,000 each) in order to maintain their profitability. Indian banks, on the other hand, can hope to maintain their profitability by focusing on revenues.

Banks everywhere will be hungry for capital following Basel 3. Indian banks' high returns on equity place them at an advantage vis-à-vis banks in the west when it comes to attracting capital. The Indian economy provides Indian banks the potential to grow; banks are in a position to attract the capital needed for growth; and growth is the key to market capitalisation. Basel 3 thus raises the enticing prospect of banks in India - and other emerging markets- catching up with their western counterparts on market capitalisation sooner than thought earlier.

September 15, 2011

8

Inclusion

An Ambitious Blueprint

India's commercial banks have been nursed back to health after a decade of financial reform. Another important component of the banking system, rural cooperative credit institutions, awaits resuscitation. Hope is at hand. Last February, a Task Force headed by A Vaidyanathan came out with an ambitious blueprint for the revival of these institutions.

The rural Cooperative Credit Structure (CCS) has three tiers comprising 112,309 Primary Agricultural Credit Societies (PACS) at the bottom, 367 District Cooperative Banks (DCCBs) in the middle and 30 state Cooperative Banks (SCBs) at the top. The SCBs and DCCBs provide refinance to the PACS.

The PACS are the lifeline of small farmers with a total membership of 12 crore. The commercial banks have 16.4 million accounts with an average size of direct loans of Rs 31,585. The PACS have 63.9 million accounts with an average size of loan of Rs 6,637.

The CCS is today badly impaired. Twenty per cent of SCBs and 35 per cent of DCCBs have eroded their net worth. Half the PACS are reporting losses. The accumulated losses of the CCS exceed Rs 9000 crore. Boards of several SCBs and DCCBs have been superseded and the sense of belonging, so critical to the performance of cooperatives, is missing in the system. The impairment of the CCS has undermined the flow of credit to the agricultural sector. One indicator is the decline in the share of cooperatives in the rural credit market from 62% in 1992-93 to 34% in 2002-03.

The Vaidyanathan Task Force wants the system to be revived at a total cost of about Rs 15,000 crore with recapitalisation being the biggest chunk of the cost. About half the cost is to be borne by the centre, a third by state governments and the rest by the CCS. This must seem a staggering sum to pour into a decrepit structure. What, then, is the case for recapitalisation and revival?

First, there is the evidence that the imposition of prudential norms, close supervision and freedom from government interference provide the necessary conditions for revival. The turnaround at public sector banks suggests that revival on such a basis is indeed possible. The Task Force would subject the CCS to stringent conditionalities. Drawing on the lessons learnt with commercial banks, the Task Force recommends that all cooperatives, including PACS, be subject to a minimum of 7% capital to risk weighted assets ratio with the ratio rising to 12% over five years.

Secondly, the gradual spread of crop insurance means that cooperatives will be operating in a more benign environment than in the past. Many of the defaults at the PACS owe to losses incurred on account of the vagaries of the weather. By creating a safety net for the farmer, crop insurance renders the CCS more viable. Thirdly, the growth of the food processing sector opens up opportunities for the CCS to diversify away from crop-related lending to lending to agri-businesses.

Interference by state governments through loan melas, waivers, provision of guarantees and the like, has wrought havoc with the CCS. The Task Force identifies the original sin as permitting state governments to have equity capital in cooperatives. So a priority in restructuring must be to return the share capital of state governments. Cooperatives are to be provided with soft loans for the purpose.

This will restore to cooperatives their intended character as organisations of members and for members, with all members having a strong stake in putting credit to good use. The Task Force also proposes legal and institutional reforms, including the enactment of a model Cooperative Law by states and an enlarged role for RBI in the regulation of the CCS.

Other committees have asked whether a three-tier structure is needed at all. It has been suggested that the DCCBs and PACS be converted into branches of the SCBs. This may not be advisable given that SCBs and DCCBs raise large amounts of public deposits whereas the PACS do not. Having an arm's length relationship between the big deposit takers and the PACS helps contain risk to public deposits. If this means higher intermediation costs, so be it.

In proposing a comprehensive overhaul of the CCS backed by capital, the Task Force has shown commendable boldness. But it, perhaps, goes overboard in asking for recapitalisation at one go. The danger is that its exhortation to cooperatives to pursue recoveries is likely to go unheeded. The experience with 'weak banks' indicates that a hard budget constraint does help in the matter of recoveries. We would be better off linking the provision of capital to cooperatives with recovery performance and phasing out recapitalisation accordingly.

April 21, 2005

Priority Sector as an Opportunity

The surge in commercial credit in the last couple of years has been one of the brighter spots of India's banking sector. Banks are no longer preoccupied with parking funds in government securities. They are eager to lend. This reflects as much the turnaround in the economy as the improved balance sheets of the banks themselves.

So far so good. But is it good enough? Neither the government nor the RBI thinks so. There is concern over the composition of credit as well as the price of credit. RBI Governor Y V Reddy gave expression to the latter concern at a FICCI-IBA seminar earlier this month. He said, "An area of concern, in terms of public perception, is that there is under-pricing of credit risk for private sector corporates while there could be overpricing of risks in lending to agriculture as well as small and medium enterprises."

The point has often been made in recent times that the priority sector today subsidises the larger corporates. The prime lending rate (PLR) is the risk-adjusted rate for the best corporates. Yet, banks lend to the best corporates at sub-PLR rates. Banks are said to compensate themselves by overcharging the priority sector.

What is overlooked is that banks seek to earn a return on capital on the overall relationship with corporates. The return includes not just loan income but fee income as well. A rule-of-thumb is that banks expect to earn one rupee of fee income for every rupee of loan income. Besides, big corporates bring to banks large volumes of low-cost deposits that lower the cost of funds. The denominator, capital allocated, is lower for fee-based services than for loans. As a result, banks can afford to price loans below the risk-adjusted rate where large corporates are concerned- the other elements in the ratio ensure that the return on capital meets the hurdle rate for the bank.

Small businesses do not generate much fee income, hence must expect to be charged the risk-adjusted rate for loans. The difficulty here is the quantification of risk. Risk may be over-estimated for several reasons. One, financial data on small businesses are not reliable. Two, the second half of the nineties was a bad period for small businesses and many banks burnt their fingers with them. The business environment has since improved and small businesses that survived are poised to do well. But estimates of risk based on past data are bound to be biased upwards and hence loan rates will err on the higher side.

There is a third reason why loan rates for the priority sector could be higher than dictated by risk. Banks think they have enough lending opportunities in the retail sector and would not like to trouble themselves with the priority sector. As both agriculture and the small-sector are crucial to growth, this needs to be corrected by regulatory intervention. But it is well to remember that the cost of credit in the informal channels is way above what banks charge. So, it is the quantity of credit, not the price, that the regulator must focus on. If a higher than risk-adjusted rate is what it takes to induce banks to lend to the priority sector, so be it.

On the quantity of credit to the priority sector, an internal working group of the RBI has just released a draft technical paper. The recent record is singularly uninspiring. Banks have failed to meet the target of 40% of bank credit as also the sub-target of 18% for agriculture. Housing loans account for 21% of priority sector loans. The RBI needs to document the record on the priority sector after omission of housing loans as also various other categories recommended for deletion by the working group.

The tenor of the report suggests that the group regards priority sector lending merely as a social obligation. That is an incorrect reading in today's context. There are clear signs of disintermediation on banks' asset side- corporates source only 30% of their funds from banks. So banks need to view agriculture and small business as areas of opportunity. And agriculture is not just about the small farmer, it includes sun-rise industries such as those driven by bio-technology.

Banks are not responding to these opportunities because of imperfect information and the absence of incentives. Where top management has short tenures, the incentive to take the long view and build institutional skills is missing. That is why regulatory action is required to push priority sector lending. Such action does not constitute a distortion, it is meant to position India's banks for competitive advantage before foreign banks gain freer entry. The name of the game has changed: priority sector lending today is about maximising shareholder value.

October 20, 2005

Five Myths about Microfinance

The microfinance bubble has burst. The AP government ordinance, the AP opposition's campaign asking borrowers not to repay and the sheer public hostility towards MFIs- all these have put the brakes on MFI activities for now. We need to rethink the role of MFIs in the rural economy. In order to do so, we must first grasp some of the myths on which the MFI sector has rested thus far.

1. **MFIs are crucial to financial inclusion:** The big impetus to financial inclusion came way back in 1969 following the nationalisation of banks. Secondly, financial inclusion is not just about giving small ticket loans. It is also about taking deposits and providing basic banking services.

MFIs are hardly the pioneers in microfinance. The early initiative came from the Self-Help Group movement started by the government of India in 1992 under the auspices of NABARD and with the involvement of banks. This is the biggest outreach programme of its kind in the world. It covers 86 million poor households and has extended credit of Rs 23, 000 crore. MFIs cover 30 million customers and have lent over Rs 30,000 crore.

Under the SHG scheme, credit is linked to savings (unlike MFI credit). There is focus on capacity-building amongst borrowers. The rate of interest is 8-10% with monthly repayment. The suggestion that MFIs are crucial to financial inclusion is only part of an attempt to give respectability to what is increasingly a profit-driven activity.

2. **MFIs have reached out to those ignored by banks:** The contention is that MFIs complement the efforts of banks by

reaching out to those ignored by banks. This too is not true. AP has an average credit/deposit ratio of over 105 per cent and a ratio of over 80 per cent in half the districts. (The national average is 63 per cent). AP does not lack credit. MFIs would have been made a real contribution had they fanned out to states where the credit/deposit ratios are low.

Instead, they have focused on AP. They have done so because AP houses nearly a quarter of the SHGs. MFIs chose the easy route of tapping into established SHGs for making loans. This was viable in the early stages but, over time, it has led to the problem of multiple lending and excessive debt burdens. It is no different from private banks in India marketing consumer loans or US banks marketing sub-prime loans.

3. **MFIs are an important mechanism for alleviating rural poverty:** Credit is only one of several instruments needed for fighting poverty. Secondly, credit can help alleviate poverty if it goes into income-generation schemes. MFI credit, for the most part, is for consumption. Thirdly, returns to agriculture are so low that it is inconceivable that it can service interest rates of 24 per cent and above that MFIs charge. Since agriculture is the key to rural poverty, it is ridiculous to suggest that MFI credit can help alleviate poverty.

4. **MFIs have substituted money-lenders who used to charge even higher interest rates:** The comparison with money-lenders is flawed. Money-lenders don't go out and market their loans as MFIs do. Besides, money-lenders make loans strictly against collateral and this is a built-in check on lending.

Secondly, MFI interest rates in AP are said to have been in the range of 24-60 per cent. At the upper end, the rates are no different from those of money-lenders. Yes, MFIs did substitute money-lenders in a way because many money-lenders found it expedient to set up MFIs themselves- they could then have easy access to bank funds!

5. **High operational costs means that small ticket loans cannot cost less than 24 per cent :** If this is true, how is lending to SHGs viable? The high lending rates of many MFIs translate into fat salaries for executives and abnormal returns. (Some have return on assets of 5%; a bank is lucky if it makes 1 per cent).

Public sector banks (PSBs) have long had branches in the rural areas. Small loans will be one element in their portfolio which will include low-cost deposits and other products. With branch costs fully written off, it is hard to see why microfinance provided by PSBs needs to be priced at 24 per cent. If indeed the operational costs turn out to be steep in some areas, then the bank correspondent and other models need to be developed.

PSBs have not put their best foot forward in respect of microfinance because they lack the incentives to do so. Most are listed now and have had to focus on earnings growth, which is easily provided by corporate and retail credit. The regulatory cap on interest on small loans was a dampener. (The cap is now gone). Lending to MFIs qualified as priority sector credit, so PSBs could not be troubled to build their own portfolios.

Many people think the recent problems with MFIs were the result of some excesses. With a little tweaking here and there, MFIs can be in the forefront of financial inclusion. They are wrong. The entire MFI model needs revisiting. At least PSBs are much better placed to pursue financial inclusion on their own. The AP ordinance and its fall-out ensure that the go-go days for MFIs are over. And that is all to the good.

November 11, 2010

MFIs: Malegam Misses the Point

Microfinance institutions (MFIs) have grown at an explosive pace in recent years. This growth has come at a steep cost: heavy concentration of loans in one state, Andhra Pradesh; over-borrowing by the poor; extortionate interest rates; and questionable recovery practices. These and the spectacle of promoters reaping huge gains in the name of uplifting the poor have caused a severe political backlash against the sector.

The RBI, which has hitherto adopted a hands-off approach to the sector, was obliged to set up a committee under Y H Malegam to go into the entire gamut of issues related to microfinance and make suitable recommendations. There were really two main issues that the committee needed to address:

One, what precisely is the role of MFIs in financial inclusion-is it to be a dominant role or a supporting one? Two, given that

MFIs have a role to play, how best do we regulate them? The committee has addressed the second at length but steered clear of the first.

The regulations recommended are sweeping in nature and will definitely have the effect of reining in MFIs and ushering in consolidation in the sector. Since RBI committees are supported by the central bank's own secretariat, they do reflect the RBI's thinking even when they mostly comprise outsiders.

The recommendations show how far quickly the RBI's own thinking has evolved on the subject. Last year, the RBI had indicated that it did not favour capping interest rates in the sector. Now, the committee wants a cap of 24 per cent. In addition, it wants to cap the interest margin.

The RBI has had to change its mind because it has found that what was being said about extortionate interest rates levied by MFIs is true. The larger MFIs have been charging an average interest rate of 37 per cent; the smaller ones 29 per cent. In addition, there have been hidden charges. The Malegam committee now wants only three components in any loan made by MFIs: the interest rate; a processing fee of not more than 1 per cent of the gross loan amount; and the insurance premium.

The Malegam committee also attempts to tackle multiple lending as well as excess borrowing. To prevent multiple lending, it stipulates that a borrower should not be a member of more than one joint liability group/ self-help group and that not more than two MFIs should lend to the same borrower. To prevent over-borrowing, it wants the aggregate value of all outstanding loans to a borrower to be restricted to Rs 25,000.

If the RBI accepts these stipulations, it could end up over-reaching itself. The issue is not the appropriateness of these norms. It is the enforcement of these norms at the grassroots. How on earth will the RBI ensure that MFIs adhere to these norms across millions of borrowers? And who is to say that no borrower should have loans in excess of Rs 25,000? Or, for that matter, that the interest rate should never exceed 24 per cent?

The best way to ensure credit discipline, whether in respect of borrowing limits or interest rates, is to mandate that all bank loans to MFIs should be through a consortium. This puts the onus for setting appropriate borrower limits and interest rates squarely on the banks.

The banks should be free to determine whether, in particular cases, borrowing can exceed Rs 25,000 or whether an interest rate higher than 24 per cent is acceptable. The onus for monitoring of end-use of funds will also be on the banks. The banks may appoint agents or assign staff for the purpose. Consortium lending to MFIs will ensure that the sort of runaway growth in MFI assets that we have seen in the recent past, fuelled by indiscriminate bank lending to MFIs, does not recur.

The more important policy question is the proper place in the sun for MFIs. In the prevalent neo-liberal philosophy, policy-makers have been more than ready to accept that the private sector is best placed to bring about financial inclusion. Some are even tickled by the thought that removing poverty through the provision of credit can actually be a profit-making activity. What better than market economics married to poverty removal?

It is the acceptance of this philosophy that must explain why the SHG-Bank Linkage programme has come to be overshadowed by MFIs in the last two years: the share of SBLP in outstanding loans has dropped from 74 per cent to 60 per cent between 2008 and 2010. MFIs have grown in relative importance not just because they are more aggressive or efficient but because of 'lazy' financial inclusion on the part of banks. Since loans to MFIs qualify as priority sector lending, banks have found it expedient to meet their targets through loans to MFIs.

This philosophy ignores the fact that banks have lower costs and hence are in a position to deliver loans at lower rates than MFIs, while also providing other financial services. Moreover, profit-oriented financial inclusion is bound to create problems, however best we try to regulate MFIs. Banks, not MFIs, must be in the forefront of financial inclusion. The Malegam committee conspicuously fails to make this point.

Feburary 3, 2011

PART – III

WORLD ECONOMY

9

Global Crisis

Puzzles about the World Economy

Several facets of the world economy today must strike many as puzzles. Here is a partial list and some explanations.

1. *High oil prices have not had much of an impact on economic growth.*

Until recently, the experts were telling us that if oil prices stayed at over $60 a barrel, they would surely begin to bite. The IMF's *World Economic Outlook* (September, 2005) believes that spot prices have been driven mainly by fundamentals, not speculation. Accordingly, it factors in a price for oil of $61.75 per barrel for 2006.

Yet the WEO projects world economic growth at 4.3 per cent for both 2005 and 2006. This would be on top of growth of 4 per cent in 2003 and 5.1 per cent in 2004. How is it that the oil shock has failed this time to derail growth?

First, unlike in the 1970s, high oil prices today are the result of a sharp rise in consumption, not an exogenous supply shock. Output has grown, so oil prices have risen. With a supply shock, oil prices rise at a given level of output, hence growth suffers. Second, global oil intensity today is 38 per cent lower than in the seventies, so the supply-side impact is muted. Third, oil prices have not fed into higher core inflation, obviating the need for higher interest rates that would slow down growth.

In 2000, the IMF had estimated that every $5 increase in oil prices would reduce output by 0.3 per cent . In today's changed world, it estimates a decline in output of 0.1-0.15 per cent. This means that the cumulative effect of the rise in oil prices since 2003 would be

1-1.5 per cent. Take this away from last year's level of 5.1 per cent and you are still left with a brisk growth rate for the world economy.

2. *Despite rising public debt and high growth, long-term bond yields are low in the industrial world.*

Real yields on long-term bonds in the US today are 1.6 per cent today compared to 3.3 per cent since 1960. The Chairman of the US Fed, Alan Greenspan, calls the low yields on long-term bonds a "conundrum".

The low yields primarily reflect what the Ben Bernanke, Chairman of the US President's Council of Economic Advisors, calls a "global savings glut". It is not that the world as a whole is saving more; indeed, the savings rate for the world economy is lower today than in the past 30 years. But global savings exceed investment because investment has declined even more than savings.

In the industrial countries, governments' fiscal position has deteriorated and reduced savings. But savings of corporates have risen to a point where they are today net savers. Corporate savings have been boosted by higher profits while corporate investment has remained low after the high-tech bubble burst. As excess capacity had been built up earlier, corporates are not in a hurry to invest. In Asia too, corporate investment has stayed low ever since the East Asian economies decided to raise interest rates after the crisis of 1997.

The low yields on long-term bonds reflect other factors as well. Asian central banks have accumulated huge reserves in their bid to stem appreciation of their currencies. A big chunk of these reserves has found its way into industrial countries' securities and this has tended to drive yields down.

A shift in institutions' appetite for securities has also contributed to a decline in long-term yields on bonds. Partly in response to regulatory requirements, pension funds and insurance companies have increased their holdings of long-term bonds and reduced their holdings of equities. Not least, markets appear to think that inflation volatility has decreased and are demanding lower premia than before.

3. *Emerging markets are today net exporters of capital.*

Rich countries are supposed to have a surfeit of capital and poor countries a lack of it. So capital tends to flow from rich countries to poorer ones. Yet, emerging markets have become net exporters of capital to the industrial world since 2000.

Some see this as a response to the turbulence in these economies in the late nineties. Private capital flows into these markets fell and local residents preferred to send their money abroad. Later, governments decided to reduce borrowings in international markets and accumulated foreign reserves in order to prevent currency appreciation. Yet others prefer to relate this phenomenon to the excess of savings over investment in these economies mentioned earlier. The excess is bound to show up as net export of capital.

4. *Gold prices are at an all-time high.*

Gold is supposed to be the classic hedge against inflation. Inflation rates are low and the markets seem to have great faith in the efficacy of central banks, yet gold prices have touched a high. Is this a case of a wave of liquidity lifting all assets? Or is there a message here that we are missing?

October 6, 2005

Market, not Economic, Crisis

The stock market may or may not determine the fortunes of the economy but it certainly determines the mood of the media and the general public. The fall in stock markets worldwide last week has created gloom all round. Many wonder whether a major economic crisis is in the offing. Fear not. Stock markets may be in for a bad time but the global economic outlook remains largely unchanged.

There is a tendency to readily associate a crash in the stock market with an economic slump. That is because we have indeed seen such a link several times in the past. The most famous is the Great Depression that followed the Great Crash of 1929 in the US. Japan went through a prolonged period of stagnation in the nineties following a crash in its stock market. In the 1997 east Asian crisis too, stock market tumbles presaged an economic decline.

But there is no automatic link between stock market crashes and an economic downturn. In 1987, the stock market dived sharply in the US but the US economy quickly shrugged off the blues. In 2000 again, the US stock market bubble burst without having any big impact on the economy. Despite the crash in the stock market last year, India ended up with a growth rate of 9.4 per cent.

Other factors are important in determining whether a stock market decline translates into a setback for the economy. The two most important factors, perhaps, are the impact on the banking sector and the policy response to a stock market crash. The Great Depression was the outcome, not of the stock market crash in itself, but of several events that followed: a failure of banks, fiscal and monetary contraction and protectionism in the US and abroad.

A crash typically becomes a broader economic problem when banks are exposed to the stock market in a big way or are vulnerable in other ways. Because of banks' role in money creation, bank failures radiate into the broader economy. In the Great Crash, in Japan in the nineties and in the East Asian crisis, weaknesses in the banking sector were central to the debilitating effects on the economy.

The US stock market crashes of 1987 and 2000 did not tell on the banking sector. As a result, the US economy remained largely unfazed. The response of the US Fed also mattered. Having learnt from its lapses during the Great Crash, the Fed switched quickly to monetary easing in both 1987 and 2000.

Cut to the present. There is much talk of the problem in the US subprime loan market spreading through the financial system and to the rest of the world. Perhaps the confusion arises because of the reference to 'loans' and 'investment banks'. This might give the impression that there are serious problems in the banking sector.

There is indeed a problem in the subprime market but a recent survey by the US Fed indicated that commercial banks' exposure to subprime loans is negligible. The entities affected are others in the financial sector- specialised lending institutions with direct exposures to subprime loans and investment banks, hedge funds and others with indirect exposures.

It is true that appetite for credit in general has suddenly shrunk and many commercial banks are stuck with low-yield loans for takeovers that they had hope to parcel out to others. This may lead to an undesirable concentration of risk at commercial banks and affect banks' profits this year. But it falls well short of a crisis in banking.

US banks have been hugely profitable for several years in a row, they are well capitalised, their risk management practices have improved and, thanks to securitisation, credit risk today is shared widely in the financial sector. The US banking sector should be able to take the present problems in its stride.

The slowdown in the US housing sector had been factored into forecasts for the US economy. The IMF does not see the problems in the subprime market as making a big difference. In its update on the world economic outlook of July 25, the IMF has revised US economic growth down by a mere 0.2 percentage points to 2 per cent.

More interestingly, the IMF has revised its forecast for world economic growth upwards from 4.9 per cent to 5.2 per cent . Evidently, the IMF is sticking to its thesis that the US slowdown is on account of problems specific to the US and not on account of factors that impinge on the global economy at large.

Key factors underpinning global growth today are intact. These are: the "savings glut" resulting from the excess of savings over investment in China, Japan and the oil exporters, a glut that has kept interest rates low; the rise of emerging markets, notably China and India, as engines of growth for the world economy; and strong domestic demand in China, India and, more recently, in the euro area and Japan.

The turmoil in financial markets may continue for a while and fools, who got carried away in their exuberance, will be parted from their money. But, in the absence of real shocks, the prospect of an economic crisis must be rated low.

August 9, 2007

Can We Prevent a Sub-Prime Crisis?

A year ago, the sub-prime crisis blew up in the US. Policy-makers in the US and elsewhere have been engaged in a grim battle to contain its fallout. Can we do anything to prevent such crises?

One view is that boom-bust cycles are integral to the free market economy and that we should stand back and let institutions fail. But the immediate consequences of such a policy-a deep and long recession-are so serious that no government has the stomach for it.

Another view is that it is hard to call a bubble correctly- we know there is a bubble only after it has burst. Once the bubble bursts, policy-makers should step in to limit the damage, as they have done in the present crisis. The danger with this approach is that public intervention to limit the damage stores up worse problems for the future ('moral hazard') so that we end up facing even graver crises down the road.

A third school looks for preventive medicine. 'Lessons from the sub-prime crisis' promises to be as rich a field for researchers as the East Asian crisis of the nineties. Robert Shiller, professor at Yale and author of a book on how irrational exuberance can create a bubble in the stock market, wades into the field with The sub-prime solution (Princeton).

Shiller proposes three types of solutions. One, better information. Two, new markets for risks. Three, new retail risk management institutions.

Some of his proposals for better information are familiar enough- more disclosure from financial institutions; an improved database on individuals' economic and medical history; a financial watchdog that will ensure consumer safety in financial products (China and India have such a mechanism but this has long been thought a sign of financial backwardness!).

Shiller has some new proposals as well. He wants low-income individuals to be provided advice on the basis of fixed hourly fees that will be eligible for tax benefits. At present, the advice they get is from people who sell products and who collect a fee from the providers of those products. Naturally, such advice tends to be biased. But how do we get people to opt for paid services when they can get free advice from sellers of products? How do we ensure that advice provided for a fee is of the right quality?

Shiller also wants financial contracts to have certain clauses that will protect consumers who cannot read between the fine print. A more interesting proposal is requiring asset prices to be quoted in inflation-adjusted terms. Shiller contends that if this had been done for housing, buyers in the US would not have thought that homes would be spectacular investments. Note that both these proposals mean more stringent regulation.

Shiller advocates the creation of new markets for risks. Housing futures, he says, would help contain a speculative bubble by creating opportunities for short sellers. But such markets, which Shiller helped launch, have failed to take off in the US. Besides, this does seem a bad time to sing the virtues of short selling- we have seen the havoc this can create at American financial institutions.

Shiller's third suggestion is the creation of new retail risk-management institutions. One is what he calls 'continuous workout mortgages', mortgages on which terms are continuously adjusted in response to changes in borrowers' incomes and conditions in the housing market.

If the borrower's ability to pay drops, the terms would be revised downwards accordingly. Shiller contends that this is what happens in bankruptcy anyway, so he is only proposing a more orderly adjustment. He thinks there are ways to address the moral hazard implicit in such an arrangement- the borrower losing the incentive to earn or under-reporting his income. Another retail institution Shiller urges is home equity insurance. By putting a floor on home prices, it would prevent panic sales of homes and sharp collapses in home prices in a downturn.

These are ideas that would go some way towards making home ownership safer for large numbers of people. But one cannot resist the impression that Shiller takes too narrow a view of the sub-prime crisis. The crisis is not just about a collapse in housing prices and people losing their homes. This is a human tragedy, of course, but in itself, defaults on sub-prime loans would not have posed a problem for the US economy. The sub-prime crisis has ballooned into a financial crisis because it impacts financial institutions that have leveraged exposures to sub-prime contracts.

Another sub-prime crisis is as unlikely as a plane wantonly crashing into a tall building in the US- the problem will manifest itself in some other form. We need to address the broader issue that underlies the sub-prime crisis: how to ensure that regulation keeps pace with financial innovation? This means the focus for reform has to be on financial institutions and the regulatory architecture, not just protection of the consumer.

Several factors have kept the world economy from keeling over. The Fed has bailed out large financial institutions and has been quick to provide liquidity even to investment banks. The US Treasury has provided a large fiscal stimulus. Central banks have coordinated their actions well. Many banks in the western world have managed to raise capital from emerging economies to offset their losses. Emerging economies, whose weight in the global economy has increased over the years, have sustained growth thanks to strong domestic demand.

August 7, 2008

From the Sub-Prime to the Ridiculous

Damn those tickers on the TV screen, the ones that record the ups and downs of stock prices. For good or ill, financial markets set the mood for the economic lives of nations. When financial markets tumble, people quickly think the world is crashing about them.

The sub-prime crisis is no ordinary financial market crisis. It has been labeled a "once a century" event. That must explain the apocalyptic headlines in the media- about "the end of capitalism", another "Great Depression" and so on.

How justified is the widespread gloom? This question raises two corollary issues. One, the general issue of the impact of financial markets crashes on the real economy. Two, the particular issue of the impact of the present crash on the US and the global economy. Since the impact of the present crash is now expected to be significant, the regulatory lessons of the crisis are the subject of considerable debate.

Let us begin with the impact of financial markets on the real economy. There is a presumption that when there is a crash in the stock market- and by this, one means a decline of, say, more than 10% in a short period- that is a warning of serious problems in the economy at large.

This presumption rests largely on the traumatic aftermath of the Crash of 1929 in the US, which was followed by the Great Depression. As students of economics know, it wasn't the Crash so much as the faulty policy responses to it that triggered the Depression.

The US Fed unwisely tightened monetary policy and the resultant lack of liquidity caused bank failures. Banks were allowed to fail- in itself a significant policy lapse. There was a failure to activate counter-cyclical fiscal policy. On top of it all, the US resorted to protectionism which caused other nations to react likewise and this again impacted trade and growth in a big way.

As the very different responses to today's financial market crisis make clear, big policy lessons have been learnt and practised since.

That is one reason why subsequent financial market crashes have not uniformly led to major recessions or even a downturn-the crash of 1987 in the US is one example. Another, more fundamental reason is that financial market crashes are not necessarily followed by economic declines.

The IMF's *World Economic Outlook* (October, 2008) surveys the evidence on financial stresses and downturns. The WEO analyses 17 episodes of financial stress in the advanced economies during the past three decades. One crucial finding is that nearly half of financial crashes do not impact in a big way on the real economy.

What is 'financial stress' and how do we measure it? The WEO has devised an index called the "Financial Stress Index (FSI)" that enables a rigorous measurement.

The FSI is constructed as an average of the following indicators:

- Three banking related variables: the "beta" of banking sector stocks, the spread between inter-bank rates and the yield on T-bills, and the slope of the yield curve;
- Three securities market related variables: corporate bond spreads, stock market returns, and time varying stock return volatility;
- One foreign exchange variable: time -varying effective stock exchange rate volatility;

Using these seven variables, the FSI is constructed for each of 17 countries in the IMF sample. An episode of financial stress is identified as a period when the index for any country is more than one standard deviation above its trend. On this basis, the IMF identified 113 episodes of financial stress in the past 30 years in the 17 countries. Of these, 43 episodes were banking-related, 50 reflected primarily turmoil in the financial markets and 20 reflected turmoil in the foreign exchange market.

The IMF went on to investigate how many of these episodes were followed by an economic slowdown and how many by a recession- and what explained the differences in the impact on the economy. It found that of the 113 episodes investigated, 29 were followed by slowdown and 29 by recessions. The remaining 55 episodes were not followed by an economic downturn. In other words, nearly half the episodes of financial stress did not have any serious economic impact.

So, we need to understand when financial stress seriously impacts the real economy and when it does not. Perhaps the most important finding in the IMF study is that about 60% of financial stress episodes that are followed by downturns are banking-related. The magnitude of slowdowns and recessions following banking-related stress is greater than that with other types of financial stress. A plausible corollary is that where financial market crashes do not impact significantly on the banking system, the real economy is unlikely to be greatly affected.

No great mystery as to why this is so. A stressed banking system means huge losses in banks and an erosion in bank capital and, quite possibly, the failure of many banks.

In either case, the supply of credit contracts. Credit contraction, in turn, leads to an economic downturn. In the event of banking failures, the credit contraction and the consequent downturn can be sharp. The message is clear: take care of the banking system and the real economy takes care of itself.

The role of banks in explaining financial stress must seem something of a puzzle in the advanced economies where the importance of banks in the financial system has receded with time. When non-bank sources of finance have become so important, why would banking stress matter so much? Where capital markets are dominant, surely banking stress should matter less?

Quite the contrary, the IMF finds. This is because banks have a symbiotic relationship with securities markets. Banks continue to fund non-bank financial intermediaries Financial stress occurs because financial institutions' leverage tends to be pro-through repurchase facilities. Banks, in turn, depend on market-based funding sources to finance their assets (such as certificates of deposit and commercial paper).

The behaviour of financial intermediaries tends to be pro-cyclical: institutions overextend their balance sheets through excess debt when the going is good; when there is a shock, there is de-leveraging. This sort of pro-cyclical behaviour is most typical of investment banks. An expansion in assets goes hand in hand with increased leverage-exactly what we saw in the build-up the of sub-prime crisis.

In theory, banks' behaviour should be less pro-cyclical because they are in the business of using retail deposits to make long-term loans and you cannot suddenly increase access to retail deposits. But, the IMF finds that in financial systems where capital markets are highly developed, banks tend to exhibit more pro-cyclical behaviour.

The WEO does not explain why this is so - and this is an important lacuna in its analysis- so let me venture an explanation. This also brings us to the second issue we raised at the outset, namely, the impact of the present financial market crisis on the US economy and the implications for regulation. Why has the financial market crisis in the present instance led on to a banking crisis?

Investors will always be comparing banks' return on equity with that of investment banks and other financial intermediaries. When investment banks ratchet up their returns through pro-cyclical behaviour, banks will find it hard not to follow suit. Banks do this on the liabilities side by resorting to wholesale funds in greater degree; on the asset side, they increase investment in securities. When banks' behaviour tends to mimic that of securities markets participants, they will be vulnerable in the same as market participants are to the ups and downs of markets.

Banks' tendency, under the pressure of investors, to indulge in the same pro-cyclical as other intermediaries, perhaps, explains why slowdowns and recessions tend to be deeper in economies with more-arms-length financial systems- that is, systems where financial markets are more developed. In the present crisis, banks have suffered greatly because they were exposed to the same securitization portfolios to which that investment banks and others were exposed.

There is a world of difference between banks having loans on their books and having securities. Loans are not subject to 'mark to market' accounting; securities are. As investment banks, dependent on wholesale funds, rushed to liquidate their portfolios, the values of securities plummeted sharply. Banks holding securities portfolios have taken a big beating.

The IMF's Global Financial Stability Report (GSFR, October 2008) has statistics on the relative risks of loan exposures with securities exposures. Financial institutions have suffered losses of $425 bn on all types of loans, including corporate and leveraged loans. Of this, banks' share is estimated at $255-290 bn. This is an order of losses that banks can easily withstand especially since banks have raised nearly $500 bn in additional capital after the crisis erupted in 2007.

It is the losses on securities that are proving harder to manage. These losses are estimated at $945 bn in October, 2008 with banks' share amounting to $725-820 bn. Thus, total losses on loans and securities amount to $1.4 trillion ($425 bn on loans plus $945 bn on securities). Drawn from the GSFR, we show only loans and losses related to the housing sector and to what might be regarded as sub-prime-related securities.

When we compute losses as a proportion of exposures, the numbers are revealing. As the losses on sub-prime loans-widely touted as the villain of the piece- are a mere $50 bn and 15 per cent of outstanding sub-prime loans. It could be argued that sub-prime loans tend to impact on other loans as well as defaults on housing loans lead to a collapse in housing prices. So, in the we have included losses on subprime, alt A, prime and commercial real estate loans together. These are together a mere 3.6 per cent of loans outstanding. Thus, loan losses by themselves cannot explain the sheer magnitude of the crisis we face today.

It is losses on sub-prime related securities that have led to matters going out of control. Asset backed securities and collateralized debt obligations on asset backed securities account for a staggering $ 500 bn in losses- or nearly 33 per cent of exposures on these. These were instruments that often had sub-prime loans as just one underlying component in a package of securities.

These securities were held in large amounts by institutions such as investment banks and hedge funds that funded themselves in the wholesale market. When defaults on the underlying sub-prime loans turned out to be higher than expected, prices of these securities fell. Institutions suffered losses on the securities portfolios they were holding. There was a rush to exit, which caused prices to fall even further.

In the panic that followed, there was simply no market for many of these securities- they turned out to be illiquid and hence no market prices were available. Many have had to be valued using rough methods that tend to exaggerate losses, meaning the prices of these securities thrown up by these methods were lower than were warranted by the default rates on underlying loans. As banks were also holding these securities, they were exposed to the same losses as other financial institutions.

Individual banks used securitisation as a means of getting loans off their books and on to other institutions. But other banks were among those who invested in these securities, so the banking system as a whole remained exposed to them. As a result, the behaviour of non-bank financial institutions exposed to sub-prime related securities has impacted heavily on banks as well.

It is somewhat misleading, therefore, to label the present crisis a 'sub-prime crisis'. This suggests that when banks make sub-prime loans, that is, practice financial inclusion, they are apt to get into trouble. Some commentators have even gone so far as to warn against political pressure for financial inclusion in India.

That would be an unwarranted conclusion to draw from the present crisis. As explained above, it is not exposure to sub-prime loans or even to housing sector loans in the aggregate that are a problem; it is sub-prime related securities that explain the sheer magnitude of the present crisis.

To complete the chain from sub-prime loans to a financial crisis, several links have to be brought in: incorrect credit rating, holding of illiquid securities by leveraged institutions dependent on wholesale funds, flawed mark-to-market accounting, poor design of managerial incentives. It is the securitization of sub-prime loans, not sub-prime loans themselves, that explains why we have a crisis on the present scale.

In light of our analysis, the WEO's comment on the role of securitisation in the present crisis must seem quite an understatement:

However, as the current crisis underscores, the trend towards securitization in more-arm's-length systems, while permitting portfolio diversification to offset the costs of monitoring the idiosyncratic risks that are inherent in traditional relationship-based systems, does not eliminate the need for banks and markets to independently assess the risk of their exposures.

We are in some ways re-learning an important regulatory lesson highlighted in the failure of the hedge fund, LTCM, in 1998. The US Fed had to orchestrate a rescue of the fund at the time. It was asked why the Fed did so when its responsibility was limited to banks. The reason given was that while the failure of a hedge fund in itself was not material, the failure of LTCM was bound to impact on banks.

Banks were exposed to LTCM in three ways: they had given loans to LTCM; they were counterparties to derivatives trades carried out by LTCM; and they held the same illiquid assets that LTCM did. A failure of LTCM, it was contended, would be the equivalent of a nuclear holocaust in the financial world. One obvious regulatory lesson was that banks' exposure to highly leveraged institutions (HLIs) must be monitored and all banks must know the cumulative exposure to a given institution.

This has been done but it is clearly not enough. Banks can contain loan exposures to HLIs but they will still be linked to HLIs by reason of holding identical securities portfolios. Either banks' investment in securities or certain kinds of securities must be limited; or HLIs themselves will need to be subjected to regulation so that they do not end up infecting and endangering the banking system.

One set of HLIs, investment banks, has already been dealt with: the bigger investment banks have either disappeared or merged with a bank or will soon be merged with a bank. A regulatory proposal that has been talked about is containing securitisation by requiring banks to hold a minimum proportion of loans on their own books. This will ensure that banks bear most of the risks attendant on loans instead of palming of these risks to others and will act as a check on imprudent lending.

But this may not be enough. Banks can still be exposed to market risks on investment portfolios. After all, the investments that posed a threat to banks in the LCM crisis were not securitisation portfolios. Clearly, we will need to expand on the regulatory lessons learnt in the LTCM debacle.

We have seen how the banking system came to be caught up in the present crisis. And we know that where the banking system is stressed, the impact on the real economy is significant. How severe can we expect the impact on the real economy to be?

The WEO compares the current episode of financial stress to six well-known episodes of banking related stress that occurred in advanced economies during the 1990s. These episodes occurred in Finland, Norway, Sweden, the UK, US and Japan. An examination of the medians and averages of selected macroeconomic variables in the US and the euro area today with those in the six episodes indicates that the current imbalances and adjustments are smaller today than in the earlier six episodes.

There are other mitigating features. One is that corporate balance sheets are much stronger. Two, the policy stance in the US has been more pro-active. Thirdly, banks have moved quickly to augment their capital. The WEO was, perhaps, written before subsequent developments that are not mentioned- moves in the US and the euro area to inject government capital into banks, more generous liquidity support and guarantees of inter-bank liabilities and deposits in the euro area. Household imbalances and the size of the US mortgage area remain problem areas.

The IMF's assessment is that the US downturn may become more severe and turn into a recession whereas the euro area could get away with a slowdown. The IMF does not say this but it is reasonable to suggest that neither the financial stress indicators nor the policy responses point to anything like another Great Depression, never mind the headlines.

Nov 8, 2008 (EPW)

Ten Regulatory Lessons from the Sub-Prime Crisis

As in the life of individuals, so also in the lives of nations, crises are manifestations of deep-rooted problems, problems that have remained unaddressed for long. The sheer enormity of the sub-prime crisis underlines the need to revisit the entire area of financial regulation and, more broadly, the management of the economy at both the national and global levels.

This is an attempt to compile an early list of possible lessons from the present crisis. It is not meant to be an exhaustive list. Besides, the lessons and prescriptions mentioned below are all the subject of intense research at the moment and will continue to be debated. One should, therefore, not presume any finality to any prescription. It is more important to flag the underlying issues. In that spirit, here goes.

1. Higher Capital Requirement: Banks and all systemically important financial institutions will need to operate with higher capital than they have done so far. This means the regulatory requirement of capital will have to be raised. When the regulatory requirement is 9 per cent, banks consider it appropriate to operate at 12 per cent.

With capital having to be provided for operational risk under Basel II and the auxiliary requirements under Pillar II of the Accord, we should expect to see banks operate at a capital of 15 per cent in the medium term.

Higher capital is the first line of defence against risk but a case for higher capital can also be made as a means of limiting incentives for excessive risk-taking on the part of managers. The lower the capital and the greater the leverage in a bank, the greater are the incentives for managers to take risks. If the risky gambles pay off, managers can show a fantastic return on equity and claim proportionate bonuses. And If the gambles fail? Well, then it's the shareholders and bondholders who are left holding the can.

2. Revisiting Basel II Capital Norms: The Basel II norms are intended to align capital requirements with banks' level of risks and to reward banks that do a better job of risk management. But this is predicated on risk assessments made by rating agencies (in the standard approach) and on the validity of sophisticated models used by banks (in the advanced approaches). There is bound to be a question mark over both, given that the credibility of rating agencies has taken a beating in the present crisis and so have the vaunted risk management models.

There is merit in the view, already adopted in the US, that the Basel II norms must be used in conjunction with conventional measures of leverage, such as the ratio of capital to total assets (without assigning any risk weights). No matter what level of capital follows from the Basel II approaches, leverage in conventional terms must not be allowed to exceed a prescribed limit.

We also need to examine whether, under the standard approach, the more reputed banks can be permitted to rely on their own ratings of borrowers rather than the ratings provided by the rating agencies. There is room to believe that seasoned bankers may be doing a better job of rating borrowers than the agencies.

3. Re-design of Performance Incentives: People are aghast at the payouts made by way of bonuses and stock options to top executives in the financial sector. 'Greed' has been cited as an important factor underlying the downfall of many firms. However, the issue is not the size of payments. In regulatory terms, we are not concerned about whether top management pay is inegalitarian. Our concern is with pay as a source of systemic risk. If performance is measured incorrectly and managers are rewarded inappropriately, that can pose serious risks to financial firms.

The nub of the issue is that, more than in most businesses, performance in the financial sector cannot be measured at a given point in time. It is unwise to reward bank managers, for instance, on the basis of loan growth or even profit in a given year. Any manager can ramp up loans in a year. But this is likely to show up as non-performing assets down the road. Performance can be measured in banking only over a long period, say, over the entire business cycle.

Once this is grasped, the design of performance incentives falls into place. First, incentives must be linked to return on risk-adjusted capital, that is, the denominator must reflect the risk that made possible the return shown in the numerator. The catch, however, is that we cannot quite know that we have captured risk accurately.

Therefore- and this is the second element in incentive design- only a portion of the bonus can be paid out in a given year. The rest goes into an escrow account. In the subsequent years, bonuses will be similarly computed. If there are losses, there will be negative entries in the escrow account. At the end of an appropriate period- say, seven to ten years- the manager collects the balance in the account. Thirdly, at the highest levels, the cash component in bonus must be small and the stock option component must be larger so that incentives are aligned to long-term performance. Following from the argument given above, stock options must vest only over a long period.

4. Widening Ambit of Central Bank Regulation: In the present crisis, the US Fed found itself obliged to offer liquidity to non-bank institutions, thus extending its lender of last resort role. It then gave a banking license to some of the investment banks so that they could convert themselves into banks. The underlying principle is that if an institution seeks or needs assistance from the central bank, then it has to submit itself to central bank regulation. Given the inter-linkages in the financial system, the distinction between commercial banks and other institutions is, perhaps, inappropriate for regulatory purposes. The time may have come to examine whether all systemically important financial institutions must be subject to central bank regulation.

5. Tread Warily on Foreign Bank Entry: The present crisis underlines that the RBI's cautious approach to foreign bank entry as outlined in its roadmap for foreign banks in 2005 is well merited. The dominant concern has been that foreign banks, with their superior financial muscle and expertise, will take away the best business, leaving domestic firms weakened. But this is a defensive argument, which some may want to brush aside on grounds of ushering in efficiency.

In the wake of the sub-prime crisis, it does appear that it is not the superior efficiency of foreign banks so much as their inefficiency or vulnerability that emerging markets may have to fear. One important regulatory issue is monitoring cross-border exposures and transactions of foreign banks. Foreign banks have been in the forefront in selling derivative products to Indian firms. This has led to an exponential rise in off-balance sheet (OBS) exposures of foreign banks. OBS assets at foreign banks are 2800 per cent of balance sheet assets compared to the banking system's average of 333 per cent. Given that OBS items have figured prominently in the sub-prime crisis, this is cause for concern.

Another issue with a dominant foreign bank presence is the potential for capital flows to reverse consequent to problems at the host country, the parent bank or the country of origin. We are only too familiar with this phenomenon in the case of capital market flows. It does not make sense to introduce such a destabilising element into financial flows intermediated by foreign banks as well.

6. Prudential Limits on Securitisation: Rampant securitisation is seen as one of the causes of the sub-prime crisis. Banks had no qualms about originating large volumes of low-quality loans because they knew they were not going to have these on their own books for long. The loans would be palmed off to other investors through securitisation. This transfer was, of course, facilitated by the high ratings that agencies were only too willing to give to the securitisation tranches.

An important regulatory issue is whether we need to restrict the percentage of loans that a bank will be allowed to securitise. The regulator could stipulate, for instance, that 75 per cent of loans should be held by the bank. Only the balance could be securitised. The 75 per cent limit would apply not just to loans in the aggregate but loans by category- home loans, credit cards, car loans, etc.

Imposing such a requirement becomes necessary because of the difficulties inherent in getting accurate rating of securitised bundles of loans. It also helps creates superior incentives for banks to monitor quality- at the point of origination as well as after the loan is made. Banks that wish to transgress the regulatory limit may be subjected to higher capital requirements.

7. Addressing liquidity Risk: The present crisis had driven home the lesson that risks in banking are not confined to the asset side. They can arise on the liabilities side as well. The quality of assets at Northern Rock was above the British average when it went under. It was lack of liquidity that destroyed the bank. Similarly, it was investment banks' dependence on short-term funds in the wholesale market that contributed to their downfall as much as their exposure to toxic assets.

One way to address liquidity risk would be to impose higher capital adequacy requirements for banks that cross stipulated thresholds of liquidity risk, measured by a number of well-known parameters. But the BIS has not favoured this approach. Instead, in September, 2008 it came out with a guidance not outlining 17 principles that might guide the management of liquidity risk. Instead of imposing higher capital requirements for liquidity risk, the BIS would rather rely on better supervision of liquidity risk at banks. It has also emphasised better disclosure of liquidity risks at banks.

8. Regulation of Derivative Contracts: Two problems with derivatives have become apparent. In the case of some products, such as credit default swaps, the contracts were a huge multiple of the underlying. A credit default swap offers protection in the event of default of, say, a bond. But such contracts came to be written even for people who did not hold the underlying instrument, in this case the bond.

These contracts thus became a form of wild betting. The seller of the protection in the credit default swap collected a fee by offering this sort of insurance to whoever was willing to buy it. Given the sheer volume of protection sold, it became impossible for institutions, such as AIG to honour their contracts when the bets went against them. One reasonable restriction would, therefore, be to limit credit default swaps to those who hold the underlying instrument.

Another suggestion is that to move certain derivative contracts to exchanges and limit over-the-counter products. This would subject these contracts to the exchanges' discipline of marking to market and meeting margin requirements on a regular basis and avoid the sort of large-scale defaults on contracts we have seen.

9. Risk management is a board function too: It does appear from the problems at several large institutions that the boards did not have a handle at all on the management of risk. This was left to management. It must be understood, however, that risk management is too important to be left to management. The board must have a role in monitoring risk at an aggregate level. If management's task at a financial firm is primarily the management of risk, then monitoring of performance along that dimension automatically becomes a board responsibility. That is why boards in India and abroad too have a Risk Management Committee as one of their sub- committees. It is not that boards need to look into the details of models. But they do need to know about overall risk exposures, exposures to sensitive sectors, whether higher returns reflect the assumption of higher risks, etc.

10. Board Composition Matters: One of the astonishing revelations from the crisis is about how little banking expertise the top financial institutions had at the board level. At Citigroup, two board members recently retired after together serving for a total of 59 years on the board. It is not as if either had banking expertise and was, therefore, indispensable. One came from the Ford Foundation and another from Chevron, the oil company. Lehman Brothers had a theatre impresario on the board. Most banks fell victim to the 'celebrity' syndrome, thinking it was enough to have a famous name, preferably a retired corporate executive or government official, on their banks.

In India, the Banking Regulation Act stipulates that at least 51% of board members should conform to certain specifications and boards are at least nominally required to have an appropriate mix of expertise including an economist, a banker, an SME expert and so on. It is a different matter that some of these norms are followed more in letter than in spirit. There is also a problem in not applying 'fit and proper' criteria that are applied to independent board members on public sector banks to those appointed by government. But the principle of limiting board tenures to a maximum of eight years is certainly a healthy one.

Mar 14, 2009 (EPW)

Crisis won't upset US Dominance

The American economy has been battered by the present financial crisis. It could take several years for it to get back to normal. Some commentators and political leaders have suggested this could be the beginning of the end of America's dominance of the global economy.

Wrong, says historian Niall Ferguson. In an article in the *Harvard Business Review* (July- August 2009), Ferguson argues that, while America's financial sector may end up weaker, American dominance of the global economy is likely to continue.

Ferguson is an unabashed Americo-phile and something of an icon to the neoconservatives in the US. He is the author of a book, *Colossus,* in which he argued that America's problem is not that it is imperialist but that it does not take its imperial role seriously enough.

Those who contend that the present crisis will be a huge setback for the US put forward several reasons:

- The US economy could take several years to come back to normal. Meanwhile, rivals like China will power ahead.
- America's national debt is set to explode and this will limit its future growth.
- The US dollar will lose its status as the reserve currency in the near future.
- The American financial system will soon be a pale shadow of what it has been.

The IMF expects the US economy to shrink by 2.6 per cent in 2009. Recovery will be slow in coming- in 2010, the US economy is projected to grow by just 0.8 per cent. Many think this could alter the race between the US and its principal economic rival, China, to China's advantage.

In 2007, Goldman Sachs had forecast that China's GDP would equal that of the US in nominal terms by 2027. If the US economy suffers low to zero growth over the next four years while China grows by 6 per cent, one would think that China could catch up with the US even earlier.

Not really. Ferguson points out that, going by the IMF's forecast (of April 2009), US growth rate will be lower than the growth rate of 2007 by 4.6 percentage points. But that of China would be lower by 6.3 percentage points. So, the present crisis could mean that China won't catch up with the US until much later than forecast earlier, say, 2040. The crisis will have stretched out America's dominance instead of abbreviating it. (The IMF's July forecast raised the growth forecast for China in 2009 but growth will still be 5.5 percentage points lower than in 2007).

This applies with greater force to America's other rivals. Growth in the European Union is expected to shrink this year by 3.2 per cent, in Japan by 5.8 per cent and in Russia by 6.5 per cent. The present crisis has highlighted how central the US is to the in the world economy. A serious recession in the US and one arising from problems in its financial sector impacts on other economies in two ways. It lowers exports to US and it reduces capital flows from the US and other advanced countries. That is why the present US crisis has translated into a global crisis. Even more perversely, many economies are hurting more badly than the US, which is the source of the crisis.

Indeed, there is no dearth of conspiracy theorists who believe the US is interested in prolonging the crisis - and may have even engineered it - knowing that its principal rivals, especially China, would be severely impacted. China has used its double-digit economic growth rate to contain discontent. A decline of five percentage points or so in its growth rate risks fuelling serious disaffection within the country.

America's public debt is set to rise sharply following the resort to a fiscal stimulus as a means of reviving the economy. The federal deficit is expected to exceed 12 per cent of GDP in 2009. Federal debt is expected to rise from 89 per cent of GDP in 2009 to 101 per cent of GDP in 2019, even on the optimistic assumption that the US economic growth rises to over 4 per cent by 2011.

India's combined debt to GDP ratio of the centre and the states was 73 per cent last March. The consolidated fiscal deficit is expected to be around 12 per cent of GDP in 2009-10. We worry, despite the fact that we can count on a long-term growth rate of 8 per cent and we know that a growth rate of this order renders the fiscal problem self-correcting. Surely, the US should have a problem given its lower growth potential?

There are differences in the two situations. The US is still regarded as a safe haven by investors whereas confidence about the Indian economy is nowhere as strong. More importantly, the dollar is the reserve currency and even America's rivals prefer to invest overwhelmingly in dollars. This gives the US enormous borrowing potential. It can simply print dollars which others will gladly pick up.

For all the talk of the dollar losing its primacy, no alternative is in sight. Indeed, the present crisis has underscored the inherent attractiveness of the dollar. The dollar rallied in the face of bad news about the US economy and has defied predictions of a steep decline since.

As Ferguson notes, there are practical obstacles to switching to the Special Drawing Rights issued by the IMF. A senior Chinese mandarin summed up the situation very well earlier this year, "Except for U.S. Treasuries, what can you hold? Gold? You don't hold Japanese government bonds or U.K. bonds... We hate you guys....but there is nothing much we can do."

Because the problems of the US economy hurt the rest of the world, the US appears set to retain its primacy in the world economy, the dollar will remain the dominant currency and the world is resigned to financing America's deficits. If there is a question mark, it is over the future of the American banking system.

For the US banking system to regain its vitality, the US government will have to assume control of the top banks at least for some time, organise the disposal of banks' toxic assets, put in place rules that rein in high leverage in the banking system and get a lot tougher with executive pay in banking. But the Obama administration has so far lacked the will to take such decisive steps.

This undermines the chances of an early recovery in the US economy and hence the world economy. But for the reasons mentioned above, it does not pose a threat to America's dominance of the world economy. When the US catches a flu, the rest of the world goes down with pneumonia and the US ends up looking stronger.

August 6, 2009

How to Respond to Asset Bubbles?

The housing bubble that burst in the US in 2007 has played havoc with the world economy. Elsewhere, stock market busts have been known to derail economies. How to respond to asset bubbles has, therefore, become a central policy issue.

The argument is often made that booms and busts or business cycles are integral to capitalism and it would be foolish to attempt to manage these. This view is most famously associated with the former Fed chief, Alan Greenspan.

Greenspan argued that it's hard to tell an asset bubble, that is, whether an increase in asset prices is driven by fundamentals or not. In responding to perceived bubbles, policy makers risked cutting off the benefits of high growth. The only sensible thing for policy makers to do, therefore, was to clean up quickly once a bubble burst.

In the period 2003-07, when the world economy boomed, this view prevailed and Greenspan was hailed as a visionary. Now, he is being reviled for not preventing the worst financial crisis of the last century.

Policy-makers will hereafter find it difficult to adhere to this laissez faire attitude towards asset bubbles and ignore the possibility of large disruptions to the economy. The idea that asset bubbles must be managed is fast gaining ground. Remember, the idea of managing exchange rates was also once unfashionable but "managed float" is no longer sneered at.

The practical questions are three. Do we have reliable indicators of future busts? Is lax monetary policy the primary culprit in the present bust? And does it make sense for central banks to have financial stability as an objective in addition to the traditional objective of price stability? The IMF's *World Economic Outlook* (October 2009) sheds light on these questions.

The answer to the first question is: yes, we do have indicators of busts but they are not very reliable. The IMF finds three significant predictors: the ratios of credit, the current account and residential investment to GDP. But these predictors are not very reliable. In the post-1985 period, these predictors raised an alarm in advance of a bust only one-third to one-half of the time. Asset bubbles are hard to predict.

To what extent has monetary policy been responsible for the present crisis, as many have contended? The IMF's answer goes against the current wisdom: monetary policy, its analysis shows, "was not the main or systematic source of the recent asset price booms". If that were the case, it would have showed in the behaviour of inflation and output. It does not. So, monetary authorities seem to have been quite successful in meeting the objective of price stability.

However, this has not helped prevent a first-class financial crisis. Which gives rise to the third question: should central banks, therefore, focus on financial stability and not just on price stability? Prior to the present crisis, economists tended not to favour multiple objectives for monetary policy. In India, the Raghuram Rajan committee argued as recently as in 2008 in favour of a focus on price stability.

The IMF's analysis suggests that it makes sense for central banks to respond to signs of macrofinancial risk. But this does not mean simply responding to sharp increases in asset prices, given that asset prices are not very reliable predictors of an impending bust. The IMF argues that you need to look closely at the drivers of bubbles: lax lending standards and rapid credit growth, overinvestment and deteriorating external balances. This seems like quibbling because you still have to work out what is rapid credit growth, overinvestment, etc.

So, the IMF's analysis suggests that it is all very well to have financial stability as a goal in addition to price stability. But this is difficult in practice because we do not have satisfactory indicators of macrofinancial risk. Still, in the near future, we should expect policy makers to respond to asset bubbles, using some rough indicators.

There are three reasons why this will happen even though the costs and benefits to such intervention are not clear. One, it has become evident that regulation by itself cannot prevent financial crises. Two, disruptions caused by banking failures are widely perceived as unfair and iniquitous and have fuelled popular outrage. In the present crisis, bank managers are perceived to have benefited from their reckless actions while shareholders and tax payers lost out.

Three, less developed countries cannot afford big setbacks to growth given their low per capita incomes. If India does not achieve a 10% growth rate, it will not been seen as a big disaster. But, if a banking crisis causes growth to fall to 4 per cent,that will become an unmitigated disaster for whoever is in power. Politicians will see clear advantages to responding to asset bubbles. The theory of asset bubbles may take time to develop but practice is likely to lead theory.

October 15, 2009

Post-crisis Regulation: A Contrarian Perspective

There is no dearth of committee reports on the sub-prime crisis. To mention a few: the Turner report in the UK, the UK Treasury's report, the US Treasury's report, the Financial Stability Forum report, the Stiglitz Commission constituted by the UN and the UNCTAD report. With the exception of the Stiglitz Commission (whose range of concerns is wider), these reports largely cover the same ground and their diagnosis and prescriptions have much in common.

So, I approached the report of the Warwick Commission on International Financial Reform, commissioned by the University of Warwick, with a certain lack of enthusiasm. Almost everything that needed to be said has been said. What more could they say? True, the Commission had more academics and representatives of think-tanks on board than many other committees. But one wasn't sure this was necessarily a virtue in an area in which application is everything.

I am happy to say that my misgivings turned out to be misplaced. The Warwick Commission does have fresh perspectives to offer. It raises a number of issues in a way that many other reports have not. And it also differs sharply in some of the recommendations it makes. In this article, I propose to highlight some of the themes that figure in the report: macro-prudential regulation, right-sizing the financial sector, regulatory capture and home country versus host country regulation.

Macro-Prudential Regulation

There is general agreement now that it is not enough to get the rules for banks and other financial institutions right. Even if this is done, the system could be exposed to risk. Worse, systemic risk could be high precisely on account of micro-prudential regulation. This arises because of homogeneity in the financial system. Homogeneity, in turn, is the result of several factors: the use of market prices as a measure of risk; failure to take into account funding and leverage in setting rules for capital; and not distinguishing between various types of risk.

Take the problem with the use of market prices as measures of risk, a problem with which we have become only too familiar in the present crisis. If all players are required to use mark-to-market accounting, then all will want to sell when the price of particular assets fall. This sets in motion a downward spiral in asset prices and leads to a huge erosion in capital in the financial system in a crisis. Similarly, the use of market measures of risk leads to herd behavior in good times as all participants want to hold assets that were regarded as safe in the past. Such herd behavior then makes the assets overvalued, risky and correlated with other assets of investors.

How do we tackle this problem? We have heard much about making regulations counter-cyclical. This would put the brakes on herd behavior in financial institutions.

The novel proposal that the Commission makes is to have different rules for different players in the financial system. Banks use short-term funding and may be subjected to mark-to-market accounting. Others, such as insurance firms, use longer-term funding and should be allowed to judge whether it makes sense for them to buy assets that banks want to get rid of.

Using the same accounting rules for both types of players does not help in a crisis situation. Rather, the Commission urges, regulations must move particular risks to institutions best capable of holding them. This is indeed a bold departure from the conventional wisdom which is to set store by a 'level playing field' for all players. More on this later.

Homogeneity in the financial system today also arises from the failure to take into account differences in funding and leverage. An institution that is heavily dependent on short-term funds from the capital markets has the same capital requirements as another that relies on deposits. The Commission proposes capital requirements that are linked to mismatches in maturities between assets and liabilities. This, however, is not something that has thus far found favour with the Basel committee.

There is one aspect of homogeneity that does not seem to have got the attention it deserves: homogeneity in ownership. Or, to put it differently, the potential benefits in terms of managing systemic risk of having different kinds of ownership in the financial sector. India and China both have this sort of heterogeneity, more so India.

We have a public sector-dominated banking sector, a fairly large room for the domestic private sector and lesser scope for the foreign sector. Their respective shares will, of course, change over time and it is possible to debate how fast this should happen. The crucial point is that the system seems to gain from having a diverse mix of ownership probably because it attitudes towards risk differ among the different owners.

Public sector banks are relatively risk-averse; foreign banks, perhaps, come in at the opposite end of the spectrum. The system as a whole avoids either extreme. In risk management, there is the regulatory issue of ensuring that all players do not use the same models because this makes for identical responses in a crisis. Can we extrapolate from this and say that the same argument holds with the pattern of ownership in banking? The Commission might have addressed this issue.

There is one significant aspect of macro-prudential regulation that the report does not touch upon: the role of monetary policy in dealing with asset bubbles. Should central banks respond to signs of asset bubbles? Is there a range for asset prices that central banks should target? These are issues that have figured in public discourse on the financial crisis.

Right-sizing the Financial Sector

I turn now to another important issue flagged in the report, namely, the size of the financial sector in relation to the real economy. The financial crisis has thrown the spotlight on how bloated the financial sector had become in economies such as the US and the UK and how certain markets, such as foreign exchange, bore no relationship to the real economy.

The Commission sees a clear need to right-size finance. It also raises an important research issue that needs to be pursued: is there an optimal size for the financial sector? Finance should not be so small that it constrains the real economy; it should not be so large that an inevitable shrinkage at a later point impacts adversely on the real economy.

What caused the financial sectors in the advanced economies to become so bloated? The report mentions several factors. One, the belief that the financial sector is the most efficient allocator of resources and hence the more developed the financial sector, the better for the economy. Two, the growth of investment banks and brokers who, it was thought, performed the role of resource allocation without putting the ordinary depositor at risk. Three, the view that market participants had developed sophisticated models that helped them monitor and manage risk effectively.

How to prevent the financial sector from being bloated? The report mentions means that have been proposed by others as well: counter-cyclical provisioning norms; mandating a ceiling on the leverage ratio for financial institutions; higher capital requirements for systemically important institutions; and a Tobin tax to limit short-term activity in the financial markets.

The fifth idea is the Commission's own: segregating different categories of finance, based on risk capacity, and moving away from a level playing field for all institutions. Former Fed Chairman Paul Volcker, Bank of England Mervyn King and former US Treasury Secretary Nicholas Brady are among those who have urged restrictions on the scope of activities of financial institutions. They would like to see a clear separation of banking from investment banking activities in order to prevent a recurrence of financial crises. Others have argued for restrictions on the size of financial institutions.

The Commission believes that a better way to handle the problem is not to have the same regulations across various types of institutions. Having an un-level playing field, they contend, will in itself prevent the emergence of financial supermarkets and the too-big-to-fail problem. This is an idea that is worth exploring because, if feasible, it could be an alternative to blunt instruments such as restrictions on scope and size.

Regulatory Capture

The Commission is forthright in laying the blame for the financial crisis where it belongs. It says, "Regulatory capture substantially contributed to regulatory failure". It makes the point that regulatory capture was not just a matter of market players coming to exercise influence- through donations to political parties and the 'revolving door' syndrome whereby people from the market go on to regulatory agencies and people in government join financial institutions.

Regulatory capture was also intellectual. There was a universal acceptance of notions of market efficiency and the consequent need for regulation with a light touch. There is also the in-built reluctance of politicians to cut off a boom- who wants to put an end to the good times?

The report draws attention to an insidious trend that we in India also need to be alert to: a growing role for the private sector in policy formulation. There is a line to be drawn always between taking inputs from the private sector - and both RBI and SEBI do a good job of this- and giving them a role in formulating policy.

The report makes three concrete suggestions for containing regulatory capture. One, regulatory policy should be more rule-based. Two, the financial sector and financial institutions should be right-sized so that they do not wield disproportionate clout when it comes to making policy. Three, we should emphasise host-country rather than home-country regulation. This is especially necessary for emerging market economies to have room to deal with cross-border flows.

Home Country Versus Host Country Regulation

Perhaps the most contrarian recommendation of the report is that the locus of regulation should be host-country regulation and not home-country regulation. The conventional wisdom underpinning the various Basel agreements tends to stress global rules in the name of creating a level playing field for players and preventing regulatory arbitrage. The Commission makes the telling point that the present system, with its global orientation, could not ultimately prevent regulatory arbitrage.

The reality is that national regulators may sign up to global agreements but will ultimately do their best to favour their own institutions-witness the expansion of US investment banks into Asia after the East Asian crisis, 'light touch' regulation in Britain, etc. Besides, global rules just cannot meet the requirements of individual countries because countries differ in their financial structure. They also differ in their political priorities. In India, the focus on financial inclusion is appropriate. Transplant this to the US and you may end up having lax regulation for the section of society that needs it most, as we saw in the sub-prime crisis.

The report states its alternative proposal in emphatic terms: "The idea is that all institutions carrying on financial activities nationally, raising funds from residents or investing in national assets or markets, must be regulated locally. An Icelandic bank could no longer operate in the UK as a branch, regulated in most party by the authorities in Iceland but must be regulated in the UK as a stand-alone bank with sufficient capital for its activities in the UK and be able to withstand the failure of its parent".

Does this imply that a subsidiary of a foreign bank will be subject to the same treatment as a domestic bank? The report suggests this would indeed be the case. Such a prescription, however, is open to question.

In India, the RBI permits foreign banks to operate either as branches or as subsidiaries. But subsidiaries of foreign banks do not qualify for the same treatment as domestic banks. This is because a host of issues related to the regulation of foreign banks do not go away just because they operate through subsidiaries. The report mentions the stability of the Indian banking sector as highlighting the advantages of host country regulation, so it would have been appropriate for the Commission to have taken note of the nuances to foreign bank regulation in India.

I would argue that it may not suffice to stop at having foreign banks operate as subsidiaries. To ensure a better convergence with host country interests, it may be necessary to require subsidiaries to list on exchanges with a requirement that, say, 40 per cent of capital be offered to host country investors.

To sum up, we in India will not have difficulty in going along with the thrust of this report and indeed will be pleased with what it says because on issues such as macro-prudential regulation and host country regulation, the RBI has turned out to be ahead of the regulatory curve and in line with what the report recommends.

The Percy Mistry report on Mumbai as an international financial centre viewed a spanking financial district as central to powering economic growth. India's growth record in 2004-08 has helped debunk this view. The Commission's emphasis on right-sizing finance should help place the issue in better perspective. The Raghuram Rajan committee report found fault with the absence of a level playing field amongst different financial intermediaries in the Indian system. The Warwick Commission report should prompt some serious rethinking on this issue as well.

Jan 16, 2010 (EPW)

Why the Greek/EU Rescue Won't Work

Greece has been dubbed the 'public sector's Lehman Brothers'. Parallels have been drawn with a large bank failure. Greece, it is said, had to be rescued because a default on its part could have lead to a wider crisis. Time was of the essence: the greater the delay in effecting a rescue, the greater the cost. As in the case of bank failure, taxpayers have to pick up the tabs.

The impact of a large bank failure on the system is understandable. Greece is a small economy. Its GDP is a little over 1% of world GDP. Why would the bankruptcy of a small economy warrant serious concern?

Again, it has to do with banks. If Greece were to default on its debt, banks in Greece as well as in other countries could be in trouble. A default would cause Greek government bonds to lose at least half their value. Many Greek banks would go bankrupt.

Banks in other countries too would be impacted. The Economist estimates EU banks' holding of Greek government bonds at •76 bn. Many of these banks have already been supported by governments following the sub-prime crisis. They can do without further losses. The rescue mounted by the EU-IMF ten days ago, it is contended, has helped stave off another banking crisis at a time when economic recovery in the EU is sluggish.

Just three weeks ago, the package required for Greece was estimated at •40 bn. The package finally pushed through by the EU-IMF amounted to •110 bn. The EU- IMF has since announced a package worth • 750 bn for all Euro-zone economies. This is a stabilisation mechanism comprising loans as well as guarantees. How much of it will be used to top up the rescue package for Greece is anybody's guess.

In a crisis such as this, the costs of rescue to governments and international agencies mount with time because private investors begin to flee. However, it is incorrect to say that the cost of the Greek rescue itself is •110 bn. This is merely the amount that the EU and the IMF have to lend to Greece to prevent an immediate default.

The entire amount is not a cost unless Greece defaults on all of it. Assuming that Greece ultimately repays this amount, the cost of the rescue would be the difference between the market rate of interest and the interest that the EU-IMF is charging.

A Greek default would have had serious consequences all round. But the basic question needs to be asked: was a rescue preferable to a default? Is it true that a Greek default would have had catastrophic effects similar to those of the failure of Lehman in 2008?

The historical evidence is that there are strong incentives for countries to default. In their book, *This time is different,* Reinhart and Rogoff document the record of sovereign defaults through history. They write, "Serial defaults on external debts are the norm throughout every region in the world, including Asia and Europe".

This undistinguished record has continued through the twentieth century in Africa, Asia, Latin America and Europe. Several Latin American countries have spent nearly 40 per cent of their time since independence in default. Greece itself has been in default nearly half the time since 1800.

Two other facts are worth noting. Today's high-income countries have made the transition from being emerging markets after a long history of default. This implies that, for the defaulter, the consequences of default are bearable. Secondly, in general, the effects of country default can be absorbed by the world economy.

In light of these facts, what is the argument against Greece defaulting today? Its primary fiscal deficit is around 9-10 per cent of GDP. This is financed by external flows. If Greece were to default, external flows would cease. This means that Greece would have to shrink its economy by 9-10 per cent at one go which would be very painful indeed.

But that is theory. In practice, external flows do not cease when a country defaults. A default leads on to debt restructuring. Lenders write off some of the debt because it is in their own interest to do so. If Greece were to default today, it is estimated that lenders would lose 50-70 per cent of their money. They are bound to negotiate a restructuring where they lose a lesser proportion, say, 30 per cent.

Going by the Economist's estimate for EU banks' investment in Greek bonds of •76 bn, a 30 per cent loss would amount to • 23 bn. This loss would have to be borne by the banks. EU governments could share half of this loss by infusing capital into banks. For Greece, there would be enormous benefit. A default or orderly restructuring could shave about 30 per cent off its external debt and make adjustment easier.

Compare these costs of restructuring with the costs of the rescue. The EU-IMF lending rate is about 5 per cent or about 4 percentage points less than the market rate on 10-year bonds for Greece. This means the cost of the rescue package of • 110 bn is around • 4.5 bn. This is the cost to tax payers outside Greece.

And the costs to Greece? Greece has agreed to fiscal consolidation of 11 per cent over a three year period. This will mean huge job losses in the public sector, higher taxes and reduced wages and pensions. That is why riots have broken out in Greece.

We can now see why rescue has been preferred to default or restructuring. Under the rescue, the costs are to be borne overwhelmingly by Greece. Under restructuring, the costs would have been borne equitably by foreign banks, foreign taxpayers and Greek citizens. The Greek rescue is all about bailing out banks using public money. The parallel is not so much with Lehman as with AIG.

Greece has gone along with the rescue because the political and economic costs of defying the EU could be steep. But we can understand why neither the Greek package nor the larger Euro-zone package has restored confidence in the markets. The markets believe that the costs of adjustment for the troubled EU economies are just too great to be politically acceptable. They believe the rescue won't work.

Banks holding EU government debt must be part of the solution. Their governments can help them bear the loss. Only a formula that distributes the costs of adjustment more equitably between the distressed economies and the healthier economies of the EU will work. The lesson is obvious: if you are part of an economic union, you end up sharing the costs, not just the benefits.

May 13, 2010

Crisis Losses and Rescue Costs

The sub-prime crisis of 2007 inflicted substantial losses on the financial sector as it unfolded over the next couple of years. These losses were estimated in trillions of dollars and so were the costs of rescue. Governments poured money into distressed financial firms through expensive rescue programmes.

These programmes were thought necessary at the time, yet have been criticised as unabashed bail-outs of the private sector. Just how big were the losses and the rescue costs? Did governments spend too much or too little in their rescue efforts? America's rescue programme provides useful clues.

Following the collapse of Lehman Brothers in September 2008, the US Congress rushed through the Troubled Asset Relief Program (Tarp). The provision made was a staggering $700 bn. Two years later, the programme has been wound up. The results should confound the critics.

Under Tarp, the US government was to buy toxic assets or illiquid assets off the books of banks and sell these once the market recovered. That didn't really happen. The Treasury realised that setting prices for illiquid assets was an impossible task. If the prices were set too high, the Treasury would be accused of favouring the banks. If they were set too low, banks in trouble would face even higher losses.

The purpose of Tarp was then modified. The funds that Congress made available were used for other purposes-injecting capital into banks and General Motors and Chrysler, providing backstop facilities to the insurer AIG, helping make the terms of some mortgages more favourable, etc. Only $470 bn of the funds made available were actually committed.

Did Tarp work? Answers differ as to how effective it was but most people believe that it did prevent the US and the global economy from going over the precipice. Tarp funds came at a time when private funding threatened to flee the banking system altogether. Once capital was infused into banks, they were able to go out and raise funds from the public and shore up their capital.

Recovery would have been faster had the US government injected more capital into banks. That would have made them more willing to lend. However, both the Bush and Obama governments shrank from stronger recapitalisation. They made sure that the capital they injected did not give them control over the banks because the American establishment is allergic to the idea of nationalisation of banks.

Instead, they attempted to expedite recovery by cutting policy rates. Banks were allowed to rebuild their capital over time by borrowing virtually at zero cost and making easy profits. As a result, recovery in the US has stretched over more than two years and even today it remains anaemic.

This is one of those things that will be debated forever but one thing is for sure. The cost of Tarp is nowhere near the figure of $700 bn that shocked the American public. As the economy recovered and banks started returning capital, estimates of the cost of Tarp began to be progressively revised downwards. The latest estimate is a mere $50 bn- or less than 0.4 per cent of US GDP.

The estimates of losses in the financial sector themselves have been revised several times. The IMF's Global Financial Stability Report estimated losses in the US at $1.4 trillion in October 2008. By April 2009, the losses had been revised upwards to $2.7 trillion. In April 2010, the estimate came down sharply to $885 bn. Global financial sector losses were estimated at $4 trillion in April 2009. A year later, they were revised to about half the figure-$2.2 trillion. How come?

The losses in the financial sector include losses on loans as well as securities. Losses on securities are estimated on a mark-to-market basis and hence fluctuate with movements in the markets. After the Lehman debacle in late 2008, prices in the markets plummeted sharply, which is why losses peaked in 2009. As economies and markets recovered in 2010, losses tended to decline.

Financial sector losses and rescue costs are not the correct way to estimate the costs of financial crises. We must look at the output lost- what the growth rate would have been without a crisis and what it was because of a crisis. But estimates of losses and rescue costs provide a rough measure of loss and they also determine the quality of government intervention.

As the experience in the recent crisis shows, these estimates can be deceptive. Mark-to-market losses at the peak of a crisis tend to exaggerate the losses and rescue costs. Markets tend to panic when they think that large financial institutions will fail. So these estimates of losses should not be used to determine the extent of government intervention.

Governments must simply do what it takes to prevent failures of large institutions. They should not be intimidated by loss estimates made at a time of panic. Had the US government prevented Lehman from failing, had it made sure that banks were quickly recapitalised, the financial sector losses would have been even lower and economic recovery faster.

October 14, 2010

G-20 Accord Needs US Policy Shift

In the wake of the sub-prime crisis, the G-20 coordinated their fiscal and monetary actions to avoid an economic catastrophe. They succeeded in averting a possible repeat of the Great Depression.

In recent months, as most people have come to believe that the worst is over, the sense of emergency is gone. Cooperation has given way to bickering. Quarrels have erupted amongst the G-20 as to how best to sustain the ongoing recovery. As a result, growth in the advanced economies remains sluggish and is becoming a drag on the global economy.

The US blames emerging markets, mainly China, for not doing enough to foster recovery. The US itself faces criticism from some of its own economists, not just from emerging markets. The meeting of finance ministers in Seoul last week failed to resolve the quarrels in the G-20 although it may have succeeded in averting a trade war for now.

"Global imbalances" are widely believed to have been an important factor underlying the sub-prime crisis. Everybody knows what is to be done. The US and other advanced economies need to export more and consume less. China and other emerging markets with large current account surpluses need to consume more and export less. Neither has happened, at least not to the extent required.

The US believes this is because China and other emerging markets refuse to allow exchange rates to rise to reflect market forces. The emerging markets say keeping the dollar weak by relying entirely on loose monetary policy is a form of exchange rate manipulation. They cannot afford to allow the dollars flooding into their economies to dictate their exchange rates as any sharp reversal of inflows could prove destabilising.

At the recent Seoul summit of G-20 finance ministers, the US changed tack in order to secure agreement on policy coordination. US treasury secretary Tim Geithner dropped the American insistence on exchange rate alignment and instead sought agreement on keeping current account imbalances within an agreed limit- say, 4 per cent of GDP.

This would allow emerging markets to contain their surpluses in ways other than appreciation in their nominal exchange rates. Emerging markets could achieve an adjustment in the real exchange rate through a rise in inflation. Or they could simply try to reduce the surplus of savings over investment which is mirrored in a current account surplus.

The proposal has a serious catch to it. As Gavyn Davies points out in the *Financial Times*, only four economies would be breaching the 4 per cent current account surplus target: Saudi Arabia, Germany, China and Russia. Of these, Saudi Arabia and Russia would be excluded because the Geithner proposal allows exceptions to be made for countries with large commodity-producing sectors.

Germany is not intervening in the markets to keep its currency undervalued and the IMF projects that its current account surplus would fall below 4 per cent by 2015. So the latest US proposal can easily be construed as targeting a familiar villain, China. Davies also notes that there are only two countries with a current account deficit of over 4 per cent, Turkey and South Africa. The US itself runs a current deficit of 3.2 per cent and would be conveniently excluded from making any adjustment!

Not surprisingly, the US proposal failed to win approval in Seoul. The G-20 merely agreed to "move towards more market-determined exchange rate systems that reflect underlying economic fundamentals and refrain from competitive devaluation of currencies". That statement fails to tell us exactly who should be doing what.

Where do we go from here? The US must recognise that it cannot shift the burden of adjustment entirely onto emerging markets. This, in turn, means it has to revisit its current approach of relying wholly on monetary policy to revive the US economy. Fiscal policy will have to play the role Keynes had famously assigned to it in a recession. An impressive array of US economists- Paul Krugman, Christana Romer, Bradford de Long, Joseph Stiglitz, to name a few- happens to think so.

It is becoming clear that monetary policy by itself cannot do the trick. Since interest rates are close to zero, the Fed has resorted to a second round of 'quantitative easing'- the infusion of money into the system through the purchase of long-term government bonds. But this is just not stimulating private demand.

Private consumption has fallen sharply in order to correct the excesses of the sub-prime crisis. Private investment is being held back by what Greenspan believes to be lack of investor confidence. It is also possible that private investment is being constrained by banks' unwillingness to lend. When banks can borrow at virtually zero interest, they can make easy money in the markets. They do not have trouble themselves with risky loans. In such a situation, government spending alone can pick up the slack in demand.

Unfortunately, the Greek debt crisis earlier in the year seems to have coloured the perceptions of policy makers. They were quick to conclude that any further fiscal stimulus was unsustainable. But there are economies and economies.

The US is not Greece. Greece had to correct its course because the market rates on Greek government bonds soared. As Christina Romer points out, even today the markets are willing to lend to the American government at the lowest 20-year interest rate since 1958. American government spending will not only revive the US economy, it will strengthen the world economy and restore the financial markets to health.

The IMF's latest *World Economic Outlook* carries the results of an internal study. The study scotches the notion that fiscal consolidation can stimulate growth even in the short-run by boosting household and business confidence. It corroborates the Keynesian view that fiscal consolidation in the short-run typically results in contraction of output.

The lesson for the US is clear: for now, fiscal and monetary stimulus must go hand in hand. At the same time, Congress can reassure the markets by approving plans for long-term consolidation. The US cannot expect China and other emerging economies to shoulder the entire burden of adjustment. Adjustment, like charity, must begin at home.

October 28, 2010

Small Economies, big Headaches

Another financial storm, another bailout. In May, it was Greece. Now, it's Ireland, an economy that accounts for just.0.3 per cent of world GDP. Over the past few weeks, Ireland has been the central figure in an unfolding tragi-comedy. The EU was pressing Ireland to accept a rescue package. Ireland insisted it didn't need one. It has finally settled for a bailout estimated to cost •80-90 bn.

The drama has not impressed the financial markets. There have been huge sell-offs in several markets, including India. You have to wonder how a country, which registers as a place where men sport skirts, can give the jitters to the world economy.

Ireland is being mentioned in the same breath as Greece. But the two situations are different. In Greece, the EU bailout was necessitated by the refusal of private investors to provide funds to the Greek government. Ireland contended that its government finances were fully funded until the middle of 2011. And yet the EU has pushed funds down Ireland's throat. Why?

The immediate problem in Ireland is with banks, not with government finances. In 2008, at the height of the sub-prime crisis, the government assumed full or partial ownership of three large banks and guaranteed the liabilities of the entire banking sector until the end of 2010. The guarantee was recently extended up to June 2011.

But these measures have not stabilised the Irish banking system. Bank losses from real estate have mounted. Corporate deposits have been fleeing Irish banks. Ireland's banks are on ventilator support- they now survive on liquidity provided by the European Central Bank.

The markets rightly believe this can't go on. Today's banking problem will become tomorrow's sovereign debt problem. The banks will require massive infusion of funds. The funds will have to come from the government. With public debt at 100 per cent of GDP, the government will find it difficult to borrow. Yields on Irish government bonds have gone up by over 200 basis points in recent weeks. That raised the spectre of a default on Irish government guarantees of bank debt.

Should this happen, two consequences will follow that could prove lethal to the world economy. One, there will be a run on banks in other troubled economies such as Portugal and Spain. Two, banks in UK, France and Germany will incur huge losses on the substantial exposures they have to banks in Ireland.

As with Greece earlier, saving Ireland is all about saving banks elsewhere in the EU. A more accurate analogy would be with the

Iceland crisis in 2008. In Iceland too, banks went bust leaving other EU banks heavily exposed. The operative word is 'contagion'.

The rescue plan for Ireland will involve a massive infusion of funds into Ireland's banks. Like any bailout, it will come at a price. Ireland will be asked to put in place austerity measures. That is why the Irish government resisted a rescue. Maybe it thought the problem would simply go away with time. Maybe it hoped it could frighten the EU into offering a rescue on terms favourable to Ireland.

Iceland, Greece, Ireland. Small economies can cause big headaches. This is happening because we are yet to find solutions to two problems: how to restructure sovereign and bank debt; and how to ensure that banks do not keep disrupting the world economy.

There has been talk of a sovereign debt restructuring mechanism ever since the East Asian crisis of 1997 but no progress on the ground. Such a mechanism must involve bond holders taking a hit. Governments would then find it difficult to run up large debts. Lenders would know they stand to lose, so they would stop lending beyond a point. Interest costs would rise sharply once debt crosses a certain level, so governments would have every incentive to curb borrowing.

The trouble is that, in a crisis, any proposal for debt restructu--ring causes bond holders to flee and destabilise the markets. Only last month, Germany and France agreed that in any crisis resolution mechanism, private creditors should share the costs with taxpayers. Many believe that is why Ireland's problems have made the markets so nervous. Arrangements for orderly default on debt can be put in place only when economic conditions return to normal.

As for systemic crises created by the financial sector, the regulation of all systemically important financial institutions (SIFIs) has come to the fore. Two important measures on the table are additional capital for large institutions and for banks with mismatches in maturity between liabilities and assets. But neither measure has secured broad acceptance. The UK and the US are keen on reining in large banks, many other countries are not.

The world needs to go well beyond these measures. The cases of Iceland, Greece and Ireland show that even banks that are not large by international standards can radiate their problems beyond national boundaries. Interconnectedness of banks is an issue even when the banks are not very large. It has to be tackled.

There has to be monitoring of cross-border borrowings of banks. It is not enough to monitor total external debt for a given country. External debt of banks in that country must be separately monitored. Secondly, there must be prudential limits on total exposure of banks in economy A to a given bank in economy B as well as to all banks in economy B. Banks routinely monitor total loans to a given borrower in their own country. The principle must be extended to their exposures to any overseas banking system. This is necessary for preventing contagion.

Lastly, as the UK and the US did on a larger scale, Ireland shows up the perils of a bloated financial sector, of relying overly on finance as an engine of growth. We need to debate whether there is an appropriate size for the financial sector in relation to the overall economy. As for any individual or firm, so also at the level of the aggregate economy, diversification has its virtues.

When a large economy such as the US keels over, the world is dragged down. That is bad but understandable. What is worse is small economies causing disruptions in the world at large. If we are to contain these, debt restructuring and tighter bank regulation are issues that can no longer be brushed under the carpet.

November 25, 2010

Who Says it Doesn't Pay to Default?

The European Union is today the sick man of the world economy. The global economic outlook is more promising than thought a year ago. The world economy will grow at 4.5-5 per cent in 2011. Emerging markets will grow at around 7 per cent. The US is poised to grow at 3-3.5 per cent. The EU will be stuck at 2 per cent or less.

EU growth matters less to the rest of the world than its capacity to destabilise the world's financial system. Last year, the EU orchestrated a rescue of Greece and Ireland. What if Portugal, Spain, Italy and Belgium were to require rescue this year? Would the stronger economies of the EU, Germany and France, have the stomach to effect a bigger rescue if required? And if they didn't?

These are questions that trouble the world's financial markets today. The rest of the world needs to worry less about exports to the

EU than a disruption of financial flows as happened during the sub-prime crisis.

The EU is contemplating moves to reassure the markets. Support to the European Financial Stability Fund (EFSF), the bail-out fund created to prevent the break-up of the Euro, is to be improved. The EFSF was advertised as a • 440 bn fund but not all of this is available for lending.

Lending capacity is said to be around • 250 bn with the rest being held in cash to ensure that EU bonds get triple A status. The EU is inclined to top up lendable capacity itself to • 440 bn. The quality of support is to be improved by buying bonds in the secondary market. This will help moderate interest rates for distressed economies.

These are useful steps. But they may not suffice if contagion spreads to some of the larger economies. The bail-out extended to Ireland is already proving inadequate. Greece will miss the budget targets set for it under the bail-out target. It's clear that the standard approach of providing a support package in exchange for austerity measures will not solve the problem of solvency in EU's distressed economies.

When faced with a debt problem, you can grow your way out of trouble or run a budget surplus or lower your debt burden through debt restructuring or default. High growth is not an option for EU's distressed economies. Running a budget surplus will require a decade or so of austerity on a scale that no electorate will tolerate. That leaves debt restructuring or default as the only realistic options. The first is an orderly resolution. The second is a messy one. Investors must choose.

It is not investors in sovereign debt alone who must accept losses. Today, banks hold substantial amounts of sovereign debt thanks to huge recapitalisation by governments. As sovereign debt gets marked down, so will bank debt. Investors in bank debt too must accept losses. It is only when the costs of adjustment are shared by domestic taxpayers, investors and foreign taxpayers that the costs will be acceptable to electorates and the distressed economies have a reasonable chance of returning to solvency.

The alternative is a default. Sovereign default is not favoured because it is said to impose substantial costs: loss of access to financial markets, trade sanctions, political costs. But these costs can be exaggerated. As Reinhart and Rogoff have documented in their book, This time is different, many of today's developed economies have a long and undistinguished history of default on sovereign debt. But this did not come in the way of their transiting from emerging to developed economy status.

Between 1300 and 1799, England, France, Germany and Spain were among those who defaulted on external debt. England led the way with eight defaults. The champion defaulter in Europe in the nineteenth century was Spain with seven defaults. Russia and Germany too figure in the list as do several countries of Latin America. In the twentieth century, eight countries in Europe defaulted. China has defaulted twice but that has not prevented it from becoming the second biggest economy in the world.

In recent years, Argentina's economic recovery since its tumultuous default of 2002 has been spectacular. As Joseph Stiglitz noted recently (ET, January 14), the Argentine economy grew at nearly 9 per cent in 2003-2007. By 2009, national income was 75 per cent above its pre-crisis peak.

The Economist has compared the records of Iceland and Ireland. Iceland let its banks fail and their creditors took huge losses. Its GDP fell by 15 per cent from its highest point before it reached bottom. Ireland rescued its banks and saw its GDP fall by 14 per cent. Iceland's growth in the last quarter was better than Ireland's. It is also not true that Iceland did better because it could let its currency depreciate. Its trade balance improved more due to a fall in imports than a spurt in exports.

Sovereign default carries substantial costs. But, as the examples cited above and the longer historical record show, the costs are not always higher than those entailed by continued servicing of debt. Debtors will choose the less costly option.

There is evidence to suggest that capital markets may be more forgiving than is supposed: access to financial markets often becomes available after just three years. Investors will demand a higher risk premium on defaulting countries. But Paul Krugman thinks the current yields on Greek and Irish bonds already price in the probability of default or restructuring.

Governments are terrified that restructuring proposals or a default announcement will cause an exodus of investors. This fear is entirely valid when only one economy is involved. Today, sovereign debt has soared across developed economies, including the US. Investors must deal with the possibility of losses in several economies.

Are investors ready to dump sovereign and bank debt as asset classes and move elsewhere? If yes, where will they go? They cannot get exposed to emerging markets or other asset classes beyond a point. Faced with collective action from the EU, investors will have to accept the benefits of orderly restructuring vis-à-vis serial defaults. To put it bluntly, the EU should call the investors' bluff.

Whatever the resolution, the irony of the present situation should not be lost on us. Debt restructuring or default was supposed to be an emerging market problem. Today it has become an advanced economy problem. How the mighty have fallen!

January 20, 2011

Learning from IMF and Other Tales

Through the nineties, the IMF preached the virtues of free capital flows. It has learnt since, from the East Asian crisis as well as the recent sub-prime crisis. In 2010, the IMF made something of a volte face. It discarded its long-standing hostility to capital controls. It took the position that countries would be justified in responding to temporary surges in capital flows.

The IMF is still learning. In recent months, it has come out with another staff paper and a policy framework that shows that its position is still evolving. The paper goes further than the one last year and argues that countries may be justified in responding to surges in flows that are of a permanent nature as well. The policy framework presents recommendations that arise from the paper.

The IMF outlines a three-step approach to dealing with capital flows. The first step is to get macroeconomic policies right. Where the exchange rate is undervalued, it should be allowed to appreciate through increased inflows. Where forex reserves are not adequate, countries can respond to inflows by building up reserves and limiting the impact on liquidity through sterilisation. Fiscal policy should be tightened and monetary policy eased where there is scope for doing these. In other words, in dealing with capital flows, countries should first exhaust these macroeconomic options. Only then should other options be considered.

The next line of defence is what the IMF calls prudential measures. These measures are of a long-term nature and may not be deployed only in response to a surge in capital flows. They could be measures aimed at increasing the capacity of an economy to absorb foreign inflows (eg strengthening the bond market). Or they could be measures that increase the resilience of financial institutions (eg. higher capital adequacy norms or loan-to-value norms). They may not have an immediate impact on capital flows but they help limit the damage to the financial sector that can be done by volatile flows.

Suppose the currency is undervalued, forex reserves are inadequate and monetary policy can be eased. In the face of a surge in capital flows, would prudential measures suffice? The answer is not obvious. You can do what you like to protect the financial sector but there is no getting away from the fact that the financial sector is exposed to the real sector. If there is rapid appreciation in currency, it could undermine the competitiveness of firms in the real sector and that is bound to impact on the financial sector.

Moreover, the whole problem with capital flows is their fickleness. Capital that flows in easily can flow out just as easily. There is huge volatility in the exchange rate and this can undermine stability in the economy, including financial sector stability. If a large portion of flows bypasses the regulated financial sector, prudential measures may not suffice. Some resort to capital controls may become unavoidable.

That would explain why many countries, such as Brazil and Peru in recent times, have thought it necessary to use controls to deal with capital flows. The IMF finds that 9 out of 30 countries it surveyed met the macroeconomic conditions it specifies for the use of capital control measures.

Unfortunately, the jury is out on the effectiveness in the long-run of such controls. The IMF makes a distinction between capital control measures that distinguish based on residency and those do not. It indicates a preference for the latter. Then again, countries may have to choose between price-based bases (such as taxes on inflows) and administrative measures (such as outright bans on certain types of inflows).

However, even well-designed capital controls may not work. Capital has a way of bypassing barriers. Moreover, there could be costs to the economy of erecting barriers. The IMF policy framework suggests that capital controls should be temporary and should be scaled back at the earliest opportunity. But this assumes that surges in capital flows are of a relatively short duration. It does not tell us how countries are to cope with sustained surges in capital.

For emerging economies, capital flows are not a function only or even mainly of their growth prospects. Global economic conditions are an even bigger determinant, especially what happens to US interest rates. In other words, however well emerging markets may manage their economies, they will be at the mercy of volatile flows of capital, based on what happens in advanced economies. This is the nub of the issue.

It has become even more relevant in the world economy after the sub-prime crisis. Monetary easing in the US and Europe is causing a flood of liquidity in emerging economies. The point, as some emerging markets have pointed out, is not how well emerging markets manage their economies but how well advanced economies manage theirs. From preaching to emerging markets, the IMF has begun to learn from them. This is one lesson it still needs to absorb.

April 28, 2011

Can Greece Jolt the World Economy?

The world economy came through 2010 without the 'double-dip' recession that many economists had forecast. It grew at 5 per cent, the pre-crisis growth rate. The advanced economies grew at 3 per cent. But the numbers flattered to deceive.

In 2011, the IMF projects growth to slow down to 4.4 per cent, with the advanced economies crawling at 2.4 per cent. Emerging economies in India must brace themselves not only for slower growth in the advanced world but with uncertainties in capital flows caused by jittery financial markets.

Two important risks to growth are the high level of government debt in the advanced economies and high oil prices. A third factor, one that promises to be the most troublesome of the lot, is the crisis in the Euro-zone. The IMF's *World Economic Outlook* (April 2011) believes that if the crisis gets out of hand, it alone could depress global output by 1 percentage point.

Last May, as the possibility of a Greek default on sovereign debt loomed, the European Union (EU) and the IMF put together a $110 bn rescue package. But the terms of the rescue clearly indicated that the problem had only been postponed, it hadn't gone away.

Greece's debt to GDP ratio is expected to rise to 160 per cent of GDP this year. Faced with this huge wall of debt, private investors are in no mood to finance Greece. If private money is not forthcoming and Greece is not to default, official money must come in. That is what the EU-IMF rescue last year was all about.

At the time, however, the hope was that official support would be temporary. Nobody now believes this is possible. The better off nations in the EU, led by Germany, will have to support Greece indefinitely. Taxpayers in these countries are in no mood to permit this.

If Greece is to have some chance of accessing the markets, some of Greek's debt must be written down, that is, investors in Greek government bonds must accept some loss on their investments. European banks are said to be holding around $150 bn in Greek government bonds. To the extent that a 'haircut' (bankers' code for losses) is imposed on investors, European governments will have to recapitalise their banks and also provide capital to Greek banks.

Restructuring entails other complications that analysts have pointed out. The EU has lent $ 34 bn under last year's rescue package. This debt is on the same footing as government debt. So, a 50% debt write off will impose an immediate cost of $19 bn on the EU. The European Central Bank too faces losses on Greek government bonds it holds.

So, here is the unappetising choice the EU governments face: if Greek debt is restructured, they have to fork out money to support their banks; if there is no restructuring, they still have to fork out money to keep Greece going. The problem appears a lot worse than thought earlier. Some analysts warn that restructuring is not an option at all. It would prove to be a 'Lehman event', unleashing chaos in the financial markets and destabilising the world economy.

Heavy as the immediate costs of restructuring are, they might still be acceptable if they produced solvency in Greece. Not so, it appears. One economist, writing in FT (May 12), estimates that even if half of Greece's debt is written off, and with all the austerity it can practice, Greece would not be able to bring its debt to GDP ratio down to the 60% mandated by the Maastricht Treaty.

It would still need to borrow from abroad in order to keep going. Its exports lack the competitiveness needed for it to grow its way out of trouble. The only way out, then, for Greece would be to exit the EU and devalue its currency. If that happens, investors in Greek debt would again face steep losses. There appears to be no happy ending in sight.

The leaders of Germany and France are inclined to do what politicians everywhere prefer when faced with a crisis: temporize. They want, not restructuring, but 're-profiling'. Greek government debt would not be written down nor would the interest rate on it be lowered. Instead, some of the existing bonds would be replaced by longer maturity bonds. The idea is that Greece gets more time to work out its problems.

But this is just evasion and it won't fool investors. In present value terms, Greek bonds would be worth less, so investors would have to accept losses. The consolation is that, for banks, re-profiling does not technically constitute a default. Banks will not have to cough up enormous sums towards credit default swaps written by them. To that extent, re-profiling entails lower costs than restructuring.

Whichever course is accepted, re-profiling or outright restructuring, Greece is not likely to return to solvency in the near future. Investors, including banks, will continue to face losses and the financial markets will remain in a state of suspense. Other troubled economies- Ireland, Portugal and Spain- will contribute to the general nervousness. It does seem bizarre but, in today's globalised financial markets, a handful of small countries can keep the world economy off the tracks for a long, long time.

May 26, 2011

A Continuation, not a Repeat, of 2008

Standard & Poor's downgrading of US government debt from AAA to AA sent shock waves through the markets last week. Is it a sign that American economic conditions are worsening? Does it presage another 'Lehman moment' for the world economy? Will it cause a huge setback to India's growth prospects? Let me spare you the suspense and state my answers upfront: no, unlikely, no.

A lowering of the credit rating signifies an increased probability of default. S&P is one of three leading rating agencies; the other two agencies have not changed their rating of US debt. Any suggestion that American creditworthiness has declined was emphatically rejected by the markets.

Equities tumbled all over the world but prices of US government bonds rose and the dollar itself appreciated. When a bond is downgraded, you expect investors to sell it. Investors responded to S&P's downgrade by flocking towards US government bonds! They see global economic conditions deteriorating and they affirmed once again that, in bad times, US treasuries remain a safe haven.

As several commentators have pointed out, the US is uniquely privileged to be able to issue debt in its own currency. This gives it the ability to repay debt simply by printing more currency. As long as the dollar remains the reserve currency- and this will be so in the foreseeable future- there is little probability of the US defaulting on its debt.

We in India should know how unfair sovereign ratings can be. We were rated below investment grade through the nineties and are rated only BBB even now, inspite of being the second fastest-growing economy in the world, with a very small component of foreign debt.

In September 2008, the US government's decision to let Lehman Brothers fail in 2008 set off a wave of panic in the markets and plunged the world economy into a full-scale crisis. Can the S&P downgrade cause a similar outcome by undermining confidence?

Today's economic situation is not as bad as that in 2008. By 2008, banks had run up huge losses. There was enormous uncertainty as to how financial institutions would be impacted through their exposures to Lehman's derivative contracts. Banks in the US as well as in Europe were heavily dependent on short-term funds. These funds fled the banking system following the collapse of Lehman. This exacerbated banks' losses and created a serious financial crisis. Financial crises lead on to economic downturns. And these downturns can be steeper and more difficult to climb out of than downturns caused by other shocks.

Banks today are much better capitalised than at the time of the Lehman collapse. According to the IMF's Global Financial Stability Report (April, 2011), capital adequacy of US banks in 2010 was 15.3 per cent compared to 12.8 per cent in 2007; in the UK, the numbers were 15.9 per cent and 12.6 per cent respectively. Banks in Germany and France too have improved capital adequacy.

The downgrade of US by S&P has very little impact on banks. The regulatory authorities have conveyed that banks will not have to provide additional capital against their stocks of US government securities. Growth in the US will be slow but a recession appears unlikely.

However, banks could be significantly impacted by any default of countries within the Eurozone. Government debt is high in several countries of Europe and banks are heavily exposed to it. Thus, the serious threat to the world economy today arises from the Eurozone, not the US.

Any solution will require, among other things, a combination of debt forgiveness and lower interest rates. The solution worked out for Greece recently suggests that Europe's leaders are getting there. The prospect of a full-blown global crisis has finally concentrated minds in Europe.

True, the mood in financial markets can turn at the drop of a hat. At the moment, however, neither is there any indication of a Lehman-like shock nor is the financial system as vulnerable as it was in the run-up to 2008. Slow growth, rather than a global recession, thus appears the most likely outcome.

What we are seeing at the moment is a continuation of the 2008 crisis, rather than a repeat of it. Fiscal and monetary stimuli have failed to return the advanced economies to their normal growth rates. For once, not just the political leadership in the advanced world but the fraternity of economists appears at the end of its tether.

From India's point of view, the present conditions in the world economy may be just what the doctor ordered. Policy makers have been looking to lower growth by way of tackling inflation. A global slowdown and falling commodity prices may obviate the need for any further increase in interest rates.

There are calls from various quarters to 'press the accelerator', 'grasp the moment' and so on. Policy makers must eschew the temptation to make dramatic gestures. Some of the issues that are slowing down decisions today do require the utmost deliberation and consultation: the trade-off between environment and growth, land acquisition and rehabilitation, the sale of public resources, etc. Others that might have a reformist air about them are fraught with serious implications, for instance, the issue of bank licenses to industrial houses.

India's gradualist approach towards reforms has served it well, not just in terms of producing accelerated growth but in ensuring a broad consensus in favour of outcomes. There is no call to discard this approach in pursuit of some illusory growth target in a challenging global environment.

August 18, 2011

IMF's Bold Recipe for Recovery

How to prevent a slide into another recession is the question that is engaging the world's policy-makers. At the meeting of central bankers at Jackson Hole in the US last week, all eyes were on the holy trinity of international economic policy- the chairman of the Fed, the president of the European Central Bank and the managing director of the IMF. Surprise, surprise, it was the head of the notoriously conservative IMF who came up with the boldest proposals for tackling the present crisis.

At the same venue last year, Bernanke had indicated plans for another bout of quantitative easing. Many expected a similar indication this time. The Fed chief disappointed them. Bernanke said that the Fed had committed itself to "exceptionally low levels" (meaning, close to zero) for the short-term interest rate until mid-2013, implying he did not intend to do more right now. To those looking for a way out for the faltering world economy, Bernanke's stark message was, "Hang in there".

The president of the European Central Bank, Jean-Claude Trichet, did not offer any comfort to nervous investors either. Trichet's discourse on the long-term factors that drive economic growth, structural reforms and price stability may have enthused students of Economics 101 but one could not see investors cheering wildly.

Enter the recently appointed IMF chief and former French finance minister, Christian Lagarde. The IMF chief outlined a menu of tough decisions the world's leaders need to take if the present recovery is not to be derailed - and she did so in plain English.

One item in the menu stands out: the "urgent recapitalisation" of banks in Europe. Private capital was welcome, Lagarde said, but we should not shy away from using public funds if necessary. The European Financial Stability Facility could be used to directly capitalise banks in Europe. This would "avoid placing even greater burdens on vulnerable sovereigns."

Regulators and bankers in Europe were rattled. Urgent recapitalisation? European banks have enough capital to cope with a possible crisis, they said. In the most recent stress tests, only nine out of 91 European banks tested had failed, with a core tier one capital ratio of less than 5 per cent. The problem at European banks today was lack of liquidity, not lack of capital.

This is sheer quibbling. All of us know that in a bank, a problem of liquidity can quickly turn into a problem of solvency. This happened in 2007-08 and it can happen again. There are concerns about solvency because European banks are holding large amounts of government debt. Some of this debt has to be written off if the weaker economies of Europe are to return to growth. Banks will face significant losses as a result.

Lagarde's proposal faces up squarely to the inevitability that European debt has to be restructured. It ensures that the banking system is not caught up in a crisis when that happens. The present economic crisis flows from a financial crisis. It is the prospect of another financial crisis that is giving the markets and businesses the jitters and stalling the recovery. Lagarde's proposal thus provides a basis for recovery in Europe while containing the fall-out on its fragile financial sector.

Lagarde was equally forthright in addressing the issue of reviving the US economy. The key was "halting the downward spiral of foreclosures, falling house prices and deteriorating household spending." This would involve writing off some of the debt of mortgage owners, again with help from the government.

Thirdly, governments in both Europe and the US must balance long-term fiscal consolidation with the need for short-term fiscal stimulus. The two are not contradictory, indeed they can be "mutually reinforcing". The long-term fiscal risks are rising pensions and healthcare. If these are tackled, there will be space to support growth in the short-run.

One element is common to the three proposals made by the IMF chief: public spending. Most people are of the view that fiscal stimulus has run its course; whatever little can be done for shoring up the recovery falls in the realm of monetary policy. Lagarde has taken a refreshingly different line. She clearly accords primacy to fiscal policy in the present scenario.

This is interesting. The IMF, which was a staunch advocate of fiscal austerity not long ago in the East Asian crisis, favours public spending as the answer to the present crisis. In recent years, the IMF has moved away from its long-held position on the free flow of capital. Are we now seeing a shift in its position on fiscal austerity in times of crises?

The head of the IMF is a lawyer and politician by training, not an economist. And yet she has come out with a clearer enunciation of steps needed to bolster the global economic recovery than the heads of the world's two leading central banks and indeed most professional economists. Whatever happens to the world economy, it does look as though the world of economic policy-making is in for a shake-up.

September 1, 2011

10

International Banking

Coping with Tsunami-like Risks

Every big disaster gives rise to the question: is it worth making the investment necessary to prevent the rare event that imposes huge financial costs?

Do we spend huge amounts in order to ward off all of the dangers that lurk in the recesses of the cosmos?

The question is by no means new to financial institutions. They can always provide for the exceptional disaster by allocating capital equal to the anticipated loss in value in extreme events.

Do this, however, and you lower the return to your shareholders most of the time. So you have a trade-off between not staving off a disaster that might occur once in hundred years and generating high returns for the remaining 99.

Institutions tend to opt for the latter. This reflects society's acceptance of the fact that not all disasters can be prevented - or are worth preventing. The best we can do is mitigate the consequences thereof. But are societies doing enough even by way of cushioning the impact of disaster?

The task of alleviating suffering today devolves overwhelmingly on governments. But governments can do only so much. We need stronger buffers against calamity. In the industrial countries, social security helps. So do life, health and unemployment insurance.

However, as Robert Shiller argues in his book, *The New Financial Order*, the time may have come to give a push to more comprehensive markets for risk insurance.

Shiller, professor of economics at Yale, is the best-selling author of *Irrational Exuberance* in which he correctly called the high-tech bubble of 2000.

In his more recent work, he shows how technology and superior access to information provide the basis for dealing with a wide range of risks to which people are exposed. Threats to livelihood come not just from natural disasters but also from man-made ones.

For many, the disappearance of a firm or the disappearance of whole industries is the equivalent of a tsunami.

A key insight of Shiller's is that, in the modern economy, individuals need to be protected not just against total loss of incomes but also against declines in income over time caused by the working of the capitalist system.

It may be more efficient, therefore, to think of livelihood insurance instead of just life, health and unemployment insurance that offer protection against extreme threats to livelihood. Under livelihood insurance, whenever there is a decline in economic value, the policy-holder collects; the cause of the decline is not material.

Erosion in earning power can be measured by constructing appropriate occupational income indices.

An individual could buy an insurance policy against an erosion of income of people of his occupation, against erosion of income of people with his characteristics (in terms of job history or education) or against erosion of incomes of the particular income group he belongs to.

How does one deal with moral hazard, the danger that an individual takes it easy in the knowledge that livelihood insurance is available? No problem: individuals will be insured against an index of the risk of a whole group over which no individual has any control.

This is just one of the many forms of protection against risk possible in Shiller's financial order. A bolder idea is income-linked loans, an idea that Milton Friedman mooted way back in 1962.

This would be a significant departure from fixed interest loans that push borrowers into bankruptcy if their earnings drop. Friedman did not pursue the idea because of the high transaction costs involved; by lowering costs, technology renders the idea feasible.

To deal with moral hazard, lenders would link future payments to an index of average incomes of similar loan recipients (say, doctors). Alternatively, future payments could be linked to both individual and group incomes.

The idea is not altogether novel: there have been sporadic applications of it in the past. In 1994, Citibank made a $1.9 billion loan to Bulgaria at an interest rate linked to its GDP growth rate.

Shiller extends the concept of risk management into areas in which government will have a role: the trading of claims linked to economies ("macro markets"), using inequality insurance to maintain a certain distribution of incomes and viewing social security in terms of sharing intergenerational risk.

The industrial countries invested heavily in safety nets and are now trying hard to prune these. As latecomers to risk management, less developed countries may have an advantage.

Safety nets could be reserved for the poorest. For the vast majority of people, it would make better financial sense to use comprehensive markets for risk along the lines Shiller advocates.

January 13, 2005

Citi Citi bang bang

The US Federal Reserve Board has told the world's largest bank not to make big acquisitions until it is surer of its internal controls. The bank's CEO wants his staff to understand that short-term profit must not be put ahead of the bank's reputation. Citigroup, a bank known to go for growth with its guns blazing, finds itself obliged to relearn the basics. The bank's predicament rekindles the debate about the benefits of size and growth through merger or acquisition in banking in a world in which regulatory risks are mounting.

Citigroup is not only the largest bank in the world by market capitalisation, it is among the most profitable. The bank is the product of a series of successful mergers that welded together a commercial bank, two investment banks, an insurance company and a brokerage firm. Yet the Fed believes that management's attention should not be diverted from its efforts to improve compliance by "the demands that mergers and acquisitions place on management resources" (*Financial Times,* March 15).

Not that the bank needed to be told. It has already divested itself of its insurance business in stages since 2002. Its CEO, Chuck Prince, had made clear that the bank would rely on organic growth rather than acquisitions. The decision, reinforced now by the Fed's order, follows a series of compliance failures for which the bank is paying a steep price in financial costs as well as damage to its reputation.

Citibank has had to pay or put aside nearly $10 bn towards settlements in the cases of World Com and Enron where investors are suing banks for their role in the collapses of these companies. Its private bank in Japan was closed down by regulators for breaches of law. It is under investigation in the European Union over a controversial bond trade. The bank faces probes in South Korea and Italy and has been rapped on the knuckles in India as well.

Mr Prince wants to change the bank's culture. His initiatives in recent weeks include screening a film on the bank's values, setting up an 'ethics hotline' that will facilitate anonymous feedback on managers and 'franchise training' for managers. Such measures have their uses but it would be naïve to suppose that training or moral exhortation can by themselves result in better compliance.

Weak compliance at Citigroup undoubtedly has to do with its size and the diverse activities it houses. The larger and more complex you get, the more difficult it is to maintain controls. Partly because more volumes mean more monitoring. But also because the pressure to sustain growth on a large base and the incentives that go with performance today inevitably lead to cutting of corners.

Having under the same roof activities with varying cultures and inherent conflicts of interest, as Citigroup does, makes things even worse. What is aggression in investment banking is imprudence in banking. An argument for banks getting into investment banking was that fees from investment banking would make it possible for banks to offer loans more cheaply to corporate clients. But this also means that banks raking in investment banking fees end up providing loans where they should not be doing so- as was the case in World Com and Enron.

This may not have mattered in an earlier era but with tougher regulation and more litigious shareholders, it can prove costly for banks. Take away the $10 bn in litigation costs that Citigroup faces and its profit of around $18 bn in 2003 does not look impressive.

Mr Prince has announced a compensation plan that will link employee rewards to the group's performance, not just that of individual businesses. It is not clear how this will help. It does not address the fundamental problem in banks, namely, that the results of decisions become known with a significant lag. Great performance today turns out to be disaster five years later.

Banks need to devise schemes whereby rewards and penalties both accrue over a long enough cycle. In a given year, only a portion of the reward will be handed out, not the full amount (whether cash or stock options). At the end of the cycle, pluses and minuses will be totaled and the balance paid. But who will bell the compensation cat? Certainly not management that stands to gain from short-term performance.

Citigroup is a sophisticated operation with highly skilled people and the best risk management systems. Yet, it is grappling with the issues of size, diversity and incentives. There is a lesson in this for those pushing for consolidation of India's bigger banks. Tighten risk management, improve human resources, think through incentives – and then contemplate mergers. Remember, better people have messed up.

March 24, 2005

Sorry, You can't Touch my Bonus

Head we win, tails we don't lose. That's the rule for Wall Street employees. The financial market crisis is still unraveling. Shareholders have seen a steep erosion in their wealth. But Wall Street's top five firms are set to distribute $38 bn in bonuses this year, up from $36 bn last year. Bonuses in a year as bad as this one? Elsewhere, that would regarded as a cruel joke. Not on Wall Street.

Firms such as Goldman Sachs that have done well through intelligent hedging of risks are clearly in a different category. Just under a half of this year's bonus will likely be accounted for by Goldman. According to one estimate, bonus payments at Goldman will be large enough to finance the acquisition of another top five player, Bear Stearns, whose stock has been battered in recent months.

At other firms, bonuses will be justified in relation to divisional performance, no matter that the firm as a whole has not done well. Investment banks such as Merrill Lynch may have run up huge losses due to exposures to sub-prime mortgages but that is the problem of the divisions concerned. The other divisions will insist on being rewarded.

On Wall Street, it is understood that total pay has a large variable component and this helps keep base pay down. The variable component has largely to do with individual performance. If an individual does well, he or she would have to be rewarded even if the firm does not do well. Wall Street would argue that if variable pay does not match individual performance, base pay would have to be uniformly higher in order to attract bright people. Potential non-performers would be rewarded along with those who perform. Shareholders would be even worse off in that situation.

What is it about Wall Street firms that permits large bonuses to be paid even when the firm has not done well? Unlike in many manufacturing firms, divisional performance and, in many cases, individual performance are easily measurable. Traders' profits are known. Revenues from IPO deals brought in by investment bankers are transparent. Fees related to mergers and acquisitions are obvious. Every individual is a profit centre.

In manufacturing firms, revenues and profit are the result of the efforts of several groups and hence isolating group and individual performance is more difficult. At an automobile company, if a new model of car fares well, does the credit go to product development or manufacturing or to marketing? If it goes to all these divisions, then in what proportion? This is hard to determine.

The investment banking compensation structure has not been without flaws. Until a few years ago, investment bankers were paid for bringing in revenues and profits without the associated risks being taken into account. This is like a commercial banker being paid for a big increase in loans without factoring in non-performing assets that will show up down the road.

With the development of models of risk-adjusted return on capital (Raroc), this problem has come to be addressed. Greater revenue may come from higher risks and higher risks translate into higher allocation of capital for a given division. Investment bankers these days tend to be rewarded in relation to return on capital. The denominator, the capital allocation for a given level of risk is also taken into account, not just the numerator, profit.

A more fundamental problem is that, in activities that require the allocation of firm capital, investment bankers rake in huge rewards when they do well but are not adequately penalised when they inflict losses on the firm. At worst, they may get zero bonus or they may lose their jobs. But the firm does not recover money from them in proportion to the losses they have caused.

The classic example is that of a star trader at one of the top firms who was paid more than $100 mn for extraordinary performance in a given year- his total pay exceeded that of the firm's CEO by a wide margin. In the next year, he ran up a huge loss. He happened to be cruising around in his Lamborghini when word reached him that he was in for a pink slip. From his superbly equipped vehicle, he shot off two faxes. One, a letter of resignation intended to pre-empt his dismissal. Another, a covering letter and a CV to another firm seeking a position on the strength of his previous year's performance.

Ideally, Wall Street firms should have a system that tracks employee performance over a business cycle. Only a portion of the rewards for a given year should be paid out. The rest should be credited to the employee's account. Losses over the business cycle should require deductions from credits for profits made. Over, say, a five year period, there will be credits and debits in the employee account. The balance must be paid out at the end of the period. Sounds fair? Maybe. But there is a fatal flaw in the scheme. Top management too would be subject to such a scheme and they would be the last people to want it.

Nov 29, 2007

Banking's Governance Disaster

UBS, one of the world's largest banks and among the biggest losers in the sub-prime crisis, is replacing four of its directors. The bank's objective, according to its new chairman, is to strengthen the board with independent members with top class financial or audit experience. The departing members include three outsiders with experience respectively in rail equipment, chemicals and information technology.

So, it has taken a loss of around $38 bn for one of the world's foremost banks to conclude that it needs significant financial expertise on its board? UBS is in good company. Earlier, Citigroup had declared its intention to look for directors with a financial background.

According to the *Financial Times* (June 25), more than two-thirds of board members at the world's top eight financial institutions lacked significant experience in banking. Less than half had any financial services experience.

Lehman's audit committee and risk committee has a theatre impresario as member. Citi has a former head of the CIA in the same roles- no doubt, the bank believes that experience in surveillance gained at the CIA has broader applications. Northern Rock's chairman at the time of its collapse was a zoologist - presumably, this was meant to guard against wild bets on the part of management.

One of the big improvements in corporate governance in recent years is said to be the institution of independent director. Boards are expected to have independent directors who will act as a check on management. But the idea that management, in its wisdom, would assemble the required expertise has taken some hard knocks. Many banks, it turns out, have big names aplenty. Banking expertise is sadly wanting. Many ask whether adequate expertise on bank boards would have led to very different outcomes. Can the best of experts monitor risks at complex financial institutions? It is safe to suggest that they can certainly do a better job than those innocent of finance or banking.

Whether the levels of certain exposures are acceptable; whether higher returns in a given year merely reflect a shift towards greater risk; whether yields accord with underlying risk; whether executive pay is properly aligned with long-term performance; yes, it is possible for boards with appropriate expertise to seek answers to questions such as these. Unfortunately, these questions are not asked often enough.

To be sure, board expertise does not ensure that tough questions will be asked. Board members may have expertise but they may be unwilling to challenge and confront management. Anybody who has sat on boards knows that any attempt to probe or criticise can inject a jarring note into the proceedings. The superannuated souls who grace many a board prefer the quiet life.

Which brings us to a fatal flaw that lies at the very heart of the present notion of independent director. The present definition of an independent director as somebody who has no pecuniary relationship with the company is inadequate. A more rigorous definition would be a director who does not owe his position to management. Such a director alone can act as an effective check on management.

In the private sector, "independent" directors are those invited on to boards by management and handsomely compensated for their services. For many retirees, earnings from directorships constitute the biggest chunk of their incomes. They would have to be saints to vigorously challenge management.

We need a radical rethink of the notion of independent director. At the very least, not all "independent" directors can be invitees of management. At least half must be nominees of financial institutions and minority shareholders. Private equity and venture capital firms insist on having their nominees on the boards of firms in which they invest. Why should things be very different in publicly listed firms?

India's public sector companies can lay better claim to having truly independent directors. Independent directors are appointed by the parent ministry or the department of public enterprises. As they do not owe their positions to management, they are better placed to speak their minds freely than their counterparts in the private sector.

As in many other aspects of bank regulation, one finds that the RBI has done a better job in the matter of board composition than many other regulators. It requires banks to have at least half the board members with expertise in specified areas. This was criticised as "micromanagement" on the part of RBI. In light of the governance disasters elsewhere, it does appear that the RBI got the idea right.

The governance of bank boards is one of many issues highlighted by the sub-prime crisis. Banks certainly could use better expertise on their boards. But the overhaul of governance must go farther than that. We need to revisit the very notion of independent director.

July 10, 2008

Wall Street Model Crumbles

Three of America's top five investment banks have disappeared over the past six months, two of them last weekend. Bear Stearns went last March. Now, Lehman Brothers and Merrill Lynch have followed.

At least Bear and Merrill found buyers, the former with support from the Fed. Lehman has suffered the ignominy of having to file for bankruptcy. Only Goldman Sachs and Morgan Stanley are left standing. Many will wonder: for how much longer?

These are (or were) no ordinary firms. They represented the pride of America's financial system. They attracted the brightest from the top business schools. They were held up as models of good management, producing returns on equity that were the envy of their counterparts in other sectors.

Today, Wall Street's reputation is in tatters. It is legitimate to ask: how on earth did the boards, the top management and the collection of brains down the line manage to bring three of the top firms to their knees?

As somebody who worked for one of these now defunct investment banks, I will first let out a little secret: I wasn't bowled over by the talent at these places. Much of the research was mediocre-no more than a rehash of numbers and arguments provided by the firms themselves. Investments were made or recommended with a casualness that took one's breath away considering the sums involved.

Today, most of the blame is being laid at the doors of the CEOs. Bear Stearns' Chairman, Jimmy Cayne, and Lehman's CEO, Richard Fuld, have gone swiftly from being iconic figures to arch villains.

But the commentators have been less than consistent. When Bear Stearns collapsed, many were quick to contrast Cayne's laid back style (he was away at a bridge tournament without his mobile while Bear was unraveling) with Fuld's supposedly hands-on approach and his ability to communicate with the markets.

Last April, *The Economist* carried a profile of Fuld in which it gushed:

> Lehman was no Bear: it relied far less on fickle overnight funding from wholesale markets, or on clients' cash balances to fund its own trading positions. Nor was the work-obsessed Mr Fuld much like the boss of Bear, Jimmy Cayne, who spent more time playing bridge than playing the markets. ...Quickly, it called key clients and trading partners, giving them unprecedented detail on its ample liquidity position. Rating agencies and the media were wooed, too...

Famous last words, huh?

Others ascribe the investment banks' collapse to the autocratic styles of their CEOs. This too is glib. If the CEO's autocratic style is indeed the problem, most corporations the world over should be failing, not just investment banks.

No, with Wall Street, the cause of failure lies elsewhere: the basic business model had come to be seriously flawed. Investment banks started off as brokerages and then branched off into underwriting of securities and advisory services. None of these businesses requires large amounts of funding.

When commissions on these businesses declined, investment banks started setting aside bigger and bigger sums for proprietary trading. From proprietary trading, investment banks moved on to private equity. In other words, investment banks started betting their own capital on risky assets- and illiquid assets at that. Worse, they chose to increase leverage to stratospheric heights. In August, even after fresh infusions, Lehman Brothers had a leverage of 20:1. The one deal that killed Lehman was the acquisition of a property investment company at the height of the property bubble.

The investment banks thought they had the expertise to manage asset risks. But there are two problems with this model. One, the assets are funded in the wholesale markets. The moment there is uncertainty about the value of assets, access to funds is cut off- and this triggers a collapse. Two, in the presence of high leverage, managers have every incentive to take huge risks. If the gambles work out, managers get big rewards. If they fail, it is shareholders who get wiped out. Fuld's own pay vaulted to $40 million in 2007 from $12.5 million in 2002.

The demise of three top investment banks has several implications. First, it calls into question the standalone model of investment banking. For most capital market activities, a stable base of funds makes sense. Banks, with their access to deposits, are better placed to succeed. That is what the acquisitions of Bear and Lehman by J P Morgan Chase and Bank of America respectively signal. In other words, 'financial intermediation', on the wane for many years, is back with a bang.

Secondly, leverage in banking itself may have to fall from the present levels. Thirdly, when investment banks come to be part of banks, investment banking too comes under the purview of central bank regulation. Wall Street, they say, reinvents itself every few decades. This time round it's not so much reinvention as disappearance.

Sept 18, 2008

Wall Street fact and Fiction

In the barrage of comments on the collapse of Wall Street's investment banks, it's sometimes hard to distinguish fact from fiction, the grey areas are easily overlooked. Here's a guide to some of the issues that are in the spotlight:

1. **The top investment banks have vanished as a class because they were highly leveraged:** This is only partly true. In financial institutions, leverage or the ratio of debt to total assets, can be misleading as a measure of financial risk. The management of asset risks is equally important. A financial institution can be highly leveraged but if its assets are of high quality or are highly diversified, the institution is not exposed to high risk.

Investment banks may have had a leverage of more than 20:1 but some high-profile banks in Europe today have even higher leverage. What counts is leverage after adjusting for the risks of various assets. The European banks in question would not be allowed to operate if their leverage was not in conformity with regulatory norms.

The trouble with the investment banks was not so much leverage as poor asset quality and heavy dependence on short-term funds. Lehman's problem was not that it had $600 bn in assets at a leverage of 20:1. Its problem was that it had (by one estimate) around $80 bn in toxic assets and it raised funds in the wholesale market. The moment the market sensed that it had more toxic assets than thought, confidence fled and nobody was willing to provide finance-in other words, it faced the equivalent of a "run" on a bank.

2. **Short-sellers were right on Lehman, so short-selling should not be banned:** Yes, short-sellers were right in sensing that Lehman had more problems than it had disclosed. But, in times of crises, it makes sense to ban short-selling because a fall in share prices sets off a vicious spiral that pushes an institution quickly into bankruptcy.

A fall in the value of equity causes leverage to rise which causes the debt rating to fall. This, in turn, prompts demands for higher collateral, which forces distress sale of assets, which erodes equity value..... before you could say 'Hank Paulson', the firm is gone. In financial crises, as in times of war, the normal rules of information must stand suspended and this applies to price discovery effected by short-sellers.

3. **Goldman Sachs and Morgan Stanley were issued banking licenses because they can survive only as banks:** Correct. But it does not follow that the two firms can become successful banking operations by themselves. Access to retail deposits requires a large branch network and this is not created overnight.

The decision to issue banking licenses to these two firms over the weekend was intended to tell the world that they had access to unlimited liquidity at the central bank as distinct from the limited liquidity facility the Fed had created earlier for investment banks. In other words, the Fed move was meant to spare them the fate of Bear Stearns and Lehman Brothers. That is good news for shareholders of these firms. But it does not follow that the two firms can succeed as banks on their own. The odds are they will have to be acquired by banks.

Incidentally, whatever happened to the Fed's due diligence process? Indian banks seeking to enter the US have been kept waiting for years but it takes only a weekend for troubled investment banks to get a banking license!

4. **The disappearance of the top investment banks shows that there is no future for investment banks:** Wrong. It only shows there is no future for full-scope investment banks of the Wall Street variety. There is room for investment banks that specialise in the traditional activities, such as underwriting of issues, advisory service, brokerage and custodial services. The top firms came a cropper because they ventured in a big way into proprietary trading and private equity. (Some of India's top investment banks derive less than 10% of their income from proprietary trading).

5. **Wall Street investment bankers were a talented lot whose risk-taking skills will be missed:** We know now how well they managed risks. Much is made of the talent at the top

investment banks. They did have some highly qualified people. But it's interesting that the people at the top at these banks tended to come from trading, a field that requires little formal training or educational background. A waiter, a bridge player and a karate expert could qualify for a trader's job- provided they created the right impression in interviews.

Trading is about taking risks. In the presence of leverage, the incentives to take excessive risks are high. If the gambles work out, there are millions to be made in bonuses. If they don't... well, we can see what happens. For jobs that often did not require very high skills, investment bankers ended up getting paid astronomical sums. Seldom in history has so much money been made by so few with such little talent.

Oct 2, 2008

Managing Risk in Today's World

One of the telling stories in the sub-prime saga is about how Citigroup's former CEO woke up to the bank's problems. In September 2007, Chuck Prince asks his CFO, Thomas Maheras, if everything was ok. Yes, everything is fine, Maheras reassures him.

That's what Maheras has been saying for a while. Rather belatedly, it occurs to Prince to get the position double-checked. A risk management group is asked to examine the bank's mortgage-related holdings. The truth soon comes out tumbling out and Citigroup announces billions of dollars in losses.

So, this is how one of the top banks in the world managed risk? By relying on the word of one executive? According to a story in the *International Herald Tribune,* the senior risk officer and Maheras' deputy were close pals, so the hard questions were not asked. That says something about the culture of the bank. If a man at the top keeps quiet, nobody else is supposed to ask questions?

At Lehman Brothers, the CEO, Richard Fuld, left risk management to a trusted deputy, Joe Gregory. Gregory apparently relied on 'instinct', not hard analysis, when it came to managing risk. A senior executive, steeped for years in the real estate business, warns him that things are getting out of hand. Gregory's 'instinct' tells him he should get rid of the troublesome guy. Fuld goes along. The rest, as they, is history.

Just think of it. Citigroup had over $2 trillion in assets; Lehman Brothers $640 billion. And the decisions on risk or even information about risk exposures were confined to two or three people! Leave aside the board, even the people working in these firms had no clue what they had got into.

The problem with firms in distress today was not just that they had the wrong risk management models. It was not lack of talent either. It was that life-and-death decisions about risk were concentrated in a few people at the top. Autocratic decision-making is what destroyed many of the biggest financial firms in the world.

So let's get this straight: risk management is not about fancy models or employing rocket scientists. It is an aspect of firm governance. If risk is to be properly managed, it is absolutely essential, first, that a large number of people within the firm should be involved in the risk-taking decisions. An even larger number should have the information on risk exposures.

When you see how the mighty have fallen in the present crisis, you begin to understand why a firm's processes need to be democratic, why it is necessary to actively foster diversity and dissent. Doing so is not a matter of practising virtue. It is simply a condition for a firm's long-run performance. That was the theme of a magnificent business book that came out in 2004, The Wisdom of crowds (James Surowiecki). And yet, as the failures in the present crisis clearly show, the modern firm remains one of the most undemocratic institutions in the world.

Secondly, risk management is not just an executive function but a function of the board. Most of the boards at today's troubled firms abdicated this function. For a board to perform this function, we must get the composition of the board right. We need institutional investors to nominate independent directors. Having 'independent' directors who serve at the pleasure of management won't do.

We also need representation on boards for employees and minority shareholders. One reason India's public sector banks have a reasonably good handle on risk is that internal processes in the public sector are more democratic and employees are represented on boards. There is no better check on management than an officer and staff cadre that is duly empowered- these are people who are well clued in to what is going on.

Thirdly, the design of compensation matters. Since performance in a bank shows up over a long period, incentives must be linked to long-term performance. Much has been written about this.

Fourthly, it is vital to get the scale of operations right. Is it possible for any CEO, however talented his team, to manage $2 trillion in assets? Talk to the CEO of a commercial bank in India with $30 bn in assets. He will tell you that he is fully stretched in monitoring risk. We know that some banks are too big to fail; many are also too big to succeed.

Fifthly, risk management is too important to be left to firms. Regulators have a vital role to play- in specifying capital requirements, in defining exposures to sensitive sectors, in bank supervision and in laying down norms for entry.

Risk management is not just about rigorous modeling of risk. The secret of risk management lies elsewhere- in embracing precepts of good management and regulation. Make firm processes truly democratic. Involve the board in risk management. Think through the design of compensation. Make sure the scale of operations is manageable. Don't allow financial innovation to run ahead of regulation.

December 11, 2008

Will Banking Become Boring?

For quite some time now, many of those who have headed for some of the best known business schools in India and abroad have done so in the hope of making it to one of the top banks- or "shadow banks"- of the world. Commercial banks apart, investment banks, hedge funds and private equity have hogged the lion's share of graduates from these places.

Part of the motivation has come from the mouth-watering presentations made by the world's leading financial firms. At top b-schools in the US, some firms were known to lay out a career path for graduates that led up to a million dollars in three years flat and up to ten million dollars in ten years' time.

That path may have been strewn with 18-hour workdays seven days a week but it has still proved irresistible to many. The other element in the lure of financial firms has been the sizzle and fizz of innovation, the opportunity to dream up and sell exciting, new financial products.

This is set to change in the years ahead. Some of the change was already in evidence in the recent placement season at the leading b-schools in the country. The great names in investment banking that used to swoop down on some of the best talent failed to show up-because many are now history. At IIMA, one of the biggest recruiters this year was not Lehman Brothers but our own Union Bank of India. You could call it a revolution of sorts.

There is more change along the way. One of the few things that are certain in these uncertain times is that financial innovation, risk-taking and the profits and rewards that went with them will be reined in. That should cause the financial sector itself to shrink in relative importance in the advanced economies.

Financial regulation is in for a sweeping overhaul. In particular, three key elements of regulation are poised to change the face of the financial sector. The first is that capital requirements for banks and other financial intermediaries will go up. This will undermine one of the key sources of abnormal profitability in banking- extraordinary leverage. One of the revelations of the present crisis is that many banks and investment banks were operating at a leverage of 30 or more.

Hereafter, banks will find themselves subject to a regulatory minimum of capital that will be above the 8 per cent required currently under rules framed by the Bank for International Settlements. This is the capital that is required to be set aside against "risk-weighted" assets. It is very likely that, on top of this, banks will be subject to a limit on leverage as conventionally measured.

As equity capital is costlier than debt, an increase in capital requirements (or a decrease in leverage) is bound to push up the cost of funds for a bank. This will impose a cost on bank customers-a lower deposit rate or a higher borrowing rate or both. Higher borrowing costs, in turn, will tend to depress output.

But financial instability carries its own costs: the loss of output as a result of a financial crisis can be anywhere between 5-45 per cent of GDP. The judgement today is that the latter outcome is less preferable. Higher capital is seen as crucial to stability. Once capital requirements for banks go up, we should expect bank profitability to fall. The halcyon days of return on equity of 20 per cent or more in banking may well be over.

Secondly, regulators are going to be far more sceptical about the supposed benefits of financial innovation. It is clear that the explosive growth in one innovation, securitised credit, laid the seeds for the present financial crisis. Moreover, as a report prepared recently by the head of UK's Financial Services Authority (*The Turner Review*) points out, innovation has spurred growth in the financial sector in ways that were either illusory or harmful.

Financial sector value added as a proportion of GDP in the UK rose from 5 per cent to 7 per cent in the period 1995- 2007. Partly, this reflected the illusory gains in a rising market arising from mark-to-market accounting. The Review suggests that the surge in value added was also harmful in so far as it arose from rents from complex financial products.

The Review notes, "Wholesale financial services...... grew to a size unjustified by the value of its service to the real economy". There is talk of excesses in the financial sector. It would be more accurate to say that the financial sector itself constituted an excess both in terms of its relative size in economies and the sort of returns it generated. It is unlikely that banks will hereafter be able to launch product innovations at will.

Thirdly, we must expect constraints on bankers' pay. Regulators will insist that incentives for bankers be based on measures of performance that better reflect risk and the long-term performance of banks. More importantly, higher capital requirements and lower profitability in banking will limit rewards in the financial sector. Outsized bonuses will not be passé but they will be more difficult to come by.

This is greatly welcome and somewhat overdue. Thanks to absurd compensation packages, financial firms (along with IT in India) have created huge distortions in the labor market. They have tended to lay a disproportionate claim on the pool of human talent to the exclusion of manufacturing and other sectors.

Will these changes in regulation- higher capital requirements, constraints on financial innovation and tighter norms for incentives- make banking a 'boring' sector rather like some regulated utility? Not really.

The management of risk that is or ought to be the core of banking will remain challenging and exciting. Besides, innovation is not just about product innovation, it is also about process innovation, finding ways to deliver products more efficiently to customers and broadening financial inclusion. While pay packages in banking will be less extravagant, bankers won't exactly be starving.

What the emerging direction of regulation will do is strip banking of some of its hype, the glamour and danger that one associates more with adventure sports. Actually, the comparison is inapt. In adventure sports, it is the sportsman who pays dearly for his mistakes. In banking, it is the audience that has all too often ended up paying the price.

April 16, 2009

Gold-mine Sachs is an illusion

Hopes of an early banking recovery in the US soared last week following impressive profit figures for the second quarter unveiled by Goldman Sachs and J P Morgan. But these hopes were short-lived. Later in the week, Bank of America and Citigroup could show profit only through the sale of businesses. Savvy investment banks may be profitable in the present environment but the traditional banking business remains in trouble.

Goldman Sachs clearly stands out. It showed a return on equity of 23 per cent in the second quarter. That is the top end of the range for return on equity in the boom period, 2003-07. When a bank makes that kind of return in a crisis environment, it can only point to one or more of four things: lack of competition, excessive risk-taking, superior access to information, the ability to influence regulation.

Goldman has clearly benefited from the demise of two major players, Lehman Brothers and Bear Stearns, and the big blows to other competitors. But its gains come at a cost to the system, namely, the risk posed by survivors who will emerge larger than before.

Large banks pose a problem that we have become painfully familiar with in the present crisis. They are deemed too big to fail and have to be bailed out by the tax payer. Knowing that the institutions they preside over will not be allowed to fail, managers have every incentive to take excessive risk.

One lesson from the present crisis is that abnormal returns to equity arose from banks not setting aside enough capital to cover risks. Is this true of Goldman today? Goldman's leverage(asset to equity ratio) of 14.2 today is just half what it was in 2008. Its profit of $3.4 bn in the second quarter is driven, not by proprietary trading where the firm uses its capital for taking bets, but by client-driven trading. Its tier I capital of 13.8 per cent under Basel I is way above the US Fed's regulatory requirement of 6 per cent.

But one should not get carried away. Goldman's tier I capital adequacy of 15.6 per cent in 2008 was even higher than the regulatory requirement. But it proved inadequate and the US government had to infuse $10bn in capital, since repaid. Regulators everywhere are agreed that capital requirements for banks need to go up. The key issue is whether Goldman is adequately capitalised in relation to the higher capital requirements that we can soon expect.

The trouble is that, while regulators are agreed on raising capital requirements for banks, they are yet to spell out precise numbers. One reason is that it does not make sense to ask banks to increase capital in the midst of a downturn as that would worsen the credit crunch. Another is that it will take time for regulators across the world to agree on common capital requirements.

But this could mean that Goldman's return is exaggerated by its having less capital than would be appropriate for a bank with its risk profile in the post-crisis world. However savvy they may be, it will be difficult for the likes of Goldman to sustain the sort of returns that investors have got used to expecting of them, once higher capital requirements kick in.

The revival in Goldman's fortunes naturally means big bucks for its employees. If Goldman can replicate its present performance in the second half of the year, average pay to employees is expected to cross $700,000. Here, we have the ultimate gold-mine for employees.

Alas, that would mean that another big lesson from the present crisis has been quickly forgotten: compensation must be paid strictly on a risk-adjusted basis. It would be sensible for Goldman to pay bonuses to employees only after allowing for the possibility that ordinary commercial banks will soon have to operate with total capital of around 15 per cent. Banks with large trading books will need an extra cushion and the bigger financial institutions even more.

That leaves us with two other factors that might explain Goldman's abnormal returns: superior information and the ability to influence regulation. In his book, *The Greed Merchants,* Philip Augar, a former investment banker, argues that large investment banks benefit from superior information gained from the sheer scope of their operations. Knowledge about clients gained from underwriting or advisory business, for instance, can be deployed in trading and private equity.

Others argue that Goldman has an influential network of former staffers everywhere in government and that it taps into this network at will. Goldman benefited from government capital in the present crisis and also from the bail-out of insurer AIG which was a counter-party in several trades. But, then, so did other banks.

We may not give credence to all the conspiracy theories about Goldman. But, we do know that sustained abnormal returns are something of an illusion created by serious market imperfections. These imperfections must be fixed as they entail a huge cost, the cost of recurring financial crises.

July 24, 2009

Banks that can be run by idiots

In the present crisis, the collapse of Lehman Brothers in September 2008 is widely seen as a tipping point. It was too big to fail and yet it was allowed to fail. Whether the crisis would have been as severe as it has turned out to be had Lehman not been allowed to go under is one of those issues that will for ever be debated.

Thereafter, the US government moved quickly to ensure that other big financial institutions did not fail, as did other governments. Large amounts of capital were infused into these institutions and guarantees offered.

But the regulatory headache remains unresolved: how do we deal with the systemic risks posed by the failure of large financial institutions? The immediate outcome of the crisis has been to make the problem worse. In their anxiety not to allow weaker or failed institutions to endanger the system, regulators have arranged mergers of these institutions with relatively stronger ones. The result is the creation of even larger institutions than before and greater concentration in the financial sector.

This may have been unavoidable in a situation of acute crisis but it also means that the too-big-to-fail problem will need to be tackled as soon as normalcy returns. The present thinking involves two elements: a resolution regime for large institutions in the event of failure; and higher capital requirements to guard against failure in the first place. It is doubtful that this approach will suffice.

The US Treasury has proposed that all systemically important institutions prepare a resolution regime for approval by the regulator. But winding down a large bank in a crisis is always difficult. It is even more difficult for banks that operate in several countries because it requires a high degree of cooperation among regulators.

Higher capital requirements for banks in general and even higher requirements for large institutions are appropriate. But even if capital requirements are doubled from the present 8 per cent to 16 per cent, banks would still be highly leveraged and prone to failure. Higher capital is the first line of defence against failure but it does not follow that it is adequate defence.

The real benefits of higher capital requirements are that they reduce the chances of failure by reducing managers' incentives for taking risk. The higher the leverage, the greater the incentives for risk-taking. If the gambles pay off, managers make huge bonuses; if they fail, shareholders and debt-holders are left holding the can. Reducing leverage helps by altering managerial behavior.

But neither a resolution regime nor higher capital addresses the too-big-to-fail problem adequately. We need to face up to a basic truth: beyond a certain size, banks are impossible to manage, likely to fail and cannot be protected by having more capital than they do today. The idea that any CEO can manage the risks of a bank with a trillion dollars or more in assets is ridiculous. Not even a managerial genius could manage the feat for long.

Financial Times columnist, John Kay, points out that managers at the helm of British banks in trouble, such as RBS and HBOS, were exceptional people with significant achievements to their credit (July 7). If they failed eventually, it was because the task was fundamentally beyond them.

In its latest annual report, the Bank for International Settlements identifies the problem and the solution correctly:

A large, integrated financial institution today has hundreds of subsidiaries... it is impossible for any individual to understand what all the parts of such an organization are doing.... Enterprise-wide risk management would seem to be an impossibility in such cases. ... in the future, a financial firm that is too big or too interconnected to fail must be too big to exist.

Modern banks can be rendered more manageable either by limiting their scope or their size or both. Limiting the scope could mean losing out on valuable synergies and the potential for lowering risk through diversification. Imposing regulatory limits on size seems the lesser evil.

How do we do this? Switzerland's central bank has proposed a maximum market share or a balance sheet-to-GDP ratio. In the top 10 economies of the world, we could specify that no bank should be larger than, say, 5-10 per cent of GDP. In 2007, that would have disqualified Citigroup and SBI (both 13 per cent of their respective GDPs).

Such a size restriction may seem to place banks in smaller economies at a disadvantage with respect to banks in larger economies. Not really. The benefits of size taper off beyond a certain absolute size and smaller banks often outperform larger ones, including in India.

Kay quotes a terrific aphorism from the legendary investor Warren Buffett: invest only in businesses that an idiot can run because sooner or later an idiot will. We need banks that can be run by idiots- and that means imposing a cap on the size of banks.

August 20, 2009

Tame the Economy, if not the Banks

The G-20 heads of government, meeting in Pittsburgh, made all the right noises on reform of the banking sector. Banks will be required to hold more capital. Compensation policies in banks must not encourage excessive risk-taking. Large banks must be subjected to stricter standards than the rest. So, are we about to see a brave new world of banking? Any celebration would be premature.

There are at least three reasons why progress on the ground may not match the rhetoric of the G-20 meet. The first is a sense of complacency as the global crisis shows signs of bottoming out. The second is the difficulty in reaching a common understanding among regulators on precisely what new rules should be put in place. The third is that banks that are too big to fail are likely to be with us even after the crisis blows over.

It is hard to miss the signs of complacency as the world economy shows signs of recovery. Last July, the IMF revised its forecast for world economic growth for 2010 from 0.6 per cent to 2.5 per cent . Several banks have seen their stock prices recover smartly and are poised to post obscene profits this year.

Why 'obscene '? Because profits in the present environment have flowed from a combination of unusually favourable factors. Monetary policy aimed at stimulating economies has lowered banks' cost of funds. Banks have benefited from infusions of capital from government. Government guarantees have allowed banks to raise funds at lower cost than otherwise. Large banks that have survived and gobbled up those that failed are reaping the advantages of market dominance.

Banks in the US are taking every opportunity to repay public funds so that they are freed from restrictions, especially restrictions on compensation. Goldman Sachs is set to declare its highest bonuses ever- the betting is that average bonus could touch a million dollars this year. There are also reports that Goldman is planning to surrender its banking license.

Governments need unusual resolve to overcome any sense of business as usual and push ahead with measures to prevent the next big crisis. The one solid assurance we have is that capital requirements for banks will go up. But how much more capital banks will have to hold is yet to be spelt out.

Most regulators will be wary of taking unilateral steps for fear of putting their domestic banks at a disadvantage. So, we need regulators to reach agreement quickly on what is an appropriate level of capital. Indian banks are operating today at a capital adequacy of 13 per cent against the regulatory norm of 9 per cent. If the regulatory norm goes up to, say, 12 per cent, Indian banks should plan for capital in the region of 15-20 per cent. Public sector banks, where government shareholding is close to 51 per cent, please note.

Some regulators want a special allocation of capital against the trading book. There is also a broadly held view that there must be an additional capital requirement for large banks, given their greater potential for disruption. Regulators have their work cut out in harmonising these perceptions and arriving at common norms for capital.

Some believe that higher capital requirements will have the perverse effect of pushing managers to take more risk because of the pressure to earn returns on a higher capital base. This is not necessarily true. When leverage in banking declines, managers' incentive to take risk is reduced. Indeed, we need more capital in banks not because it provides a better cushion when failure happens. We need more capital to prevent failure in the first place by reining in appetite for risk.

Higher capital is an indirect way to rein in excessive risk-taking. The direct way is regulating managerial pay. The G-20 mentions a number of measures: deferring variable compensation; paying such compensation in stock rather than cash; and clawing back compensation when bankers run up losses. But it may not be enough to get the design of compensation right. Some caps on compensation may be inevitable. In India, the RBI has not hesitated to step in to regulate pay of private bank CEOs, using certain norms. The G-20 communique waffles on this point.

Lastly, there is the issue of 'systemically important' institutions that are too big to fail. Higher capital cannot address this problem. Plans for orderly resolution of these institutions in the event of failure may be of little avail in times of crisis. This problem needs to be tackled head-on either by limiting the scope of banks, say, preventing deposit-taking institutions from having certain types of activities. Or it may require limits on the size of banks. But such measures are considered too radical even in today's context. We need an even bigger crisis before such solutions find acceptance.

Whether it is capital requirements or executive pay or the problem of large banks, solutions will be slow in coming and will be in the nature of compromises worked out by politicians, regulators and powerful banking lobbies. Moreover, by its very nature, financial innovation is likely to find its way around many regulations - witness the huge 'shadow banking system' where the present crisis originated.

It would be unrealistic, therefore, to expect stronger regulation of financial institutions by itself to stave off the next crisis. Better macroeconomic management must supplement regulation. Perhaps the biggest gain from the present crisis is a wider acceptance today of the importance of 'macro-prudential' surveillance, including the notion of leaning against asset bubbles. This will require, among other things, monetary tightening or counter-cyclical measures targeting particular sectors and a moderation of volatile capital flows as bubbles build up.

Again, there is work to be done on identifying the trigger points for such actions. But at least, the Greenspan thesis that policy-makers do nothing in the face of asset bubbles no longer has as many takers as before. Booms and busts are, of course, integral to capitalism. But policy-makers have an obligation to limit the frequency and intensity of disruption. This applies especially to crises resulting from banking failures, where the sins of a managerial aristocracy are visited on the hapless multitudes.

October 1, 2009

Banks, Relax - Until the Next Crisis

Every economic crisis gives rise to suggestions for radical reform . But these suggestions typically last only as long as the crisis. Once the crisis has blown over, it is business as usual.

In 1987, the steep fall in the US stock market prompted calls for rethinking capitalism itself. The US economy quickly shrugged off the stock market fall and the pundits were left looking foolish. In 1997, the east-Asian crisis evoked several radical proposals - an international bankruptcy mechanism, an overhaul of the IMF, an Asian reserve fund. These too were quickly forgotten once the east-Asian economies began to recover.

In 2001, the internet and telecom bubble was followed by demands for rethinking the investment banking model. The storm passed and investment banks carried on with only cosmetic changes in their practices. The one big reform was the passing of the Sarbanes-Oxley Act in the US, which sought to make top management more accountable.

Following the sub-prime crisis, there has been an avalanche of proposals for reform of banking. A record number of committees has gone into the causes of the crisis and made proposals. Some three years after the crisis began, it is beginning to look as though it will be a case of a mountain of labour producing a mouse.

The sub-prime crisis laid bare the problems in the banking sector. Banks have too little equity and too much debt. In the advanced economies, they rely excessively on short-term funds. They tend to invest in large amounts of illiquid securities. Bank creditors think governments owe it to them to bail them out when a bank fails. Many banks are so large that they just cannot be allowed to fail.

After three years of debate, what do we have? A half-hearted attempt to tackle the first two of the issues listed above. The Bank for International Settlements (BIS) will soon unveil proposals for bank capital as part of what is being called Basel-3 norms. (Global rules for bank capital known as Basel 1 were instituted in 1988. Basel 2 was introduced in 2007). The indications are that tier one core capital requirements will be pegged at 3 per cent compared to the present requirement of 2 per cent.

Banks will have time until 2013 to meet even this modest increase. Most of the bigger US and European banks have tier one core capital of around 10 per cent so they are hardly likely to even notice the new proposals. We still do not know how much the total capital requirement will go up from the current level of 8 per cent. Nor how much additional capital will be required for banks with a high level of trading activity or banks above a certain size. Banks can relax for now.

September 2, 2010

Occupy Wall Street Lacks Focus

Protests under the banner of Occupy Wall Street, which started in New York city, have spread to other cities in the US and Europe. Like the Anna Hazare anti-corruption campaign here, it has kindled hopes of a mass movement against certain excesses in the western system.

The Anna campaign succeeded in giving a certain impetus to the Lok Pal Bill. Occupy Wall Street does not promise to deliver anything comparable. Unlike the Anna campaign, it has neither a leader nor the support of the media. Worse, it lacks focus. Although it is said to target Wall Street, its website talks about the 'greed and corruption of the 1 per cent' and World Revolution, and it invokes the imagery of the Arab Spring.

A general lashing out against capitalism and its elites will achieve nothing. If the campaign is to be effective, it must focus on what it purports to be, a campaign against the banking oligarchy. It must ensure that the ongoing reform of the banking sector ends up addressing the central issue: the ability of bankers to inflict misery on society at large and get away with it.

It was a financial sector crisis that led on to the economic crisis of 2007. To prevent banks from failing, governments in the US and elsewhere infused large amounts of public funds into them. Many bank CEOs, who were responsible for these losses, left with handsome terminal payments. Ordinary people reckon correctly that there must be something wrong with a sector in which people at the top are largely immune to the problems they create for society at large.

Any solution must attack three problems in banking: banks' potential to wreak havoc on the economy; the compensation structure in the industry; and banks' ability to influence public policy.

In response to the crisis of 2007, regulators plan to introduce higher requirements of capital for banks. What is called 'core capital' is to rise from 2 per cent to 7 per cent. Assuming that the higher capital requirements do materialise, that may not still not make banking safe enough. An overall capital level of 15-17 per cent is better than before but it may not suffice. We will still have a handful of big banks whose failure can cause a crisis. Occupy Wall Street must turn the heat on big banks and ask that they be broken up.

This will also help address the second problem in banking, namely, outsized incentives that cause bankers to take excessive risk. Bankers complain that higher capital requirements will result in a decline in returns to equity in banking. That, in turn, will make it difficult for banks to access capital. This is true. But bankers fail to mention that returns to equity will decline sharply because they want to pass on the cost of higher capital in full to shareholders. They are not ready to accept that some of the cost of higher capital should be borne by bank employees.

Shareholders appear powerless to ensure the latter. Employee costs remain stuck in the range of 50-65 per cent of revenues. Bonuses continue to account for the bigger portion of bankers' salaries. There has been some attempt towards deferring bonuses over the long-term but 'claw-back' clauses that would cause bankers to compensate for losses on their account still lack teeth.

Banks justify the present compensation structure on the ground that it is required in order to 'retain talent'. To ordinary people, this sounds like an excuse for top managers to pay themselves exorbitant amounts. Vikram Pandit of Citibank has got approved for himself a pay packet of over $20 million. This includes an incentive for meeting earnings targets for 2011 that are way below those for 2010.

Goldman's CEO Lloyd Blankfein gets a hike in his wage from $600, 000 to $2 mn and a bonus for 2010 worth $12.6 mn. What are regulators and bank directors trying to convey? That they can't find a capable CEO willing to tumble out of bed for a mere $10 mn?

Outsized pay at the leading banks distorts pay in the sector as a whole and creates problems for the broader economy. Neither falling returns to equity nor public outrage at compensation levels will cause this problem to go away. It does appear that the simplest way to deal with outsized pay at the large banks is simply to cut the banks to size.

Bankers have got away with light touch regulation, they have got rules bent in their favour partly because banks are big contributors to political parties. The nexus operates in insidious ways as well. In the US, heads of banks and investment banks go on to important positions in government. Banks can offer lucrative jobs and assignments to the kith and kin of politicians. The capacity of banks to influence policy also arises partly from the fact that many of them are so large.

Thus, size is the one factor common to all the reasons that banks are feared and despised today: the havoc they create when they fail, systemic risk posed by incentives, and the capacity to influence policy. Occupy Wall Street risks ridicule if it is seen as a rant against capitalism. It would be more effective if it had a one-point agenda of seeking the break-up of large banks.

October 27, 2011

Boards can't Check Bank Failure

What were the boards doing? That is one question that keeps popping up whenever the sub-prime crisis is discussed. We are talking of the boards of some of the best known names in the business-Citibank, Bank of America, Lehman Brothers, Bear Stearns, Merrill Lynch. And, one might add, Royal Bank of Scotland (RBS).

RBS' failure was not a pretty sight. It had emerged as a symbol of British prowess in banking, a bank that had moved into the list of the top 20 in the world by aggressively growing its balance sheet. Sir Fred Goodwin, its CEO, was beginning to be hailed as a genius. When the bank nearly keeled over in 2008, the UK government injected £45 bn in capital. (Its value has since eroded to £25 bn).

Were there deficiencies in governance that contributed to RBS' failure? In a comprehensive report, the UK's Financial Services Authority suggests there were, even if it lists these as a tentative seventh factor in the failure. By governance, one means here the role of the board and the culture of the bank.

The six factors of which it is more certain are a mix of regulatory, supervisory and management failures. The regulatory and supervisory issues are being addressed in one way or another. It is the report's focus on governance that invites attention. If indeed faulty governance was a factor, then addressing it might help prevent such failures in future. Read the report, however, and you find yourself wringing your hands in despair. It doesn't look as though the problem of governance can be fixed at all in the present scheme of things.

The report makes a couple of things clear. There was nothing the RBS board did that exposes it to enforcement action. In other words, you can't pin any illegality on the board. You can't fault it for non-compliance with regulatory norms either. It had the right mix of skills. It met often enough. It discussed all matters it was supposed to discuss. The chairman allowed all members to express themselves freely. This was clearly a board that ticked all the boxes.

The one decision for which the board can be clearly faulted is the acquisition of ABN Amro. The acquisition, billed as the biggest bank takeover ever, was financed heavily by debt and was one of the important reasons for the bank's failure once the global crisis erupted. Since it was a hostile acquisition, very limited information was available- 'two lever arch folders and a CD'.

How did the RBS board approve a large and complex transaction with such limited information? Well, RBS had earlier acquired Nat West in a hostile bid and had managed to make success of it. RBS had been going great guns for several years. It all comes down to one thing: who wants to argue with a successful CEO?

The lessons from the ABN Amro acquisition are obvious and the FSA has drawn them. It proposes that all major takeovers by banks be subject to regulatory approval (which is already the case in India). Further, hostile takeovers must be approved subject to an additional capital requirement for the acquiring bank.

The broader lessons for governance at banks are not as obvious. The FSA faults the board for not challenging the CEO's single-minded focus on profit growth. The board did not quite understand the risks posed by the furious pace of growth at the bank nor did it change the incentive structure for the CEO, which was aligned with profit growth.

But these limitations are by no means unique to the RBS board or even to banks. One wonders whether any board exists that would challenge the CEO when things are going right. That is simply not part of the board room culture we have today. Board members are drawn from the same mutual admiration society of retired corporate executives and bureaucrats and, in many cases, exist solely to collect the fee and commission available (extremely generous in some cases, as it was at RBS). If they were the dissenting sort, they would not be on the board in the first place- management would never invite them.

The FSA report suggests that minutes of board meetings be recorded in some detail so that the FSA can judge whether management is being challenged at all. In preparing its annual inspection report, the RBI does go through board minutes. Here is a suggestion: let the RBI check, in how many boards, there is active questioning of management or dissent in the board. If the proportion exceeds 5%, that would be a surprise.

This culture can change only if we have a radical change in the method of appointment of independent directors. Not more than 50 % of independent directors should be chosen by management. The rest should be appointed by institutional investors, minority shareholders and employees.

The way boards are constituted today, they can, at best, ensure that laws and rules are complied with. They are incapable of the critical scrutiny that is needed to prevent bank failure or even under-performance. That is possible, if at all, only through more stringent regulation. The good news, as the FSA report documents, is that some of it is happening.

December 24, 2011

11

Corporate Governance

Taming the Despots

Fixing the problem of governance of the modern corporation is, perhaps, the central challenge of the market economy today. Efficient financial markets are part of the solution. So is tougher regulation aimed at penalising fraud.

But an equally important requirement is changing the near monarchical status of the CEO within the corporation. Power has to be distributed more equitably- between the board and the CEO and between the CEO and other managers in the corporation. The forced exits of some high-profile CEOs in the US suggests that we may be seeing the beginnings of a shift in the balance of power in the American corporation.

In recent weeks, boards have sought and obtained the ousters of such legendary CEOs as Michael Eisner of Walt Disney and Maurice Greenberg of the insurance giant AIG. This would have been considerably unthinkable even a couple of years ago, so complete was the identification of these CEOs with their respective firms.

Boards are able to flex their muscles today because reforms in the boardroom such as the increase in the number of independent directors that followed the collapse of firms such as Enron and World Com allow them to do so. They are willing to flex their muscles because not doing so could prove costly-in path-breaking settlements of class action suits, outside directors in both firms had to pay shareholders damages out of their own pockets. It would seem that the Sarbanes Oxley Act of 2002 that ushered in a slew of corporate reforms in the US is beginning to bite.

PART – IV

MANAGEMENT AND GOVERNANCE

What regulation and litigation have achieved is to erode the absolute powers that CEOs have tended to enjoy thus far. This is a welcome development. It is incredible but true that most corporations are despotisms where the writ of the CEO runs unquestioned. Within the firm, the CEO can do pretty much what he likes- as long as he delivers 'performance'.

There are serious problems with this view of the CEO's responsibilities. Performance (especially measured by stock prices) could reflect a general boom in the economy or in the stock market. Various measures of performance could end up over-emphasising short-term performance at the expense of long-term sustainability. Besides, corporate performance is mostly the result of group effort and of strengths built up over time, not the work of a solo artiste, much as CEOs would like to pretend otherwise.

The exclusive focus on stock performance has meant that CEOs can throw to the winds all principles of fairness and natural justice in the exercise of their power. A CEO may hound out a promising colleague who threatens his position; he can hand out punishment and reward without regard for merit; his authoritarian approach may stifle creativity and talent. But there is no recourse. As long as the firm is ticking along, he reigns supreme.

Ah, you may say, but no CEO in a competitive market can afford to be like that. He needs to attract and retain talent. If he acts in arbitrary ways, the firm's performance is bound to suffer. You would be surprised. Large corporations can take a lot of damage before the results start showing- and by then the CEO is gone. Talented people may leave but they can also be replaced.

At the investment bank, Morgan Stanley, some of its best executives have just been shown the door by the Chairman and they have since gone public about the damage the Chairman's high-handed ways could cause to the firm. The Chairman has moved quickly to find replacements. If the board is ruffled at all, it is not showing it. You can be pretty sure that Morgan Stanley's results for the next quarter will remain unaffected. In the bureaucracy and in the army, there are checks against abuse of power by superiors in the form of appellate processes. In most corporations there are none.

The assertion of board power in the US in the face of non-performance or misdemeanour on the part of the CEO is welcome because it is the first step towards the democratisation of the modern corporation. But this process needs to be carried further. One way to do so is for boards to commission a 'management audit' along the same lines as financial audit, a proposal mooted by Peter Drucker many years ago. Such an audit would examine the internal processes of the firm and enable boards to develop a more rounded view of performance than is provided by a single measure such as the stock price. It would also provide a check on the arbitrary exercise of power within the firm.

The export of democracy to places where it does not exist is said to be one of the paramount objectives of American policy today. A good place to start would be the modern corporation. American success in the area could prove infectious.

April 7, 2005

Only First Among Equals

Morgan Stanley, the bluest of blue-chip investment banks in the US, recently decided to ask its CEO, Philip Purcell, to leave. Nothing extraordinary about that. In corporate America, CEOs get fired all the time. Except that Mr Purcell's departure was forced by a systematic campaign carried out by former executives of the firm

This should make those interested in corporate governance sit up and take notice. It is almost unknown for boards to take cognisance of complaints against a CEO emanating from those below, much less from former employees, unless these relate to violations of the law. As unusual as it is for people below to go to the board with complaints about the CEO- everybody knows the price to be paid for such impertinence. Boards are content to take the view that they will be guided by performance, however nebulously defined. What goes on between the CEO and his underlings is as, they say, an 'internal matter'. Rumblings within the firm are always the work of 'disgruntled elements'.

The board at Morgan Stanley, including 'independent' directors mostly handpicked by Mr Purcell, initially did what most boards tend to do. It reflexively sided with the CEO. It turned out that Mr Purcell could not still dissent nor staunch high-profile departures. To top it all, the group of eight ex-employees announced that they would wage a proxy war against Mr Purcell ahead of the next annual general meeting. At this point, both the board and Mr Purcell threw in the towel.

Morgan Stanley's performance in recent months has been below expectations but not so bad as to warrant the CEO's exit. It was the impact on future performance that got the board worried. Unlike, say, automobile companies, investment banks are overwhelmingly people-driven organisations and can quickly implode once employees start deserting them in droves. Investment bankers and analysts take their clients with them; traders take their skills. More than in any other business, the inability to hold on to employees can prove fatal to an investment bank. Morgan Stanley's board had to squarely face up to this fact.

In the process, the Morgan Stanley board may have unwittingly underlined a hitherto neglected principle, namely, that the CEO is not everything in a firm, he is merely the most important face of the firm. There are other faces as well. But you would not think so, seeing how far the cult of the imperial or charismatic CEO has been carried in recent times.

Not just boards but also the media and the public at large have, in recent years, bought into the idea of visionary and charismatic corporate leaders who can transform organisations through the sheer force of their personality. As we have seen, many of these "visionaries" in corporations such as Enron, World Com and Tyco have ended up with jail sentences or are on their way to doing so. Harvard Business School professor Rakesh Khurana has written a book, *Searching for a Corporate Saviour: the irrational quest for charismatic CEOs,* and several articles in which he argues that the cult of the charismatic CEO is a recipe for corporate disaster.

This is because charismatic authority tends to discourage criticism, concentrate authority and pursue grandiose visions in disregard of legal or ethical norms. Such leadership thus carries within itself the seeds of future disaster. The implication for corporate governance is that boards must act to curtail such tendencies in any CEO, ensure that there is a chain of succession and that power in a firm is widely dispersed.

Corporate performance is the result of collective effort, not the work of one superman. The hype over personalities ignores this reality and leads to a distorted view of the corporation.The charismatic CEO is but an extreme example of this distortion. It needs to be corrected.

Boards must recognise that they cannot be guided by the CEO alone in matters relating to the corporation. They must take soundings from other senior executives as well. One of the healthier innovations in corporate governance in recent years is for boards to meet and take stock of issues without the CEO being present. It makes sense for boards to meet senior executives as well, again in the absence of the CEO. That would better enable them to judge whether internal processes and systems conduce to sustainable performance.

The success of the democratic ideal rests on the belief that the pooled wisdom of many is superior to that of any one individual. If this applies to nations, it applies to corporations as well. Ensuring that the CEO is only the first among equals, not an absolute monarch, is crucial to the health - and wealth- of corporations.

June 30, 2005

Reinvention of Family Business

Ratan Tata says he is worried about the adverse market reaction to Tata Steel's acquisition of British steel maker, Corus. His worry is understandable. In acquisitions, analysts generally tend to buy management's claims about synergies and the acquirer's stock price rises. It is only later that reality catches up. In as many as two-thirds of deals, the acquirer's shareholders see an erosion in value. In Tata-Corus, the markets are negative from the word go. That sounds like bad news.

Go through the typical analyst report on the acquisition and you understand why the analysts are sceptical. The acquisition will cause Tata Steel's leverage to rise steeply. There will be equity dilution as well.

The projected increase in operating margin at Corus from 8 per cent to 25 per cent is a tall order. Much of this will arise from Tata Steel supplying slabs at lower cost to Corus. But this will be possible only three or four years down the road after Tata Steel has augmented its slab-making capacity. In the intervening period, any decline in steel prices will badly impact the combined entity. Like Dr Spock, the irritatingly logical Vulcan in the TV serial, Star Trek, the analysts seem to have all the reasoning on their side.

And yet like Dr Spock was on occasion, they could be proved wrong. Remember, the Tatas are not new to cross-border acquisitions: there is a solid integration capability that has been built up across their tea, software and automobile businesses.

Besides, the benefits may be larger than expected. The restructuring on which the Tatas have maintained a discreet silence- job cuts, sale of low-margin plants at Corus- could happen after a couple of years. Iron ore exports from India may become possible down the road. Demand for steel may exceed expectations.

But the Tatas may not be betting only on imponderables such as these. There could be gains to the group that would not figure in the analysts'computations. Group companies could get a piece of Corus' orders. Besides, an acquisition of this kind has the potential to improve the market's perception of the group. No longer will the Tatas be perceived as a laid-back group. This could translate into better valuations for Tata companies.

So, while the acquisition looks dicey when viewed as a standalone proposition for Tata Steel, it begins to look attractive when one factors in the gains for the group as a whole.

You may ask: what do Tata Steel shareholders get in the bargain? Well, it would not be difficult for the group to funnel gains of the group back into Tata Steel through transfer pricing and other ways.

But there is a message in the analysts' response to Tata-Corus. Professional managers would have thought likewise and shied away from the deal. Most managers are slaves to quarterly results. If they summoned the nerve to go ahead with such a deal, they would be suspected of indulging in a dangerous gamble at the expense of shareholders.

No such suspicion attaches to an industrial house with large stakes in the company in question. When it comes to strategic thinking, family managed businesses have an advantage over professional management: the former can take risks that the latter would be averse to.

This advantage has traditionally been offset by major failings. One is the temptation, in a low growth environment, to make money by siphoning off funds. But this is weakened by the sea-change in growth prospects in India as also improvements in governance.

Another failing has been the inability to attract high quality talent in a work culture where power was concentrated in the hands of the owner. This is changing in the better-run businesses. A new generation with strong professional credentials has ceded powers and sought to create a culture that professionals are comfortable with. As a result, some of the best-known MNCs of yesteryear are no longer the automatic first choice for professionals these days.

The Tata group itself did not have these failings but it had others: inadequate accountability on the part of professionals and the absence of a strong central direction. Ratan Tata has tried hard to address these.

We are thus seeing the reinvention of family businesses in India. These new businesses will be a force to reckon with for they can combine the long-term thinking that is the strength of family ownership with the systems and talent that go with professional management.

India's unfolding growth story brings revelations by the day. We have just woken up to the easy availability of international finance to fund acquisitions. A more potent revelation, perhaps, is the reinvented family business with its potential to take the world by storm.

February 8, 2007

The Fading of Public Companies?

The public company is said to be one of capitalism's great achievements. Yet, the advantages of being a public company are today no longer obvious. Taking public companies to private is all the rage today.

Private equity funds today sit on equity of nearly half a trillion dollars. Around 150 of these have more than $1 bn in funds. The size of companies being bought by private equity is getting bigger and bigger. Top managers prefer to work for private equity firms rather than for public companies. One other indicator of success: private equity firms are among the most preferred recruiters at US business schools.

What accounts for the growing popularity of private equity? Do they add value? And how might public companies replicate the remarkable performance of firms under private equity? A roundtable organised by the conference *Journal of Applied Corporate Finance* (Summer 2006) with leading academics Michael Jensen and Steven Kaplan and top practitioners provides answers.

Private equity is a success. The average return on private equity funds was about the same as on the S&P 500 over 1980-1995. But this comparison is deceptive. The return on private equity funds is net of fees paid to those running the funds. These fees are a minimum of 3 per cent of the funds managed. Gross of fees, private equity funds beat the S&P. Moreover, the returns to the private equity funds do not take into the huge gains to sellers- the people from whom private equity funds buy businesses at huge premia to market values.

Private equity is successful, first, because there has been a huge governance failure in public corporations. This may come as a surprise. Haven't we had a governance revolution in recent years? Alas, the changes seem to have been largely cosmetic. 'Independent' directors, selected by management, cannot provide effective monitoring.

We need investors, especially institutional investors, to be directly represented on boards. This happens with private equity; it does not in public corporations. Boards at firms managed by private equity tend to be smaller and less unwieldy than those at public companies and discussions more intense and meaningful. Directors appointed by private equity firms have superior operational expertise.

But there is more to private equity than institutional activism. The structure of private equity firms is crucial to its success. Like the erstwhile US conglomerates, these firms manage a portfolio of businesses. The difference is that each business has its own allocation of debt and equity and stands on its own feet unlike in the conglomerates where there was a common pool of debt and equity at the corporate level.

Thirdly, in private equity, the operating heads of each business have a significant equity stake in their own businesses, much higher than in public companies. Some of the equity stake is money that the executives themselves are asked to put in. The equity stake is illiquid until management has proved that it has created value. The incentive structure in private equity is thus better designed than in the typical public company.

Fourthly, the funds raised by private equity firms for particular investments have a finite life- say, seven to ten years. At the end of that period, investors have to be paid back. So, those running the private equity firms must deliver performance if they want to stay in business and raise fresh capital. The time frame is reasonably long so that the businesses do not have to be managed from quarter to quarter.

Fifthly, private equity-run businesses are highly leveraged. The tax benefit of debt apart, management is under pressure to service the debt. This addresses the 'free cash flow' problem that was said to be at the root of underperformance in companies.

For public companies, the success of private equity poses huge challenges. An obvious course would be for them to go private. The alternative is for public companies to replicate the sources of success in private equity: take on debt where there is excess cash, invite large investors onto boards, improve managerial incentives and use financial structures that help allocate capital and track stock price separately for each business unit in the company. Failing these, we may well see a fading of public companies.

Private equity started off in the 1980s as leveraged buy-outs of public companies. These often hostile takeovers were fiercely resisted and corporate raiders were famously characterised as "barbarians at the gate". Today, it is management of public companies resisting private equity buyouts that is seen as uncivilised. We cannot but marvel at capitalism's ability to reinvent itself.

April 5, 2007

Time to Rethink Governance

Why on earth would they want to do that? Over the past month, bewildered investors and media analysts have been asking the question of Satyam's aborted attempt to use about Rs 7000 crore in cash to acquire equity in two property companies.

The lack of synergy between the companies, the conflicts of interest, the issue of valuation- all these were so glaring that it was a mystery why a businessman of the stature of B Ramalinga Raju would have attempted such a move.

Well, it's all falling into place now. There was no cash pile waiting to be transferred out. It was a fiction created through some incredibly creative accounting. Revenues, profits, reserves, cash were all cooked up over the years leading to an inflation of the balance sheet by around Rs 7000 crore.

It was becoming difficult to keep up the fiction. That's where the proposed investment in the two property companies belonging to Raju's family came in handy. If Rs 7000 crore could be shown as having been used to finance the acquisition, the gap at Satyam would cease to exist. Of course, Raju's sons, who ran the property companies, would have received from Satyam a cheque that was worthless. But that's all in the family, you know.

This is the merest sketch of a story that has the hallmarks of a thriller. It will take a while for investigators to fill out the details. A whole slew of questions will need to be answered. How did the auditors fail to discern any sign of wrongdoing? How did all of it escape the audit committee? If cash of around Rs 7000 crore was not there, how was it corroborated by bank statements? And so on.

Investor fury over Satyam's failed attempt at diversification is now giving way to more universal shock and horror over a scandal that could turn out to be India's own Enron. Following the terrorist attack in Mumbai last month, the incompetence of politicians was contrasted with the supposedly high standards of performance in corporate India. The Satyam affair has now dealt a severe blow to the pristine image of business in post-reform India. As the economic environment worsens, expect more skeletons to come tumbling out.

In the US, the corporate scandals at the turn of the century prompted much agonising over governance. The Sarbannes-Oxley Act followed, fresh rules for auditors and board members were framed. And yet the collapse of financial firms in the sub-prime crisis revealed gaping holes in governance. Clearly, the Anglo-Saxon model, which we have broadly tried to imitate, is inadequate and we need to rethink the mechanisms of governance. Here are a few ideas:

- It is not enough to rely on statutory auditors. In the public sector, the CAG provides an additional layer of audit. Similarly, for the private sector, we need a public institution, the Board of Audit and Surveillance (BAS), with the authority to carry out surprise audit of any listed company above a certain size (say, turnover of over Rs 500 crore). The audit can also be triggered by requests made by independent directors of a company or large institutional investors. The Board should develop a scale of 1-10 for evaluating the quality of financial statements. The Board can be funded by fees collected from companies.

- The posts of chairman and managing director for large companies must be separated.
- Management cannot select all independent directors. At least, half the independent directors must be appointed by institutional investors. There should also be employee representatives on boards.
- No independent director should be allowed to serve on more than five boards. There should also be a limit on the cumulative turnover of the five companies. It is impossible for independent directors otherwise to do justice to their jobs. Besides, why should board memberships at the top companies be limited to a small coterie? Let us democratise the working of corporate boards.
- Cross-directorships- the back-scratching syndrome- must be prohibited. This applies not just to companies but also to non-corporate organisations. Businessmen serve on the boards of academic institutions. They get academics from the same institutions to serve on their boards. Who is monitoring whom?
- No independent director should be permitted to quit a listed company without furnishing reasons. The reasons should be made available to the stock exchanges and to SEBI.
- The BAS or SEBI should maintain at its website a list of directors associated with companies that have had serious governance issues, rather the list of 'defaulters' made available by RBI. Analysts and investors can come to their own conclusions about other companies with which these directors may be associated.
- Above all, let us all learn to beware the company that is centred on one individual. We have learnt to appreciate the virtues of the democratic process in the political realm. Alas, we are yet to apply the lesson to the corporate world.

January 8, 2009

A New Paradigm for Management?

There is talk now, as in previous economic crises, of having to reinvent capitalism. What this generally means is that we need to redefine the roles of state and market. But there are people who think this is not enough. The time may also have come to remake key institutions of capitalism.

One institution that is under siege today is management. There is a sense everywhere of having been let down by managers at some of the most prestigious corporations in the world.

The world's leading financial companies were held up for long as role models of management- efficient, innovative and nimble. Now, these very institutions and their CEOs are being pilloried for having messed up in a big way. Management has got discredited and in the process it has given capitalism a bad name.

What sort of changes in management practices are needed to build companies that are truly fit for the future? Thirty five scholars and practitioners met in California to debate this question. They came up with 25 ideas for reinventing management. Gary Hamel summarises them in a recent *Harvard Business Review* article titled, 'Moonshots for management'- moonshots to signify that management should be aiming high. Hamel contends that if management does not reinvent itself by using these ideas, companies cannot survive.

Alas, many of the ideas will evoke cynicism if because they have been around for a while now. Eliminate formal hierarchies. Reduce fear and increase trust. Exploit diversity. Expand employee autonomy. Unleash human imagination. Encourage passion among employees. Use lofty goals such as truth, love and justice to inspire employees instead of mundane ones such as differentiation or focus. And so on.

There are two problems with the list. One, no management would quarrel with it. Indeed, all managements will profess to practise virtues such as the ones listed above. ("We believe in transparency and empowerment.") Except that in most organisations, people down the ladder have difficulty believing this to be true.

Two, if the benefits to implementing the list are so obvious- if the business imperative is indeed so strong- why is it that these precepts appear so distant, almost Utopian? Clearly, management does not practise these precepts because the incentives to do so are missing. Or, to put it differently, the incentives to continue on the existing basis are stronger.

The incentives, in turn, have to do with the way performance is measured. Today, performance is all about maximising shareholder value. CEOs in the US are lucky if they last five years. Their incentives are tied to producing shareholder value in the short period they are in office, not to sustaining performance over a long period.

As management guru Peter Drucker pointed out long ago, concentration of stock ownership in financial institutions also generates pressures for 'short-termism'. It is very difficult for a pension fund not to accept a takeover bid at a higher price than the prevailing share price. If the share price falls a year or so after the takeover- as happens more often than not- the pension fund could end up being sued by its client companies.

If we are to move to a different management paradigm, two key issues will need to be addressed. First, the measurement of management performance. Secondly, the design of incentives. As long as performance is measured as short-term shareholder wealth maximisation and management incentives are linked to this objective, there isn't much hope for change.

The goal that Hamel puts at the very top of his list is that management should serve a higher purpose than shareholder wealth maximisation. But managers are not going to focus on "socially significant and noble" goals of their own accord. They will do so only if their performance is measured differently.

How do we define and measure performance in today's world? Drucker himself was dismissive of shareholder value as the sole measure. He wanted performance to be measured on other dimensions such as innovation and market standing. The presumption, of course, is that the capital markets are not all that efficient and that the share price does not capture these dimensions adequately.

But if the market's judgement is not to be trusted, who is to carry out the task of enforcing performance? Drucker himself did not provide an answer to this question. Perhaps the answer is simply one of providing better information on managerial performance to the markets. Maybe boards, investment banks and rating agencies need to do a far better job of this than they have so far.

Hamel and his colleagues do not address the central issue of defining and measuring top management performance. Theirs is a largely moralistic exhortation to managers to raise their sights. If such exhortations could change the world, we wouldn't be having today's problems in the first place.

February 19, 2009

Reining in Rogue Bonuses

Goldman Sachs is set to pay record bonuses this year. Word of the impending bonus-which could take average compensation per employee to close to a million dollars- has sparked outrage in the US and elsewhere. Goldman CEO, Lloyd Blankfein, said in an interview that his firm was "doing God's work". On innumerable blogs, the statement drew immediate comparisons with Satan.

Politicians have expressed their displeasure over outsized bonuses being made in the present conditions. There has been harsh comment in the media. Protesters gathered outside the Washington headquarters of Goldman carrying wanted signs bearing the face of Mr Blankfein.

Outrage over executive pay is not new. But it is interesting that two of the biggest votaries of market forces, *Financial Times* columnist Martin Wolf and the Economist, are among those who argue in favour of curbing banking bonuses in what they regard as today's exceptional situation.

What is different this time? Many things. First, the taxpayer's safety net for banks, which exists even in normal times, has since been extended to non-bank players, including Goldman. The net itself has grown bigger and stronger net. It has included not just lender of last resort backing from the central bank but guarantees for various liabilities.

Secondly, some players, notably Lehman Brothers and Bear Stearns, were allowed to fail while others were rescued through capital infusion and other means. This meant that the survivors stood to prosper in a more concentrated market. Thirdly, banks have benefited from attempts to stimulate economies through sharp reductions in interest rates. In other words, bankers have gained from policy measures that were required to clean up the mess that they had created in the first place.

It is hard to make the case that booming profits today at banks such as Goldman are the result entirely of sound risk management or superior investment banking skills or even a favourable trading environment.

So, what is to be done? Two sets of solutions have emerged. The first addresses the problem of 'unfair' bonuses in today's conditions. The other addresses the long-term issue of systemic risk posed by bankers' pay.

The short-term solutions proposed are:

- A 'windfall' tax on bonuses: Mr Wolf wants a "windfall" tax on bonuses. He argues that bonuses have resulted from fiscal costs incurred in saving banks and economies. It is only fair that some portion of it is recouped by government. Mr Wolf would like the tax to be imposed on the bonus pool. But then banks are not the only institutions to have benefited from easy money; so have other institutions and also ordinary investors. It is not clear why banks alone should be subject to a "windfall" tax. Moreover, no government can impose such a tax by itself when others are not- it would only cause financial services to relocate to places where there is no such tax.
- Recover 'funding premium' from banks: *The Economist* points out that state guarantees have lowered banks' costs of funds. Assuming that they would pay two percentage points more without state guarantees, the costs of the top five banks would rise by $36 bn. Central banks should levy a 'funding premium' just as they charge a premium for deposit insurance. The difficulty here is in quantifying the 'funding premium'. It is bound to vary across banks.

The long-term solutions proposed are:

- Ensure bankers' compensation is strictly on a risk-adjusted basis: This is the solution favoured by the G-20 and most committees that have looked into the sub-prime crisis and it involves linking compensation to return on capital allocated to a business unit. The snag is that capital allocated may not be commensurate with risk and this may become known only over a long period.

  Several other things need to done to ensure that bankers are not rewarded for short-term profits: paying bankers mostly in the form of stock options that vest over a long period; minimising cash bonuses; including 'claw-back' provisions whereby bonuses paid in times of profit are suitably adjusted when bankers inflict losses. Many doubt that such measures are feasible in a competitive market for talent.

- Link bankers' pay to the value of all bank liabilities, including preferred shares and bonds: The conflict in any firm is not just between the interests of managers and shareholders. There is also a conflict between the interests of equity holders and bondholders. This conflict is particularly acute in banks because banks are more highly leveraged than the typical industrial firm.

Any design for pay must also address the second conflict, Lucian Bebchuk and Holger Spamann of Harvard Law school argue (Discussion paper no 641). They would like executive pay to be linked to the value of not just equity shares but all securities including preferred shares and bonds. But this assumes that the market has correctly estimated the value of preferred shares and bonds. This does not always hold true- we know how badly flawed credit ratings can be.

How far do these solutions take us? Not very far. The problem is fundamental. One aspect of it is abnormal returns in banking made possible by a unique combination of high leverage with implicit government backing in the event of failure. This problem must be tackled head-on. First, leverage in banking must be brought down by mandating higher capital requirements- this is on the cards but nobody has spelt out the details. Secondly, we may need regulatory limits on the scope or size of banks or both in order to address the "too big to fail" syndrome.

Another aspect of the problem is the sheer futility of expecting governance reform to bring about a better alignment of interests between managers and providers of funds. To be sure, this problem is not confined to the banking sector, it is a malaise that cuts across industries. But it is less affordable in banking.

The time may have come to regulate and monitor executive pay in banks. This may be jarring to many ears but it must been seen as part of the effort to contain systemic risk. The RBI approves bank CEOs' pay. In this area, as in so many others, the RBI may have something to teach other regulators.

November 26, 2009

Peter Drucker Lives on

Peter Drucker, the acclaimed management thinker, was widely remembered on his centennial last month. *Harvard Business Review* ran a feature titled, *What would Peter do?* The reference was to the present economic crisis in which managers and businesses have come under a cloud.

Well, first Drucker would have rubbished any characterisation of him as a 'guru'- he famously said that newspapers used the word only because the word 'charlatan' was too big to fit the headline. Drucker did write some books of the 'how to' variety. But he was not the sort to prescribe 'six easy steps to brand-building' or 'eight rules for go-getting CEOs'.

Drucker was a business philosopher who sought to establish broad principles for successfully managing businesses over the long run. His focus would have been on what managers might do to prevent situations that give business a bad name.

One of the articles in HBR mentions some of the things he would have done in today's situation. He would have exhorted top managers to work together to rein in excesses in executive pay. He would have reminded businesses that in order to retain the loyalty of knowledge workers, businesses must create a larger purpose that such workers could relate to. He would have re-emphasised the need for businesses to work closely with civil society and non-profit organisations.

Some of Drucker's ideas have been so widely embraced that they have become commonplace. The purpose of a company is to create a customer. Every company must define clearly the nature of its business. Discarding the old is as important as focusing on the new. Knowledge-based organisations need fewer levels than the traditional industrial firm. Managers routinely practise these tenets without even knowing where they came from.

Is there anything in Drucker's work that remains relevant and is not fully reflected in managerial practice? I combed through Drucker's writings and found at least three areas where his ideas could make a difference: the role of a CEO; the functioning of corporate boards; and the larger responsibilities of management.

Most people think the CEO is one man's job. No doubt, many CEOs find it convenient to have it that way- the imperial CEO lording it over all he or she surveys. Yet, as Drucker correctly points out (and this was in 1955!), the CEO's job involves three distinctive functions: planning for the future, responding to every day problems, being the organisation's face to the outside world.

It is impossible, Drucker asserts, for any individual to successfully handle more than any two of these three functions. Hence, the CEO's role cannot be discharged by one person, it can be done only by a team. And the team should comprise at least three members. How many businesses can claim to do this?

Drucker is emphatic as to the need for effective boards. "It is an organ of review, of appraisal, of appeal". The last function, appeal, that Drucker mentions is striking if only because it is defunct today. Drucker says of this particular function of the board, "Somebody has to discharge the final judicial function in respect to organisation problems, has to be the 'Supreme Court'". We all know the drab reality that obtains today. Most boards do not even want to take cognisance of appeals from managers- that would be 'interfering in operational matters'.

Drucker argues that it is in the interest of the top management team to attract outstanding individuals to the board and to make the board effective. An effective board is crucial to the success of top management. Yet, most CEOs tend to regard boards as decorative at best and a nuisance at worst.

Lastly, the responsibilities of management. One is self-evident and has been placed on the altar- making profits. Drucker is not dismissive of profits. Indeed, he sees it as the first responsibility of business. But, management has other responsibilities towards the enterprise as well: making sure of tomorrow's management; not claiming special allegiance from its employees over and above the contractual obligations; allowing the freest mobility from the bottom to the top; developing a capital expenditure policy that counteracts the business cycle.

Beyond these, management has a larger responsibility towards society. This is not what passes these days for 'corporate social responsibility'. It is much loftier than that. Drucker inverts the free market slogan, "What is good for the enterprise is good for the country". He contends that management must strive to make whatever is good for the country become good for the enterprise. Business must make this rule "the lodestar of its conduct".

There is so much wisdom in Drucker's writings. Yet, it is possible to go through an MBA programme without even having heard of Drucker. It is possible to be a professor in a business school without having read Drucker. That is, perhaps, why so many managers are like the blind men in the parable who feel out an elephant's parts without knowing the elephant.

December 10, 2009

Board Memberships as Careers?

Corporate governance was supposed to be the great fix for lack of accountability in management. A decade or so after the governance revolution, how to fix corporate governance is itself the issue.

We know that corporate governance isn't working. *The Economist* (October 28) recently cited a study that covered 296 financial institutions in 2007-08. The findings are damning. Directors who knew finance didn't do better than those who knew nothing of finance. Separation of the posts of CEO and Chairman did not matter. Shareholder returns were inversely related to the proportion of independent directors!

The challenge remains: how do we make boards effective? An article in the latest *Harvard Business Review* (December 2010) suggests that the answer may be making an independent directorship something of a career in itself.

The author, Robert Pozen, lists reasons why boards are ineffective. They are too large (the average size of the top 500 companies in the US was 11 in 2009). Members lack domain expertise (only one of Citigroup's directors at the time of the sub-prime crisis had ever worked at a financial services firm). Members are not able to spare enough time for the boards they serve on.

The answers follow. First, have professional directors, that is, people for whom directorship is a primary, not an ancillary, vocation. Secondly, cut the size of boards to seven, the CEO plus six independent directors. Thirdly, of the six directors, make sure four are people with domain expertise. The fifth should have expertise in accounting and the sixth could be a generalist.

Professional directors would not serve on more than two boards. They should spend at least two days a month at the company, apart from board meetings. Since independent directors would be expected to work a lot harder, they should be paid better. Most of the pay should be in the form of long-term stock options.

Since this sort of time commitment would be beyond working professionals, the choice of professional directors would be restricted to retired persons. Pozen thinks this pool is large enough to meet the requirements of companies. Regulators could make professional directors mandatory for banks. Institutional shareholders should push for professional directors in other companies.

What do we make of this proposal? Some flaws are obvious. Independent directors may not work harder just because they are paid more or because they serve on only two companies. Spending two days a month at a company make not may such a big difference to their knowledge of it.

Besides, how do we define domain expertise? 'Electrical goods' covers a wide range of products; somebody who has worked with in the electrical cables industry may not be knowledgeable about motors. 'Consumer goods' covers refrigerators, washing machines, ceiling fans, etc. and these may not have much in common. To be truly knowledgeable about a company, one must have worked for a competitor. Finding enough of such people who also meet other requirements for a board directorship would be a tall order.

But there is a more fundamental fallacy in Pozen's formulation. The effectiveness of a director is not so much about knowledge of a company. It is more about sincerity and commitment. The questions that need to be asked are often very simple ones. Why are we losing market share? How does the company propose to reverse the trend in declining profit margins? Which divisions have failed to meet budget targets? Are succession plans in place? Why are star performers leaving?

Asking these questions, indicating that one is not satisfied with the answers and demanding accountability for lapses does not require great insight or ability. It requires commitment and a willingness to rock the boat. These are qualities not commonly found in boards or, for that matter, anywhere else in institutions.

It is sad but true that conformity comes naturally to the vast majority of people. Silence and collusion are more rewarding than standing up to what is right. Making a career out of board memberships will not make people non-conformists. Least of all if it is management that has provided them with a plum post-retirement career.

In the name of corporate governance, companies have enacted a huge farce. Management selects 'independent' directors and often heaps big rewards on them in the form of fee, commission and stock options. In exchange for this munificence, the worthies on the board are expected to question, challenge and even oppose management. I don't know if such people exist on this planet- I haven't met any in my lifetime.

No, independent directors can be effective, if at all, only if they are not selected by management. To begin with, let management select no more than 50 per cent of independent directors. The rest must be appointees of institutional investors, employees, minority shareholders and other interest groups. Then, there is at least a fighting chance that we will see the commitment that is sadly missing now.

December 9, 2010

It's Ok to Keep it in the Family

Ratan Tata will soon step down as the head of the Tata group. There is talk of somebody from outside the family succeeding him. Some people cheer this. They see it as setting a fine example of the professionalisation of India's family-managed businesses (FMBs).

One is not so sure. India's FMBs have transformed themselves in order to meet the challenge of competition. Several professionally managed companies worldwide have badly let down shareholders over the years. It is no longer obvious that India's FMBs are better off passing on the baton to professionals from outside the family.

Mr Tata's own record is instructive. When JRD named Mr Tata as his successor, many doubted JRD's choice. Mr Tata's record at the electronics firm, Nelco, had not been particularly inspiring. And yet he has gone on to remake the group in ways that would have then been regarded as unthinkable. Mr Tata will leave behind a group that is bigger and more competitive than when he took over. When Russi Modi, one of the group stalwarts ousted by Mr Tata, says that the mantle should go only to another Tata, he is expressing a widely felt sentiment.

The Tatas are not alone in transforming themselves. Several other FMBs have done likewise. The Aditya Birla group has paid a great deal of attention to human resource issues; today, it has a younger and more cosmopolitan top management team. The Mahindra group has broadened the scope of its activities and made foreign acquisitions.

The Rahul Bajaj group made a historic decision to exit scooters and focus on motor-cycles. Mukesh Ambani has shown that he has imbibed his father's spirit of thinking big. Other family businesses-the various TVS groups, RP Goenka, Thapar, those in the media - too have forged ahead.

This is not what was expected 20 years ago. FMBs typically come under stress from the third or fourth generation onwards. They disintegrate or pass into other hands. One would have expected liberalisation to accelerate this process in India. This hasn't happened. FMBs have adapted remarkably to the transition from a controlled economy to a competitive one. It is one of many unanticipated consequences of reforms.

There are two shortcomings that have typically beset FMBs. One is the lack of alignment of the interests of the family with that of minority shareholders. A low-growth, high tax environment affords incentives for siphoning off funds for private benefit. It has incentives for FMBs to grow by exploiting rents in a controlled economy.

The high-growth, low tax environment of the liberalised economy has made for a better alignment of the interests of the controlling family and minority shareholders. It has created incentives for FMBs to invest in growth opportunities, become more competitive and reap the benefits through an increase in market value of firms. FMBs have responded well to the change in incentives.

The second shortcoming in FMBs has historically been lack of competence at the top. The CEO position goes by ownership rather than merit. For this reason and also because professionals believe they will not have enough freedom, FMBs tended to lose out in the race for talent. In the new economic environment, FMBs have shown a willingness to tackle this problem.

Many have allowed a younger, better-trained generation to take over. They have also shown themselves willing to give professionals more freedom and to match compensation provided by professionally managed firms. Some professionals have found that they have greater operational freedom in an FMB than in MNCs where many important decisions are made overseas.

True, an FMB can be undone by the wrong person from the family getting to call the shots or by fratricidal wars. Provided, however, these two risks are managed, there are several reasons why FMBs have the potential to fare better in the Indian context.

Professional managers deliver where institutional shareholders demand performance and there is an active market for corporate control. Neither obtains in India. Giving managers stock options is useful. However, in a favourable environment such as we have today, the family's large shareholding makes for a stronger alignment between the interests of top management and shareholders. Short-term thinking is the bane of professionally- run firms everywhere; in an FMB, long-term thinking comes more naturally. Continuity in a firm's values is better achieved in an FMB.

At some FMBs, a new generation is getting ready to take over. Aziz Premji is grooming his son, an MBA with international exposure, for the top job. Venu Srinivasan has inducted his daughter, who has a doctorate in engineering, on to the board of his company. Nobody is complaining. Mr Tata is entitled to judge that a professional from outside is best placed to guide his group today. However, if he chooses to entrust the reins of his group to a family member, one suspects the move will be well received. That too is a sign of how much India has changed in the last 20 years.

August 4, 2011

How to Pick a CEO

Infosys Technologies initiated a much-publicised search for a chairman and CEO, which ended a few months ago. Deutsche Bank's recent search for a CEO too was widely publicised. In both these cases, the process began long before the incumbent was due to step down and the boards were said to be involved.

Selecting a CEO is one of the most important functions of a board- some believe it is the second most important function after monitoring CEO performance. And yet it is among the most neglected. A 2009 survey by the National Association of Corporate Directors in the US revealed that 43 per cent of US public companies had no formal succession plan and 61 per cent had no emergency plan.

Boards tend to ignore succession planning until close to the retirement of the incumbent. This is because, all too often, the incumbent's idea of succession planning is to prevent any succession in the first place. When the CEO finally decides to move on, the board lamely accepts his recommendation on a successor.

These days, CEO departures can be both abrupt and frequent. In these situations, boards turn to a headhunter. The headhunter's list mostly comprises outsiders, as the headhunter lacks knowledge of the inner workings of the company.

Research shows that the selection of outsiders generally leads to inferior performance compared to the selection of insiders. In other words, there is little to beat a planned succession from amongst a set of inside executives whom the board has had the opportunity to watch over a long period of time.

A recent article in *Harvard Business Review* (October 2011) by A G Lafley, a former CEO of Proctor & Gamble, shows what succession planning at its best can be. Lafley decided that the search for a successor would begin at the very beginning of his term. He also decided that one out of six meetings of the board would be devoted to CEO succession and leadership development.

Lafley helped the process along in two ways. First, he ensured that the company's directors had first-hand exposure to a range of future leaders. Every director was encouraged to meet at least twice a year with business or functional leaders without any corporate P&G managers present. In addition, before and after every board meeting, the board was given an opportunity to meet P&G's senior executives on any subject of their choosing. Once a year, the directors and the management team would go to an international business location to meet directly with regional and local leaders.

Secondly, in collaboration with the directors, Lafley developed criteria for the CEO's job, scenarios for the company in the future and a list of experiences that would prepare candidates for the job. He measured candidates against these criteria and scenarios and provided his inputs to the board from time to time.

Lafley took upon himself the task of identifying and training the top 500 executives in the company. In addition, every month he had one-to-one conversations with 15-20 high potential leaders.

These leaders were put through several tests. The person who finally succeeded Lafley had been on every single list from 2001 to 2010.

It is possible to be sceptical about some of the things that Lafley talks about. For instance, he mentions 10 criteria that his successor was expected to meet. It was not enough for him to have character and demonstrate business performance. He would have to be compassionate, inspiring, courageous, visionary, etc. It would appear that P&G was looking, not for another CEO, but the Lord Almighty himself !

Still, one must grant that P&G's succession planning process is as thorough as can be. The most striking feature is the board's involvement in the process. The advantage of involving the board so deeply is that the board gets to know the company and its senior executives a lot better.

This has the potential to transform corporate governance. Most boards tend to be cut off from the companies they are supposed to manage. The only information they have is whatever the CEO chooses to make available. By getting the board to interact with several levels of management in a structured way, succession planning can become a means for improving the effectiveness of the board itself.

Indian companies would do well to emulate the process followed by P&G. The larger industrial groups do need CEOs for their various businesses. In the listed companies in a group, it is possible to involve boards in a rigorous search. Ditto for the few professionally managed businesses we have.

It is in the public sector that succession planning is most lacking- witness the vacuum at the top today at LIC and UTI. This is a pity because a couple of factors make it possible for the public sector to score on this account. There is a healthy turnover at the top, thanks to a fixed retirement age for the CEO. Secondly, the boards have directors who are truly independent of management as they do not owe their jobs to management.

It is legitimate for the government to want a say in the selection of public sector CEOs. There is a way in which it can both have its say and improve outcomes. The government must constitute a permanent search committee for PSUs (along the lines of the Public Enterprises Selection Board) in which its nominees are in majority but which co-opts independent directors from the companies whose CEOs are to be selected. PSU boards are among the most ineffective boards. Getting them involved in succession planning could be a way to put some life into them.

October 13, 2011

Managing Without Managers

Morning Star is a tomato processing company based in California, with revenues of $700 mn and over 400 employees. These unremarkable facts would not qualify for a cover story in *Harvard Business Review* by management guru Gary Hamel (December 2011). What makes the company remarkable is that it has no bosses, titles or promotions.

Anybody can spend the company's money, jobs responsibilities are negotiated among peers and compensation is peer-based. It is a company that has dispensed with 'management' as conventionally understood, that is, a set of chosen people in whom decision-making is concentrated.

Does this make sense? Can it work? Well, Morning Star claims it has had double-digit growth in revenues and profits; the industry's rate is 1%. It is said to have funded its growth entirely through internal resources. It says it is the most efficient tomato processor in the world.

One reason firms exist is that markets cannot coordinate amongst the sort of complex activities that are required in, say, a manufacturing operation. Within a firm, the coordination happens through a hierarchical structure. Those at the higher levels of the hierarchy direct and monitor the ones below. Morning Star defies this assumption.

The idea is not entirely novel. Way back in the mid- 1960s, Peter Drucker had propounded the idea of the modern organisation of 'knowledge workers' (as distinct from manual workers) in which it would be necessary to reduce the levels of hierarchy. Drucker argued that people with highly developed skills or expertise can give of their best only through self-motivation, not through guidance from above. He forecast that, with the rise of 'knowledge workers', firms would tend to become flatter. He was proved right.

Investment banks, which have a high concentration of knowledge workers, have very few levels. A large investment bank has hundreds of managing directors. A star trader could be designated managing director without having anybody report to him. However, while the number of levels has fallen steeply, few firms have been able to dispense with them entirely. Morning Star's achievement is that it has been able to abolish hierarchy altogether and, that too, within a manufacturing context.

How does it all work? Who takes decisons, sets targets, reviews performance? The answer, it turns out, is: everybody. A key element in Morning Star's model is what is called the Colleague Letter of Understanding (CLOU). Every employee negotiates his CLOU with all those affected by his work. This letter sets out what each employee is to accomplish in a given year. Similarly, the company's 23 business units negotiate CLOUs with each other.

Staffing decisions are done entirely by colleagues working together. There are no promotions: people take on greater responsibilities after persuading their colleagues they can deliver. Disputes are settled through discussion, mediation or decisions taken by groups of six people. Performance is measured through feedback from colleagues on one's CLOU. Compensation is decided through elected compensation committees.

Can this model be replicated in a company with a lot more employees? Hamel thinks it can. He doesn't mention this but there is a celebrated example of self-management in a company with a lot more employees. A Brazilian firm, Semco, has 3000 employees, a turnover of over $200 mn and has been growing at 20-30 per cent every year. Semco does have managers but employees have more freedom than elsewhere. They can choose their hours of work, decide their salaries and pick their bosses. Managers are anonymously evaluated every six months by their subordinates. Semco has practised this philosophy for 25 years now.

Ricardo Semler, the owner of Semco, has questioned the whole mystique of 'leadership' which implies that the ability to take decisions or lead is a gift that a few people have; those down the line must look up to these great men and women for guidance. In reality, leadership qualities are to be found at all levels. And when decision-making is spread across more people, you end up getting better results.

For all the talk of 'empowerment', it is hard to see top management in hierarchical companies embracing any of this. Those at the top do not want to lose power and control. Besides, we are all conditioned on the notion of 'moving up' in life. For the most part, companies still cling to the command-and-control model that was originally borrowed from the army. Even the mannerisms of corporate bosses mimick the ways of the army: the stiff demeanour, the curt nod, the abrupt dismissal.

This presents us with a jarring contradiction. Modern democracies harbor within themselves corporate organisations that are fundamentally undemocratic in character. The prevailing corporate model is sought to be justified on grounds of performance. And yet, as Morning Star and Semco have shown, it is possible to resolve the contradiction while delivering performance.

February 16, 2012

12

Education and B-Schools

Discontent of Summers

Larry Summers- tenured professor at Harvard at 28, scion of Nobel Laureates Kenneth Arrow and Paul Samuelson, Treasury Secretary under President Clinton- would be regarded as an adornment by any university. Harvard evidently does not think so. Summers, who took over as president of Harvard five years ago, put in his papers last month ahead of a planned vote of no-confidence by the university's Faculty of Arts and Sciences.

Summers came to Harvard determined to change things. It didn't help that he advertised his intentions: that is not a message that faculty anywhere wants to hear. Surprisingly for someone who had taught at Harvard himself, Summers underestimated the political skills required to usher in change in a university and overestimated the power of the president's office.

Summers got into numerous spats. He lashed out at senior faculty who he thought were taking it easy. His remarks about women having less "intrinsic aptitude" for math than men touched off a furore. He labelled those asking Harvard to disinvest in firms in Israel "anti-Semitic".

But it was one of his cherished reforms, getting faculty to take undergraduate studies more seriously, that finally cost him his job. The top American universities are focused on research and regard teaching as a necessary evil. Faculty are judged overwhelmingly by their research output. Teacher ratings provided by students mean very little. Undergraduate studies are a neglected stepchild in this scheme of things. Summers' attempts to shake up the system were bound to be fiercely resisted.

Summers' ouster is important for what it says about governance in the modern university. Managing a university that houses assorted schools or even a school in a university is the ultimate HR challenge. Tenured faculty can't be fired, indeed they have no legal retirement age.

Faculty are brilliant minds with formidable reputations and huge egos. They believe they can best manage their jobs themselves and do not like to be told what to do. They are apt to behave as though the lofty norms they preach-about accountability, transparency, conflicts of interest and the rest-apply only to lesser mortals not to themselves. How on earth do you enforce accountability in such a system? How do you usher in change?

Business schools have provided some answers. The Dean cannot wield the stick but he has carrots to dispense. Performers can be given huge salary increases or chair professorships. New faculty can be hired on terms vastly superior to those of senior, non-performing faculty.

Business schools can do these things because their links with the commercial world enable them to raise vast sums of money. This has, in fact, created a situation where power at business schools has drifted away from faculty and towards the office of the Dean. The Dean leverages the school's performance into endowments. He uses endowments to raise performance. Faculty may mutter about Deans behaving like CEOs but, as long as the carrots keep coming their way, they will not revolt.

Other schools are not as fortunately placed when it comes to raising resources, so the Dean's job is a lot trickier. A university like Harvard will not lack resources for any of its schools and Summers did try to exert influence by channelling funds to favoured Deans. But the system proved too strong for him. Maybe prosperous faculty at Harvard don't have to look to the President for pecuniary opportunities, maybe they will not surrender power at any cost. Summers was reduced to flailing against the system of tenure itself.

Some might wonder whether there is any urgent need for reform at places such as Harvard. The short answer is that the quest for improvement must be unending and no institution can be exempt from accountability. And self-regulation will not suffice. It is important to uphold first principles: somebody delivers performance, somebody else asks the hard questions. Board monitoring is necessary, of course, but it needs to be supplemented by periodical external audits by committees of eminent persons.

As for leadership in academic institutions, whatever the carrots available, a soft touch is essential. Coaxing rather than cajoling, persuasion rather than dictation is what will eventually work. This is true wherever you are dealing with highly skilled people but it is especially true of academia. The late Peter Drucker was fond of saying that in the modern organisation of knowledge workers, the CEO's role is that of the conductor of an orchestra. If universities can uncover what it is to produce music, they will have invaluable lessons to offer the rest of the world.

March 9, 2006

Ravi Mathai the Living Legend

IIM Ahmedabad turned 46 earlier this week. This is as good an occasion as any to recall the services of its legendary founder-director Ravi Mathai.

Ravi Mathai, son of John Mathai, finance minister in Nehru's cabinet, was appointed the first full-time director of IIMA in 1965. (Vikram Sarabhai had been honorary director until then). The choice of Mathai was in itself remarkable. He was not an "insider"- the Institute had been set up earlier. He did not have an advanced academic degree- he was a corporate executive who had only recently joined IIM Calcutta as professor. In a country that is still gerontocratic, he was obscenely young-he was 38.

It is a tribute to Sarabhai's own leadership qualities that he made absolutely the right choice. By 1972, when he stepped down as director, Mathai had not only put IIMA on the national map, he had laid secure foundations for its continued success. If IIMA has since gone from strength to strength, it is very substantially because of the strategic decisions taken in Mathai's time as well as the culture, systems and processes he put in place.

Through my nine-year association with IIMA, I have often been struck by the abiding impress of its founder-director. I remember attending the then director's welcome address to the incoming post-graduate batch soon after I had joined. In the course of a 20 minute address, the director invoked Mathai's name four times. In the initial years, I noted with astonishment how almost any significant process would be traced back to Mathai. ("Oh, that happened in Ravi Mathai's time"). Heads of institutions fade into oblivion within weeks of demitting office. Mathai is remembered at IIMA all the time.

What explains Mathai's success and his profound impact on IIMA? First, a clear sense of purpose. IIMA's concern, as Mathai put it, was "with the application of knowledge". This meant that the Institute would be involved in teaching, research and consulting. The impact "would be greatest if it were the combined result of all activities", so faculty must engage in all three activities.

Mathai saw clearly that to focus merely on business would limit IIMA. It would also expose it to charges of being elitist in its orientation. IIMA's ambit needed to be wider: it would be an institute of management, not just a business school. It would develop expertise in important sectors including agriculture.

Secondly, Mathai's conviction that academic activities can flourish only when faculty are given the fullest freedom. In an academic institution, excellence cannot be ordered. It springs forth when people are given the space to grow and to express themselves freely.

Thirdly, the idea of a faculty-governed institute where decision-making rests primarily with the faculty and not with the director or the board. An example is the admissions committee that is independent of the director. The mechanism has been crucial in insulating admissions from unhealthy influence.

Fourthly, what is, perhaps, Mathai's greatest bequest to IIMA: the principle of a single term for the director. After six years as director, Mathai stunned the community by announcing his decision to step down and stay on as professor. He gave two reasons for doing so. One, leaders of academic institutions tended to use their positions for career advancement; this was not good for the institutions. Two, it was important to establish the principle that the director's position is not hierarchical, he is only first among equals. You are professor, you become director and then you become professor again.

This one contribution of Mathai's cannot be overstated. In the present scheme of things, the director has sweeping powers. The board of governors does not quite have the monitoring authority of a corporate board. Faculty governance can work only to the extent the director is willing to let it work. Limiting the director to one term is vital to good governance. It is the knowledge that a director's actions can be looked into once he has reverted to a faculty role, the certainty that he will be cut dead in the corridors by colleagues whom he has mistreated that acts as a check, however inadequate, on the incumbent.

There is more to Mathai's enduring impact than his grasp of the principles of good governance in academic institutions. He managed the relationship with government with great skill. He was a superb man-manager with the gift of drawing out the best in people. Above all, he had moral authority: he brought to his office high integrity, a spirit of sacrifice and self-effacement.

India has been fortunate in having had great institution builders. At the national level, we had people of the make of Nehru, Patel and Ambedkar. At the organisational level, we have had the likes of Homi Bhabha, Vikram Sarabhai and RK Talwar (of SBI). In that constellation of institution builders, Ravi Mathai shines brightly.

Dec 13, 2007

Can Management Gurus Manage?

Business school professors make a living out of teaching management. Should we presume, therefore, that they know how to manage? Many people seem to think so.

R Gopalakrishnan of Tata Sons mentions some paradoxes he has come across (*ET*, May 19). A professor who specialises in conflict management happened to be going through a divorce. A professor of behavioural science simply could not get along with his colleagues. It seems legitimate to ask: what business do these people have to teach anything to others?

One could easily extend this logic to other faculty. Those who teach investment management ought to become billionaires by playing the market. Faculty who specialise in leadership should end up in the director's chair, if not the prime minister's. Marketing faculty should be able to market themselves very well- some at least should become famous "brands" themselves.

Professors who teach innovation should be flooding their institutions with breakthrough ideas. Anybody who teaches a course in business ethics should be a saint. And, of course, the combined wisdom of faculty should be producing institutions that are paragons of sweetness and harmony. We know otherwise: managing a B- school or any collection of academics, for that matter, is the ultimate administrative nightmare.

Is something wrong here? Not really. Peter Drucker, the greatest of management gurus, once confessed that he would make a poor executive- he simply could not delegate although preaching delegation came easily to him. The gulf between theory and practice is vast and it is not confined to management. Literary critics don't make great writers themselves nor art critics great artists. A dance or music teacher may not be able to perform on stage himself or herself. There are great sports coaches who have never made it to the highest levels themselves.

Alright, Mr Gopalakrishnan seems to say, b-school faculty cannot manage but at least b-schools can do a better job of teaching management. How? One solution he proposes is that "staffing of teachers at institutes should have more of them who have practised and practitioners who can teach".

This sounds eminently sensible until one gets down to practising it. Take the first part of the solution, having faculty who have been managers. Many b-school faculty, who have corporate experience, would readily admit that this experience adds little value in the classroom. I have been a banker and I teach a course in banking at IIMA. I can't say that my experience as a banker adds an awful lot.

As for practitioners coming into the classroom, the experience has not been a very happy one. Yes, practitioners offering a session or two in a course can be useful. But there are not many instances of practitioners making a success of a whole course on their own. This is because teaching, like any other craft, has its own discipline which is acquired only over time. Structured learning is not something that many practitioners are equipped to provide.

One is also not clear what is meant when people talk of bringing the "real world" into the classroom. A big chunk of coursework at b-schools comprises basic tools and techniques. These are best taught by academics. What they provide the student is an analytical way of looking at issues that managers face in their working lives.

B-schools have tried to bring in "real world" issues through the case study method. This involves going into a firm and documenting a particular problem and ways in which it was handled. The case is discussed in class and alternative approaches are discussed. Indian firms can help out by simply being open to cases being written about them the way firms in the US are.

When practitioners talk of B-schools missing out on "real world" issues, what they often have in mind are organisational and interpersonal issues- team building, motivation, leadership, etc. Whether these can be taught at all in a classroom has been debated. B-schools have experimented with ways of teaching these, not always with conspicuous success. Can practitioners do a better job? Perhaps. But, as always, seeing is believing.

B-schools are at the receiving end of endless sermons from practitioners on how they need to get their acts together. For a change, here are a couple of suggestions on how practitioners might contribute. One, please go through the course outlines of a b-school and tell us: (a) what new courses are worth offering; (b) how the content and pedagogy of existing courses might be changed in order to better reflect the "real world".

Two, identify, say, 25 aspects of an important theme that Indian businesses are facing, namely, the challenge of globalisation. Offer these aspects to B-schools for case writing. Let Indian managers not be guilty of the sin they tend to ascribe to B-school faculty- of not practising what they preach.

May 29, 2008

Crisis: Are b-schools to Blame?

Managers are in the line of fire in the present crisis, especially managers in the financial sector. Economists might argue that the crisis was caused by deep-rooted factors such as global imbalances and flawed regulation but the man on the street is in no mood to listen. He thinks greedy, overpaid managers just went and blew it.

From there, it's just a short step to arguing that part of the blame must rest with the industry that produces managers in large numbers- b-schools. Philip Delves Broughton is a journalist who went to study at Harvard Business School and wrote a lively book about his stay there. In an article in the Times of London (March 1), Broughton lashed out at his alma mater and at b-schools in general:

Time after time, and scandal after scandal, it seems that a school that graduates just 900 students a year finds itself in the thick of it. Yet there is remarkably little contrition. ....You can draw up a list of the greatest entrepreneurs of recent history, from Larry Page and Sergey Brin of Google and Bill Gates of Microsoft, to Michael Dell, Richard Branson, Lakshmi Mittal - and there's not an MBA between them.

Yet the MBA industry continues to grow, and business schools provide vital income to academic institutions: 500,000 people around the world now graduate each year with an MBA, 150,000 of those in the United States, creating their own management class within global business.

Given the present chaos, shouldn't we be asking if business education is not just a waste of time, but actually damaging to our economic health?

One can read two separate propositions into the above quote. The stronger one is that b-schools serve no particular purpose. The milder one is that b-school curricula are inadequate and in some ways responsible for much that is wrong today in the world of business.

The first proposition is easily dealt with. Whether b-schools are useful is one of those debates that will never end- like debates on the death penalty, globalisation and fashion shows. Every one of these issues was hotly debated when I was in college. They continued to be the staple of college debates even today.

The test must be empirical. If b-schools are mushrooming and if the demand for their products keeps rising, it's reasonable to infer that b-schools are serving some purpose. B-schools have been around for a hundred years now, so businesses have had enough time to find out if they add value.

It's the second proposition that is of greater interest. Is there something seriously wrong with b-school curricula and the attitudes that b-schools inculcate? Broughton cites HBS case studies that failed to pick up signs of trouble: Enron and Royal Bank of Scotland. How come a school that purports to teach general management failed to see the gaping problems at these firms, Broughton asks:

In the same vein, you could ask why many economists failed to anticipate the present crisis. Case studies at b-schools are intended to focus on a corporate situation and stimulate discussion on various approaches to it. They are not meant to be judgements on a company. Nor do b-school faculty profess to offer ideal solutions in class.

The proposition that b-school curricula and attitudes need radical revamping has takers among academics. In an article in the *Harvard Business Review* (June, 2009), Joel Podolny, a former HBS professor and ex-dean of Yale's School of Management, says he shares Broughton's anger at b-schools. He highlights major lacunae in b-school teaching:

- inattention to ethics and leadership;
- a tendency to teach management in "disciplinary silos" instead of offering a holistic view;
- a focus on theoretical models that do not clarify how organisations actually work;
- an obsession with school rankings that, in turn, leads to a focus on jobs and salaries in place of the greater good of society;

Podolny is not being terribly original-these points have been made before. B-schools do update curricula and attempt new ways of teaching all the time. No doubt, they need to keep trying. But there does seem to be a problem with expectations that people have of b-schools.

There is much talk lately about b-schools having abetted greed in the corporate world through their focus on shareholder value. There is also the suggestion that b-schools should inculcate a certain high-mindedness in their students.

Unethical behavior, it's worth reminding ourselves, is not the monopoly of b-school products nor is it confined to managers. Nevertheless, b-schools have thought it necessary to respond by introducing courses on ethics and new ones on leadership. It's, of course, great PR for b-schools to be able to say "We emphasise ethics in the very first semester of our programme". But much of the talk about b-schools creating 'ethical leaders' can be dangerous nonsense.

First, there is nothing about the focus on shareholder value that implies that managers must disregard laws or even ethical considerations. Secondly, it is absurd to think that b-schools can take students in their mid-twenties or -thirties and make better human beings out of them. As Peter Drucker pointed out long back, moral sense is formed fairly early in life and is the result of one's whole upbringing.

The exasperated layman may ask: if b-schools can't create better leaders or model organisations, what do they contribute? Well, as somebody who went through an MBA program himself, let me attempt an answer. After graduating from an IIT, I had no clue as to what business is all about. The two years at an IIM gave me a broad understanding of different functional areas- finance, marketing, operations- and a grasp of strategy. These are things that people learn over several years in a business and a b-school helps abbreviate the learning period.

That's about it. Both b-schools and society at large need to be modest about what b-schools can achieve. To expect b-schools to produce a wonderfully balanced, caring and socially responsible person is sheer delusion. You can't expect b-schools to succeed where Buddha, Jesus and Vivekananda failed.

June 11, 2009

IITs and IIMs: Yash Pal is Wrong

In India, institutions of higher learning tend to deteriorate with time. The great universities of the past- Bombay, Madras and Calcutta- are today but pale shadows of their former selves. This hasn't happened with the IITs and IIMs. These institutions have retained their attractiveness to students and employers alike. The newer IITs and IIMs lag behind the older ones but are still preferred to most institutions outside the IIT/IIM fold.

The Yash Pal committee on higher education now wants the IITs and IIMs to develop into full-fledged universities. The committee is dead wrong. The IITs and IIMs have other priorities. Besides, replicating the IIT/IIM experience at universities may be infeasible.

We have seven IITs that admit about 10,000 students into their undergraduate programme and seven IIMs that admit 1600 students for their post-graduate programme. These are pathetically small numbers in relation to the requirements of the economy. The total in any graduating batch across all IITs cannot meet the requirements of even one of our IT giants in a normal year.

So, one priority for IITs and IIMs is to scale up without compromising on quality. This is a challenge that neither the IITs nor IIMs have been able to crack so far. It required the introduction of OBC quotas to produce the first significant scaling up in years.

The IITs and IIMs say they face constraints of both physical and human infrastructure. But several proposals made for increasing capacity have not been given due importance: faculty working in shifts; creative use of IT; involvement of international faculty in teaching; reducing faculty time spent on administrative tasks; curtailing excessive time spent at some institutions on in-company training programmes.

Eight new IITs and seven new IIMs are to be set up in the Eleventh Plan. This is an acknowledgement of the difficulties in coaxing greater capacity out of the existing IITs and IIMs. Creating new IITs and IIMs may solve the problem of physical infrastructure but how can it address the faculty crunch?

Surprising as this may sound, it could. There is a large pool of NRIs keen to return to India. Many of them wish to return to their home towns, so setting up new IITs and IIMs could help. New institutions can offer better entry level positions and faster promotions than older ones. Entrenched interests at the older institutions are often an obstacle to attracting new faculty. So the new institutions hold out the promise of enhancing the faculty pool.

Still, the existing IITs and IIMs must do their best to increase capacity. This should be their first priority, not becoming full-fledged universities. Another priority is improving their standing as research institutions. So poor is the quality of teaching in higher education in India that the IITs and IIMs have made a mark through quality teaching alone. But this is not enough. They need to gain recognition in research. They must respond to emerging areas in the economy through the creation of high quality centres.

The IITs and IIMs are expensive affairs. A new IIT is estimated to cost Rs 750 crore; a new IIM Rs 250 crore. The recurring expenses are large and are sustained at the IITs and the newer IIMs through large government grants. The older IIMs have avoided taking government grants in recent years through large increases in fee. But this approach cannot be used in converting IITs and IIMs into universities. Government will find it difficult to replicate the IIT/IIM level of expenditure across all disciplines and fees would be unaffordable to students.

A better approach is to concentrate on the 14 new central universities the government proposes to set up. The government could contemplate a level of financial commitment higher than for ordinary universities but not of the same order as for IITs and IIMs.

Academic excellence is not achieved merely through higher funding. Our experience has been that unstinted financial support from government, with not too many questions asked, delivers results in areas that require focus- atomic energy, space research, defence applications, institutions of higher learning. This has helped produce excellence upto a certain level. But moving to the next level requires better governance.

September 3, 2009

Foreign Varsities as Mentors

The Foreign Universities Bill was approved recently by the cabinet and is to be tabled in parliament soon. Some hope that the entry of foreign universities will lead to dramatically improved standards in higher education. Others fear that the coming of foreign universities will sound the death-knell of India's educational institutions, including our elite institutions.

These hopes and fears are both misplaced. Opening up to foreign universities is certainly desirable and some good institutions may come in. But, in the foreseeable future, it is unlikely that a large number of quality institutions will set up full-fledged universities or even colleges in India.

In higher education, as in defence, the US leads the rest of the world by a wide margin. US firms in manufacturing and services other education may be keen to get into India but US universities are not. American firms face slow growth in the US and Europe and need rapidly growing markets such as India and China.

But this does not apply to US or other foreign universities. The top US universities, such as Harvard, Yale, and Princeton, do not lack finances. They are supported by enormous funding from private sources. They can attract some of the best faculty and students from all over the world to the US. Why would they want to set up shop in India? Oxford lacks the stature of the best US universities. Its vice-chancellor told the *Times of India* last weekend that Oxford has no plans for coming to India.

It is not just that the top US universities lack the incentives to come to India. If they did come, it would be difficult for them to be viable while maintaining quality. Quality in education comes from having the best infrastructure, the best faculty and the best students. Foreign universities will find it difficult to achieve this mix in India.

Even if land is made available to foreign universities at a concessional price, the start-up costs for a university or even for a full-fledged college would be large. Having the best faculty would mean bringing in a sizeable number from abroad. This would be an expensive proposition, of course, but even paying dollar salaries may not suffice to get faculty to relocate to India.

The best colleges in Europe, Canada and Hong Kong have for long tried to attract faculty from the US by offering a premium over what US schools pay. They have had little success. To be out of the US is to be cut off from the research network and to lose out on the ability to publish. Being in the US is, therefore, something that faculty greatly value. This would also apply to European faculty evaluating relocation to India.

High infrastructure and faculty costs will translate into high fees. A top US b-school charges about Rs 45 lakh for a two year programme. Even this fee contains an element of subsidy that is covered by endowments. In India, one can expect the fee to be somewhere in the range of Rs 25-30 lakh.

A fee of this order would mean catering only to the upper income groups. It would mean shutting out talent from the mass market, which is where the strengths of the IITs and IIMs lie. When you cannot attract the best students, you cannot have the best quality of output.

Thus, the economics of higher education militates against the entry of the best foreign universities. Foreign firms in manufacturing or services other than education can adapt to Indian conditions by hiring local talent, using technology and tapping the export market. None of these is open to a foreign university. The university is one field where technology has remained largely unchanged for centuries: nobody has found a superior alternative to faculty and students coming together in classrooms.

This explains why markets with a higher per capita income than India, such as Singapore, Israel and China, have not been able to interest top universities. It is naïve to suppose that standards in higher education in India can be miraculously enhanced by opening up to foreign universities. There is no alternative to the hard grind:

improved funding for government institutions, better governance and greater domestic competition.

Foreign universities can contribute at the margin through mentoring of Indian institutions and by sparing faculty for limited assignments. This happened at the older IITs and IIMs at their inception and it did deliver results. IIM-A and IIM-C benefited from their collaboration with Harvard and MIT respectively. The expenses were underwritten by the Ford Foundation. The collaboration was for a period of about five years, by which time IIM-A and IIM-C had acquired a certain momentum.

Yale university is said to be willing to mentor the 14 innovation universities planned. This may well be the way to go. The government would have to pay the fee for such collaborations. This would be worthwhile provided there is a clear plan for assimilation on the Indian side. Mentoring and collaboration hold out promise more than full-fledged entry by foreign universities.

This is required as much for the IITs and IIMs as for central universities. The RC Bhargava review committee on IIMs (2008) did not subscribe to the view that the IIMs are shining role models of governance and it highlighted a certain lack of accountability in the system.

Better governance is not a matter of the government abdicating its monitoring role or exiting institutions of excellence. Far from it. State presence is not incompatible with academic excellence. In the US, there are several state universities-California, Texas, Ohio- that can give the best private universities a run for their money. It is all about putting in place the right governance structures.

Here are some suggestions. The IITs and IIMs have large, unwieldy boards. The Bhargava committee had rightly suggested that IIM boards be pruned from about 26 to 11 members. We need to define an appropriate composition for IIT/IIM boards, with the right balance between government representatives and independent members.

Chairmen and independent members of IIT/ IIM boards must be selected by a distinguished Appointments Committee for Higher Education. The boards must lay down clear performance objectives for directors of IITs and IIMs and closely monitor performance. Not least, academic boards, no less than corporate boards, are prone to 'management capture'. So, board monitoring must be supplemented by periodic external audits by committees of eminent persons.

The IITs and IIMs should not aspire to become universities. They have other priorities. They must scale up as much as possible. They need to produce better research. They need to spread out into newer areas in their respective disciplines. To be able to do all this, they must first get their governance right.

September 3, 2009

Foreign Varsities as Mentors

The Foreign Universities Bill was approved recently by the cabinet and is to be tabled in parliament soon. Some hope that the entry of foreign universities will lead to dramatically improved standards in higher education. Others fear that the coming of foreign universities will sound the death-knell of India's educational institutions, including our elite institutions.

These hopes and fears are both misplaced. Opening up to foreign universities is certainly desirable and some good institutions may come in. But, in the foreseeable future, it is unlikely that a large number of quality institutions will set up full-fledged universities or even colleges in India.

In higher education, as in defence, the US leads the rest of the world by a wide margin. US firms in manufacturing and services, other education may be keen to get into India but US universities are not. American firms face slow growth in the US and Europe and need rapidly growing markets such as India and China.

But this does not apply to US or other foreign universities. The top US universities, such as Harvard, Yale, and Princeton, do not lack finances. They are supported by enormous funding from private sources. They can attract some of the best faculty and students from all over the world to the US. Why would they want to set up shop in India? Oxford lacks the stature of the best US universities. Its vice-chancellor told the *Times of India* last weekend that Oxford has no plans for coming to India.

It is not just that the top US universities lack the incentives to come to India. If they did come, it would be difficult for them to be viable while maintaining quality. Quality in education comes from having the best infrastructure, the best faculty and the best students. Foreign universities will find it difficult to achieve this mix in India.

Even if land is made available to foreign universities at a concessional price, the start-up costs for a university or even for a full-fledged college would be large. Having the best faculty would mean bringing in a sizeable number from abroad. This would be an expensive proposition, of course, but even paying dollar salaries may not suffice to get faculty to relocate to India.

The best colleges in Europe, Canada and Hong Kong have for long tried to attract faculty from the US by offering a premium over what US schools pay. They have had little success. To be out of the US is to be cut off from the research network and to lose out on the ability to publish. Being in the US is, therefore, something that faculty greatly value. This would also apply to European faculty evaluating relocation to India.

High infrastructure and faculty costs will translate into high fees. A top US b-school charges about Rs 45 lakh for a two year programme. Even this fee contains an element of subsidy that is covered by endowments. In India, one can expect the fee to be somewhere in the range of Rs 25-30 lakh.

A fee of this order would mean catering only to the upper income groups. It would mean shutting out talent from the mass market, which is where the strengths of the IITs and IIMs lie. When you cannot attract the best students, you cannot have the best quality of output.

Thus, the economics of higher education militates against the entry of the best foreign universities. Foreign firms in manufacturing or services other than education can adapt to Indian conditions by hiring local talent, using technology and tapping the export market. None of these is open to a foreign university. The university is one field where technology has remained largely unchanged for centuries: nobody has found a superior alternative to faculty and students coming together in classrooms.

This explains why markets with a higher per capita income than India, such as Singapore, Israel and China, have not been able to interest top universities. It is naïve to suppose that standards in higher education in India can be miraculously enhanced by opening up to foreign universities. There is no alternative to the hard grind: improved funding for government institutions, better governance and greater domestic competition.

Foreign universities can contribute at the margin through mentoring of Indian institutions and by sparing faculty for limited assignments. This happened at the older IITs and IIMs at their inception and it did deliver results. IIM-A and IIM-C benefited from their collaboration with Harvard and MIT respectively. The expenses were underwritten by the Ford Foundation. The collaboration was for a period of about five years, by which time IIM-A and IIM-C had acquired a certain momentum.

Yale university is said to be willing to mentor the 14 innovation universities planned. This may well be the way to go. The government would have to pay the fee for such collaborations. This would be worthwhile provided there is a clear plan for assimilation on the Indian side. Mentoring and collaboration hold out more promise than full-fledged entry by foreign universities.

April 1, 2010

Begone, Management Gurus!

Leading b-schools are looking to overhaul the MBA syllabus. Nitin Nohria, the newly appointed dean of *Harvard Business School*, is said to believe that the way management is taught in b-schools contributed to the recent financial crisis.

Srikant Datar, another HBS professor, and two of his colleagues have authored a book, *Rethinking the MBA*, that echoes this theme. It also laments the fact that MBA students are taking less and less interest in their classes and spending more time on networking and attending recruiting events.

A book that I have just finished reading: *The management myth: why the experts keep getting it wrong,* provides pointers to why students in MBA programmes may be switching off. The author, Matthew Stewart, thinks that management theories don't add up to much, so the MBA course itself means little.

Stewart's background is interesting. After completing a doctorate in philosophy, he took up a job with a management consulting firm. With no knowledge of or background in management, he found himself advising CEOs of top companies at a billing rate of half a million dollars a year.

Stewart rose to become partner at the consulting firm. The firm itself went bust a few years later. Finding himself unemployed,

Stewart decided he would get acquainted with management literature. He caught up with the books that he had acquired when he joined the firm but had never had a chance to open since.

In his book, Stewart dissects some of the more famous management theories and finds them hollow. His assault on management's claims to being a science rests on a scrutiny of key theories in two areas, organisational behaviour and strategy, and works that focus on the creation of 'excellence' in companies.

As an example of how pretentious management theory can get, Stewart cites the 'Hawthorne effect' uncovered by one of the famous names in organisational behaviour, Elton Mayo. A researcher was studying the effect of workplace illumination on worker productivity at a plant, Hawthorne Works. When the illumination was increased, productivity went up; when it was turned down, again it went up. The same thing happened with various other interventions.

Mayo concluded that the results were not due to any external intervention but to the fact that the employees found they were getting attention. This is the foundation of much that has followed in the field since- about 'empowerment', 'teamwork', etc. But Mayo's finding hardly qualifies as a dazzling insight. He was merely pointing out that, as Stewart puts it, 'If you are nice to other people, they will usually be nice to you'. This is a simple ethical construct. The danger in wrapping it up in management jargon is that students will see through the puffery and switch off- and, perhaps, this is what is happening at b-schools.

Stewart also takes on one of the most hallowed theories in strategy, the Michael Porter framework for analysing industries. Porter came up with a couple of important prescriptions based on the framework. One is that there are only three generic competitive strategies open to firms: cost, quality and focus.

Stewart points out that the Porter theory has not been tested rigorously, say, by comparing firms that adopted these strategies with firms that did not and seeing whether one sample did better than another. There are plenty of real-life examples of firms that did not pursue one of these strategies and did well. For instance, several Japanese manufacturers managed to combine quality with low cost, as US firms learnt to their dismay.

Another important conclusion from the Porter theory is that firms end up making excess profits when they can take advantage of market imperfections. But it is not a theory in the sense of having predictive power. It cannot tell you whether a firm has sustainable competitive advantage or not. The corporate world is littered with the debris of firms that, at one time, were thought to have sustainable advantage.

Other theories of strategy have not fared any better. Gary Hamel and CK Prahalad propounded the idea of 'core competence' and held up the Japanese manufacturer, NEC, as a shining example. In the years that followed, NEC turned out to be an underperformer. In *Competing for the Future*, Hamel and Prahalad gave several examples of model firms. Bill Gates said much later that, except for Hewlett-Packard, every example they gave was a 'total joke'. Hamel had moved on- he was now pronouncing Enron as America's 'most innovative company'.

Some of Stewart's sharpest criticisms are reserved for the genre of management books typified by *Excellence*, authored by two ex-McKinsey consultants, Tom Peters and Robert Waterman. The book purported to list the attributes of high-performing companies after evaluating 43 such companies. Two years later, half of the excellent 43 were in trouble. Five years later, almost all showed signs of decline. Peters responded in his next book by declaring, 'There are no excellent companies'. By then, of course, he had made a fortune out of his first book.

There are serious limitations to Stewart's examination of management theory. He focuses on a few theories in the softer areas of management and some popular books. A great deal of what is taught in the harder areas at b-schools, such as accounting, finance and quantitative sciences, is based on sound theory and finds wide application in business.

But Stewart is right in saying that most of the hard stuff at b-schools can be picked up fairly quickly. That is why companies have taken to recruiting from admission lists and hiring bright people from streams other than the MBA. They know they can themselves provide the necessary hard skills and in a shorter time.

The hard skills constitute training. It is the soft part that constitutes education and makes for a rounded manager. It is not easily imparted through courses in ethics or leadership that are the staple of b-schools. Soft skills, Stewart points out, are what the old liberal arts education or 'humanities' was all about. This indicates a way forward for remaking the MBA: combining the hard parts with the basic elements of a liberal arts programme.

July 8, 2010

Let IIT Directors Retire at 65

Over the past year or so, three leading business schools in the US - Harvard, Chicago and Stern-have hired new deans. The oldest of them is 48. Here in India, we seem to be moving in the opposite direction. The ministry of Human Resources Development (HRD) has permitted the Boards of IITs to raise the retirement age of directors from 65 to 70. This is a bad idea. The IIT Boards would do well not to implement it.

Raising the retirement age to 70, it is said, will give greater scope for a second term and even a third term for directors. Some in the IIT system have argued that this is necessary as there is a scarcity of directorial talent. Nonsense. There is enough talent within the country and amongst overseas Indian faculty willing to return to India- enough to fill the post of director in the 15 IITs we have.

We need younger leaders in this country, new leaders. One of the welcome changes in the Indian corporate world in recent years is that there are more young people at the top. Alas, other walks of life - politics, the bureaucracy, academia- have remained relatively immune to this trend. Academia must embrace this trend, not buck it.

That apart, there is a weighty reason for not having a higher retirement age and a second or third term for directors: in the IIT system (and also in the IIM system) there is very little accountability of directors. Lack of accountability of the director is the principal governance issue in our elite institutions today, not any supposed lack of autonomy. Over the years, the Boards of these institutions have failed to put in place adequate norms for accountability of the director. In the past couple of years, the ministry of HRD has tried very hard to bring this issue to the fore but we are yet to see any results.

The contrast with top institutions in the US, the Mecca of higher education, could not be starker. Competition among educational institutions in the US is fierce, unlike in India where the leading IITs and IIMs face no worthwhile competition. The deans of these institutions are, therefore, subject to a high degree of accountability.

A failure to improve the faculty profile, the departure of faculty of stature, a fall in programme rankings, a decline in the quality of research - these and other failures could easily cost the dean his job. In India, it is possible for the director of an elite institution to sleep through his tenure without evoking any response from the system.

Until the Indian system is subject to greater market discipline-say, through the entry of quality institutions from abroad- and until a rigorous system of accountability is in place, it would be most unwise to give a second or third term to IIT directors. The decision to extend a director beyond 65 would be based on the whims, not just of those in government, but those on the Boards of these institutions. We must not forget that Boards invariably tend to lean towards the incumbent. Those at the top know how to keep the Board happy.

The IIMs, in general, have followed the healthy principle of a single term for the director, although there have been occasional departures at some IIMs (other than IIMA). The man responsible for this convention in the IIM system was IIMA's first full-time director, the legendary Ravi Matthai. Matthai was all of 38 when Vikram Sarabhai and his colleagues chose him as the first full-time director. (Sarabhai had been honorary director until then).

Even at the time that he was appointed, Matthai had indicated to Sarabhai that he would not like to stay on in the job for more than five to seven years. His contract, however, did not stipulate any term. Power is addictive. Matthai could have changed his mind and stayed on as director until retirement. He did not do so. At 45 and at the peak of his fame, he chose to step down, having put IIMA firmly on the map of the country as a centre of excellence.

Matthai argued that as institutions evolve, a change in leadership is required as otherwise a system can get too set in its ways. My own sense is that he was also alive to the dangers inherent in a director's staying on for too long in a system where the director had sweeping powers but was subject to very little accountability. At IIMA, having a single term for the director has been crucial to preserving the culture and processes that Sarabhai and Matthai created. It has been an important factor in IIMA's retaining its position of pre-eminence in the country.

IIMA has adhered to this convention for the past four decades. (Those seeking to have it overturned have run into the argument to end all arguments: if the great Matthai could step down after one term, why should anybody else continue?). But not all the IIMs have remained true to it. The government would do well to codify this convention for the IIMs and extend it to the IITs as well. Not only must the IIT director retire at 65, he must stay only for one term. Where accountability is ill-defined, limiting the director to one term is eminently desirable.

September 16, 2010

A Tale of three Jubilees

Three well-known institutions in the country - IIM Ahmedabad (IIMA), IIM Calcutta (IIMC) and *The Economic Times* (ET) - are currently celebrating their golden jubilees. It's an occasion to reflect on what it takes to create and sustain institutions of excellence.

Let me take up the institutions in the order in which I got acquainted with them. I joined the two-year programme at IIMC straight from IIT Bombay. I had no aptitude or liking for engineering. I went to IIT Bombay because that is what any sensible student who had done well academically and did not want to become a doctor was expected to do. IIMC provided the perfect escape.

My first impressions of IIMC were entirely favourable. A smaller, more compact campus than IITB. Hostels that were better maintained. A large room with a balcony that gave on to an open expanse. A pond right in front of the hostel. And breakfast that was edible and filling.

The director's welcome could not have been more effusive. There was the inevitable reference to our being 'the cream of the cream'. After the hellish standards at IITB, IIMC was a relief. Attendance was not compulsory- IIMC believed in turning out ladies and gentlemen, not nerds. The quality of teaching was highly variable.

We all got duly placed and IIMC alumni are now spread all over the world, many in high positions in the corporate sector. The nagging question remains: are B-schools anything more than placement agencies? Let me attempt an answer.

Customer focus. Market segmentation. Brand building. Ratio analysis. Cost allocation. Net present value. Business strategy. Optimisation. Through the sheer power of repetition over two years, the concepts get so thoroughly dinned into you that they stay with you for a lifetime. IIMC did a good job of that.

It might have done better. IIMC was the first of the IIMs. It quickly lost ground to IIMA and, some would say, later to IIMB. Perhaps being in Calcutta became something of a handicap. But the quality of leadership has certainly been an important factor. The golden jubilee is a good time for introspection.

ET was launched in April 1961 in the face of much scepticism. Who would want to read page after page of economic news and commentary? Shanti Prasad Jain, the visionary proprietor of Bennett, Coleman & Co, was not deterred. He encouraged the hiring of specialist writers and reporters, in some cases at pay scales higher than those in the Times of India. (This caused much heartburn in TOI staff).

I have heard that it took more than 10 years for ET to break even. But neither S P Jain nor his wife, Rama Jain, ever faltered in their support to the paper. Their commitment has paid off richly. Over the years, ET has extended its coverage from the economy and the financial sector to the corporate world, politics, personalities and even entertainment. From being a niche paper, it has become a mainstream paper.

My affair with ET started when I was a doctoral student in New York in the late eighties. On a visit to Mumbai, I set up a meeting with the editor, Manu Shroff. I told Mr Shroff that there were many interesting things going on in the world economy that did not find reflection in Indian papers. He suggested I send in articles for the edit page. I started writing for ET thereafter.

Some months later, I got a letter from Mr Shroff asking whether I was willing to serve as part-time correspondent in New York. I readily agreed and began sending a steady stream of stories on international economic affairs. One day, I received a call from Mr Shroff. A finance ministers' meet was due in Montreal in connection with the Uruguay round of world trade negotiations. Could I cover it for *ET*? I was one of two Indian correspondents at the event and learnt a thing or two about reportage.

I continued to write for *ET* off and on after I returned to India. During the East Asian crisis, I commenced a fortnightly column. I have come to value the discipline as much as the complete freedom extended by successive editors of the editorial page.

IIMA, whose faculty I joined in late 1998, was founded in December, 1961. It got to the top quickly and has stayed there ever since. In a milieu in which institutions of higher learning seem almost fated to decline with the passage of time, this is no mean achievement.

What explains IIMA's enduring success? Most of the magic at IIMA was created in the first ten years. Two individuals were primarily responsible, Vikram Sarabhai, the founder, and Ravi Matthai, the first full-time director.

Sarabhai laid down key principles: a faculty-governed Institute; an emphasis on relevance and the real world; and the application of management principles not just to industry but to other important sectors such as agriculture.

Matthai translated these principles into reality. He added concepts that were startlingly innovative: administrative positions that carried responsibility but no authority; the rotation of all positions; self-regulation through norms evolved by the community instead of rules dispensed from above; a single term for the director. These principles and concepts have defined IIMA. They account for its pre-eminence. They have been elements of what might today be called a 'sustainable business model.'

To this day, IIMA gets three key things right: admissions, teaching and placement. The admissions process is completely insulated from outside interference. The Institute does not compromise on excellence in teaching. It goes all out to place its graduates with the best firms in the world.

In a speech that he made when he stepped down as director, Matthai said, "I think this is a good institution. Over the years....... this can become a great institution." The transition from good to great is yet to happen at IIMA. It is a task that today poses challenges of leadership and governance of a different order altogether.

A decade ends. It has been a transformational decade for the country. We can now look forward to a decade in which we will become the fastest-growing economy in the world, one that promises to usher in unprecedented prosperity into the lives of millions. But where are the institutions that can fire the imagination of the young? Where are the institution-builders?

December 23, 2010

Soaring Costs of Higher Education

Higher education costs have tended to soar in many parts of the world. In the elite private universities of the US, fees have reached staggering levels not only in the professional courses, such as law, medicine and management, but in undergraduate courses as well. The Economist noted recently that fees at American universities have risen five times as fast as inflation over the past 30 years.

In the UK, the government last year allowed universities to almost triple their fees with effect from September 2012. In India, there is anecdotal evidence of fees having risen sharply in professional courses. In non-professional courses, government institutions still charge only modest fees. However, in professional courses, where private colleges dominate, the total fees, including capitation charges, can be exorbitant. How to price higher education and how to ensure access are among the important policy challenges facing the country. But, first, we need to understand what is causing prices to rise so fast in the first place.

In higher education, we have three choices. One, we can have a government-dominated system where education is subsidised. Two, we can allow private universities and colleges to come up with the freedom to charge whatever the market can bear. Three, we can allow private institutions freer entry but regulate fees and make provisions for subsidising needy students.

In non-professional courses, we still have the first model. In professional education, we have attempted to move towards the third model but have ended up closer to the second one. There is regulation of fees in some areas but this only covers the official fee. The official fee is often only a small component of the overall fee, with a large component being collected under the table.

Several arguments are made for privatisation of higher education and market-driven fees. Investment in higher education has high payoffs and can, therefore, be financed by loans. Needy students can be taken care of through scholarships or interest subsidies. Subsidised education provided by the government imposes huge fiscal costs, which, in turn, come in the way of both creation of fresh capacity and quality. Competition in higher education will help moderate fee levels.

Every one of these propositions is questionable. In India, the student is not an independent entity. He is part of a family unit for which the student loan is one of several loan obligations. An education loan undoubtedly adds to the burden of the family.

Funding of scholarships is woefully inadequate. Merely letting fees rise does not lead on to superior quality- quality is poor at most private professional colleges despite the huge fees charged. It is also not true that competition helps moderate fees.

The phenomenon of soaring costs in higher education has been studied. The main explanation, it turns out, is simple enough: institutions keep raising fees because they can get away with it. The demand for higher education keeps growing briskly even in the developed world. Institutions of higher education operate in a sellers' market, so they lack the incentive to cut costs, improve efficiency or introduce new technologies.

We must accept, therefore, that where higher education is left to the private sector, fees will escalate. That is why the US has a strong network of state universities (some of which are of very high quality) alongside its renowned private universities. In the US, universities are keen to sustain investment in infrastructure and faculty as there is a correlation between investment per student and the university ranking. At least some of the fee increase can thus be ascribed to the pursuit of quality.

That does hold for India. Most institutions here are simply extracting rents from a scarce product. Higher fees in India merely reflect the commercialisation of education. B-schools are a case in point. The older IIMs have raised their fees substantially in recent years. This, in turn, has triggered large increases in fees at B-schools that do not provide comparable quality. The Anil Kakodkar committee has proposed that the annual fee for the IITs' undergraduate programme be increased from Rs 50,000 to Rs 200-250,000. If this happens, it is bound to cause fees at lesser engineering colleges to rise.

We should not be surprised at the absence of any link between fee and quality in higher education in the country. The UK too is struggling to establish such a link. The government last year allowed fees to rise from £3375 to a maximum of £9000 with effect from September 2012. The idea was that universities would raise fees in keeping with their quality. To its dismay, the government finds that all universities, irrespective of their quality, have veered towards the maximum.

Germany is one country which has sought to buck the trend towards commercialisation of higher education. Many German states have recently opted for free university education. Germany is faulted for not being able to match the excellence of the US in higher education. And yet German education is good enough to produce high quality manufacturing and to power one of Europe's strongest economies.

The German model holds a lesson for India. For us, access to higher education should be the priority. We have enough experience by now as to the limits to using regulation to ensure access. So, we need to seriously rethink the issue of public provision of higher education.

July 20, 2011

Universities as Growth Engines?

Universities are seen as producers of theoretical knowledge that others can use to create prosperity. None have traditionally exemplified this role better than the intellectual powerhouses represented by American universities.

A recent book argues that, since the eighties, American universities have transformed their roles considerably: they have embraced the practical application of knowledge in a much bigger way than before (Creating the market university, Elizabeth Popp Berman, Princeton). In the process, Berman claims, they have become engines of growth, producing research that drives new industries and products.

Berman argues that American universities' move towards the market was driven neither by ideology nor by the necessity to find new sources of funding. Rather, it came about because all the parties concerned- the government, the universities and industry- came to appreciate the overriding importance of innovation in the economy. They came to believe that universities must not just provide the intellectual basis for innovation but be in the forefront of innovation themselves.

Universities moved closer to the market in three ways: faculty entrepreneurship in the biosciences; the patenting of university inventions; and creation of university-industry research centres (UIRCs). Earlier, these activities used to be initiated by individual academics or administrators. Now, they came to be espoused by the leaders of universities.

The universities' drive towards the market got a big boost from the development of biotechnology since this was an industry that had close links with academia from the very beginning. Many biotechnology firms were co-founded by academics, had academics on their advisory boards or used academics as consultants. Initially, the biotech firms focused on pharmaceuticals and drew on academic expertise in molecular biology and biochemistry. The spread of biotechnology to fields such as agriculture, mining, chemicals and environment drew other parts of the university into collaboration with industry.

Until the late 1970s, universities were not favourably disposed towards patenting. They tended to see their research more as a public good. They changed their view by the eighties on the ground that if they did not patent their research, industry would lack the incentive to invest in it. Patenting by universities got a big boost when the US Congress passed an Act in early 1981 that allowed them to patent research developed with the help of government funding. The number of patents issued to universities increased from under 400 in 1980 to over 1100 in 1990.

The third way that universities used to bring themselves closer to the market was to create UIRCs. These were vehicles for bringing universities and industries together to work on problems of common interest. The number of UIRCs shot up from around 250 in 183 to over a 1000 in 1990 and they accounted for 15% of all academic R&D spending. Industry itself provided only 31% of UIRC funding n 1990 which meant that the larger proportion of funding came from government (both the federal and state governments) and the universities themselves. Thus, UIRCs appealed to industry because they provided subsidised research to industry.

UIRCs represent a form of university-industry collaboration that has been around for long. In the US, they took the form of industrial parks in an earlier era. Moreover, unlike patenting, they are not heavily dependent on biotechnology. They represent collaborations in older areas such as electronics, materials science, computer-aided design and manufacturing. To the extent that they are contingent on government subsidy, they cannot even be said to represent a market orientation in universities.

It does appear that American universities are doing more applied research than before but just how important has the transformation been? To answer this question, we need some figures. First, what proportion of total revenues is accounted for by these activities and by all forms of consulting? Secondly, how does academic R&D spending compare with industry R&D spending? Thirdly, what has been the impact on the US economy of the innovations coming from academia? The book does not provide any of these figures or facts. It is a little difficult, therefore, to swallow the author's contention that the universities have turned into growth engines or that they are in the forefront of innovation.

The underlying story, one suspects, is less grandiose that Berman makes it out to be. It is more plausible that, faced with cuts in government spending, America's universities saw the opportunity to augment their revenues through a range of new consulting activities. In the process, they could help faculty, who had already established their credentials as researchers, augment their income and thus attract and retain faculty of high quality. They waded cheerfully into the opportunities for applied research.

However, as Berman herself acknowledges, the focus on applied research has not come at the expense of theoretical research-publication in top journals is still the gold standard for faculty at American universities and the universities remain world leaders in theoretical research. America's universities may indeed have become more market-oriented but they have done so without compromising their basic character.

February 2, 2012

PART - V

INDIAN POLITY

13

Political Class

Beliefs that Took a Beating

As the year draws to a close, it is worth taking a look at some cherished beliefs that took a beating during the course of the year. The list that follows is by no means exhaustive but it suffices to show how wrong some of the propositions voiced in popular discourse can be:

1. Sonia Gandhi is the Congress' biggest liability. Unless the Congress jettisons her, it is condemned to oblivion.

We have been hearing this ever since Sonia took over as Congress president. And yet the pundits who proclaimed this could not have been more wrong. It is not that Sonia has been able to pull in more votes- the Congress' share of the popular vote declined slightly in the last general elections although less than the BJP's. But she has shown that, at the existing vote share, the Congress can romp home if it can stitch together the right alliances.

2. The NDA led by the BJP is the natural party of government. The combination of Hindutva and India Shining make the NDA invincible.

Well, we know better. From appearing invincible, the BJP has gone on to become an object of doomsaying. Many are now asking whether the BJP's recalcitrants such as Uma Bharti and some of its NDA partners will stay with the BJP for long. Hindutva and the Ram temple seem to have lost some of their emotive appeal. But those itching to write off the BJP had better bear in mind belief (1) above.

3. Governments are fated to fall victim to the "anti-incumbency" factor. Even a solid economic performance can't help because poor governance alienates voters.

The assembly elections in Maharashtra did not fit this glib thesis. The Congress-NCP combine was voted back to power in the face of poor governance- starvation deaths were reported in parts of the state. Think again, political pundit, before shooting off your next 1000 words.

4. India Shining is a myth. The growth rate of 8.2 per cent in 2003-04 was a statistical blip made possible by low growth in the previous year.

Not true. This year's growth is expected to be 6-6.5% on top of 8.2% last year. Most people expect this growth rate to be sustained thereafter. Say the worst of the NDA regime but, in terms of macroeconomic indicators, India is indeed shining. It is a different matter that large numbers of people remain untouched by rapid growth.

5. It was the prospect of privatisation held out by that messiah, Arun Shourie, that caused the stock market to boom. Without privatisation, the market is doomed.

Shourie was credited with having added over Rs100,000 crore to the stock market with a stroke of his pen. By penning privatisation or strategic sales into the NDA's agenda, he had brought off a miracle. When ignorant politicians stymied his plans, the market tanked irretrievably- so we were told. Shourie's fans are having to think again. The UPA government resolved not to proceed with the Shourie brand of privatisation- and the Sensex has surged past the 6000 mark. Why? Because sustained economic growth and a rise in inflation are boosting corporate earnings. Public sector units, including banks, are among those witnessing a surge in earnings. Sorry to disappoint you, folks, but profits can boom and the Sensex can ride high without privatisation.

6. FII inflows would dip with the UPA government coming to power. FIIs would be cheesed off with the retrograde elements in the UPA-Left agenda- no privatisation, heavy spending on employment guarantee and other schemes, no liberalisation of the regime for FDI, etc.

We never had it so good where FII inflows are concerned! The present year could see FII inflows touching an all-time high- and this despite interest rates in the US firming up. FIIs may not be as enthusiastic about PSU stocks- although even this is not clear now-but that is no reason for them to turn their backs on the universe of Indian stocks.

7. The days of low interest rates are over. Expect Indian interest rates to rise in tandem with rate movements elsewhere.

We are not quite there yet, there has only been a modest rise in interest rates. If forex reserves continue to rise and if the recent reversal in oil prices continues, the low interest rate regime could stretch out longer than people think.

8. India's cricketers have finally emerged as world-beaters.

Forget the poor showing against Australia, let India show they can humble South Africa on home ground.

How come so many propositions have been proved incorrect? It is not just a matter of the unexpected confounding calculations. Often, propositions are falsified because they are patently self-serving. Because the associated beliefs have more to do with people's predilections and prejudices than with the ground realities.

December 2, 2004

A Crumb or Two of Comfort

What has been a good year for the most part has ended on a grim note for the country. Amidst the enveloping gloom, the writer drew a crumb or two of comfort from a book he has just finished reading, Strobe Talbott's Engaging India: Diplomacy, democracy and the bomb.

When the Vajpayee government went in for nuclear tests in May 1998, harsh international condemnation and American sanctions followed. However, both Vajpayee and Clinton made a crucial decision: it was important for the two countries to engage in dialogue and see how to establish a better relationship than had existed over the previous 50 years.

Clinton chose as his representative Strobe Talbott, Deputy Secretary in the US state department and a buddy of his from his days at Oxford. Vajpayee entrusted the job to his friend, Jaswant Singh, then Deputy Chairman of the Planning Commission. The two emissaries met 14 times on ten locations in seven countries on three continents over a two and a half year period.

Talbott's book is about this protracted dialogue, what it

produced and also what it failed to produce in terms of reordering the Indo-US relationship. But there is a lot more to the book than that. It is the story of how the Vajpayee government dealt with one of the most serious challenges ever to Indian diplomacy and came out smiling. It is an account of how the professional relationship between Talbott and Singh evolved into friendship and set the tone for the changed chemistry between the two nations. Not least, the book is a surprising testament to the resilience and integrity of the broader Indian political system.

As the book makes clear, the decision to explode a nuclear device in 1998 marked an essential continuity in Indian policy, reflected in its steadfast refusal to sign the Non-Proliferation Treaty for nearly three decades under varying governments (a point that seems to have been lost on the present foreign minister). Talbott saw this clearly but he also sensed another motivation: a desire to be taken seriously by the rest of the world, especially the US.

The Americans were realistic about what could be achieved in the dialogue with India. They recognised there could be no rolling back of India's nuclear status, so they wisely focused on objectives they believed were more attainable: get India to sign the CTBT, to subject itself to stringent safeguards on nuclear exports and to limit its ballistic missile capability.

The Indian short-term goal was to refrain from further provocation and to ride out sanctions in the hope that the CTBT itself would collapse for want of ratification by the US Congress, a hope that was duly borne out. The larger strategy was to engage the US long enough for the latter to recognise it was dealing with a serious player, one with which the US could establish a broad commonality of interests. Talbott is generous with his verdict on the eventual outcome: "Jaswant Singh came closer to achieving his objective in the dialogue than I did to achieving mine".

If the book has any hero, it is Jaswant Singh. Talbott senses early on that he is dealing with an interlocutor of some calibre, an "Indian statesman". He never loses sight of his own brief but cannot help acknowledging Singh's dexterity in negotiation. The initial respect gives way to admiration and, finally, to affection. Towards the end of the book, Talbott and Singh are visiting each other's families. The reader is left in little doubt that Singh's equation with

Talbott as much as Talbott's own equation with Clinton contributed towards lifting the Indo-US relationship to a new plane.

The book shows other Indian political leaders too in favourable light. Vajpayee's decision to test showed steeliness of resolve, of course, but also a judgement that the country had become strong enough to withstand sanctions. To borrow an expression Singh used in another context, the country had reached a "critical inflexion point" and it was time to let the world know, to project an image of self-confidence.

Sonia Gandhi remained unbending when Talbott met her to garner support for India's signing the CTBT- "she was all charm, some diffidence and no give" and, by way of response, asked Talbott to convey her warmest regards to Clinton. L K Advani "arched his eyebrows, pursed his lips, and abruptly changed the subject". The entire Indian political leadership stood firm in the face of enormous American pressure.

The reassuring message for us all is that the Indian political system - yes, the very system we habitually rallying against- does deliver under very trying circumstances. That is an uplifting thought as we cope with the aftermath of the recent tragedy.

December 30, 2004

Crisis: Bring in the Politicians

It does appear now that the impact of the global crisis on the Indian economy could be greater than thought earlier. We knew that exports would be badly hit. We had also figured that liquidity would be impacted by a net outflow of FII money.

What was just not factored in was the impact on Indian firms of the collapse of international lending. As I argued last fortnight, one could not also have bargained for the magnitude of mark-to-market losses of Indian companies on international derivative exposures. The sharp fall in forex reserves and the unusual surge in credit since August, which I documented, both suggest that these losses are larger than is generally supposed.

Indian banks would have settled derivative transactions on behalf of their clients- this would explain the huge foreign outflows. Losses on derivative exposures of Indian corporates would show up on banks' books as loans recoverable- hence the surge in credit. This 'involuntary' growth in credit must partly explain why credit for productive purposes has suddenly become so scarce and we are seeing a slowing down of the real economy.

What sort of a slowdown can we expect? There is general agreement that the full impact of the present crisis will be felt in FY 2009-10. Growth estimates for 2009-10 are being revised downwards to as low as per cent.

Given the strengths of the Indian economy, there is no reason why the impact should be as severe as that. If this happens, it will be because of a general collapse of confidence. A comprehensive policy response can prevent such a collapse and limit the damage to the Indian economy.

The response so far has been to loosen the monetary tap and to get banks to lower their lending rates. The prime minister and the finance minister have been busy meeting captains of Indian industry. The message from government seems to be that everything will be done to ensure funds for industry. In return, Indian industry must refrain from effecting big layoffs that could prove awkward for the ruling coalition in the run-up to the general election due early next year.

This approach makes sense only if the government thinks that the crisis will blow over in six months or so. Or if the government believes that the political imperative is to ensure minimal disruption until elections are over- matters thereafter can be left to the incoming government.

This is a dangerous approach to take because half-hearted measures could result in the crisis spinning out of control. Government action must rest on the premise that the crisis will take two years to play out. Action must begin now and not be put off until after the elections. And action to arrest a fall in confidence cannot be confined to monetary policy.

We need a strong fiscal response. This does not mean cuts in indirect taxes alone. That can only have a limited impact on the economy. People may have money but they lack the confidence to spend. Confidence can be bolstered only through massive government spending and the creation of new jobs. This means spending on infrastructure.

It is argued that infrastructure projects take long to fructify and hence cannot help in dealing with the sort of crisis we face today.

But we are talking of spending over a two year period. And infrastructure is not just about airports, ports and power. We need rural roads, low-cost housing, minor irrigation, schools, warehouses, water tanks. All these create employment and can be planned and executed quickly if there is a sense of emergency all round.

All we hear are plans to route soft loans for infrastructure through banks. In today's conditions, attempts to boost infrastructure through private investment won't suffice. Government must take the lead.

But this requires the government to involve politicians in the discourse on the crisis. We need to involve the states and political parties in formulating and overseeing speedy execution of infrastructure works. This is not a crisis that can be addressed by government sitting down with businessmen in New Delhi.

The prime minister must convene a meeting of the National Development Council and ask for plans for infrastructure spending to be drawn up on an emergency basis. Let the government forge a consensus among political parties on a plan for infrastructure spending for the next two years. Forget about the FRBM Act for now.

The present crisis poses a huge challenge but it also creates a major opportunity- to address long-neglected issues of infrastructure. Tackled properly, the present crisis could turn out to be a blessing just as the balance of payments crisis in 1991 was. It could lay the foundation for much stronger growth once the crisis is resolved. All political parties have a stake in rising to the challenge because the consequences of inaction- escalating social strife in a country already reeling under terrorism- are too frightening to contemplate.

November 27, 2008

Fear not the Regional Parties

Regional parties have been a force to reckon with at the centre ever since the era of coalition governments dawned in the late eighties. Their clout has grown with each election and it promises to get stronger after the present one. There is every possibility of the next PM being from one of the regional parties.

The rise of regional parties makes a section of the Indian elite jittery. It thinks coalition governments dominated by regional parties spell instability and weak governance. Only the two national parties, the Congress and the BJP, can provide stability and governance.

Even if coalition governments are inevitable, they are best dominated by the Congress or the BJP, so goes the thinking.

On the face of it, it would appear that these beliefs are well founded. The NDA and UPA coalitions, led respectively by the BJP and the Congress, lasted their full term of five years. In the eighties, VP Singh's National Front government collapsed in just 11 months. The Chandra Shekhar government that followed fell within seven months. In the nineties, the United Front government lasted 21 months.

However, these experiments failed not so much on account of internal dissensions. They failed because the BJP or the Congress found it expedient to withdraw support. These coalitions were unstable because they came to power with a small number of seats and depended on larger parties for support.

There has been a dramatic change in the strength of regional parties since. The regional parties have increased their share of the vote from 20-25 per cent in the pre-coalition era to 45 per cent. Regional parties today rule a majority of the states.

It is not difficult to visualise a formation of regional parties in the coming parliament with a total strength of around 150 seats, equal to or greater than those of the Congress and the BJP. This changes the picture quite a bit. In the eighties and nineties, the Congress and the BJP could topple coalitions in the hope of mustering more seats in fresh elections.

Today, the two leading national parties cannot entertain such illusions. At least in the foreseeable future, there is no escape from the dominance of regional parties. The politics of caste and region needs to play out before national parties regain their ascendancy. For this to happen, we need at least another decade of growth, the swelling of the middle class and the spread of urbanisation.

The two leading national parties, the Congress and the BJP, must know this, hence will not be eager to engage in toppling games. There is thus less reason than before to suppose that governments comprising regional parties will be inherently unstable.

Critics of regional parties also say that they lack ideological coherence and a national perspective. Only the hopelessly naïve will set any store by ideology in an era of endlessly shifting alliances. The name of the game is opportunism, so forget about ideology.

As for regional parties not having a national perspective, an MIT scholar, Adam Ziegfeld, makes a distinction between regional and regionalist parties. Parties may be regional in the sense that their support base is confined to particular states or regions. But they need not be regionalist in the sense of merely catering to regional aspirations. (The CPM is a classic example.) Ziegfeld estimates that out of the 45 per cent vote share accounted for by the regional parties, the regionalist parties accounted for only 13 per cent.

There are those who believe that regional party governments will not push ahead with "reforms". Well, you could have said that of the UPA as well, with or without Left support. The Indian elite can't digest the reality that many of the "reforms" lack widespread support. If privatisation is not happening, it is not because the Left or some regional parties oppose it. It is simply not a vote-catching proposition.

Let's face it, much of the anxiety about regional parties stems from sheer prejudice. The elite is comfortable with a suave Manmohan Singh but it has difficulty coming to terms with leaders with a mass base such as Mayawati, Mulayam Singh Yadav and Jayalalitha. Do they have a view on international affairs? Can they come to grips with economic policy? These are some of the questions that are asked.

Only a profound ignorance of the mystique of leadership can explain such anxieties. It requires no ordinary ability to run a state. Some of the regional leaders may not be conversant with the jargon of international affairs or economic policy. But they certainly would not lack the judgement to choose from options presented by competent advisors.

There is enough anecdotal evidence to go by. The English media unfailingly projects Deve Gowda as a schemer and bumbler. Yet, those who have watched the former PM from close quarters have a different view. I once asked a distinguished bureaucrat which PM had impressed him the most. Without a moment's hesitation, he replied,"Deve Gowda". He added simply, "Man of the masses".

In his memoirs, former cabinet secretary TSR Subramaniam speaks highly of Mulayam Singh's administrative abilities. On a recent TV discussion, a journalist quoted former US ambassador Lalit Mansingh as saying that Mayawati, speaking in Hindi, had impressed her US audience during a visit as CM.

Yes, there is a load of talent among regional leaders waiting to be given expression. For much too long, policies have been framed by Delhi-centric politicians, be they from the Congress or the BJP. Bureaucrats sitting in New Delhi have dreamt up centrally-sponsored schemes for the states. Regional leaders are closer to the grassroots. There is every reason to expect a new orientation to emerge with regional leaders coming into their own in New Delhi, one that will strengthen Indian federalism and is more in tune with the imperative of inclusive growth.

Indian democracy, which has held the polity together, empowered the weak and helped lift the nation to a new growth trajectory, seems poised to work another miracle. So, fear not the rise of regional parties. The only thing we need to fear is the fear of change itself.

May 14, 2009

Don't Demonise the Politician

There was great jubilation last week over the government's decision last week to concede Anna Hazare's demand for a joint committee to draft the Lokpal Bill. The political class had been humbled, the ordinary citizen had won- or, that's how a section of the media and the middle class saw it.

The episode raises issues that we need to debate dispassionately. One, as some commentators have pointed out, whether it is legitimate for groups outside parliament to ask for a say in the framing of laws. A broader issue is whether it makes sense to denigrate the politician and look to non-political actors for solutions to political problems.

In the present case, the activists insisted on a say in the drafting of the Lokpal Bill on the ground that the present version does not adequately address corruption. But, then, that is a point that can be made about any piece of legislation. Unions can ask for a say in the framing of banking laws; environmental activists in laws pertaining to the environment; academics in laws related to education; and so on.

Drafts of legislation must certainly be made available for public comment. But what happens when every interest group seeks to encroach on parliament's power to frame laws? Is it legitimate to ask that those interested in or affected by legislation seek to frame it? How do we choose from amongst several groups that lay claim to framing legislation?

The democratic answer to such a situation is to assume that parliament represents the will of the people and to vest it alone with the power to make laws. Whichever way we look at it, the recent episode cannot be treated as a precedent. In general, the drafting of legislation must be the sole prerogative of parliament.

The finalisation of the Lokpal Bill is likely to prove a contentious affair. The Jan Lokpal Bill, drafted by the activists, envisages sweeping powers for the Lokpal. One wonders whether any set of individuals, however exalted, qualifies to be vested with such powers. Abuse of power is not the monopoly of the politician.

At the root of solutions such as an omnipotent Lokpal is the belief that the politician is the arch-villain in our system and that we must look to non-political actors to solve our fundamental problems, including corruption. This is an offshoot of the neo-liberal ideology that government is evil and all is best left to the market. If government is evil, then so are those who run government.

The majority of people see the politician as the most venal element in Indian society. They are wrong. The fountainhead of corruption is more likely the businessman. As a friend, who happens to run a business put it to me, 'In any illicit deal, the politician gets a cut of only 10-15 per cent. It's the businessman who appropriates the bigger chunk.' It is ridiculous that today some of the loudest rants against corruption should emanate from businessmen.

Corruption in the corporate world would not be possible without the participation of the middle-class. The middle-class is happy to both abet the corrupt practices of businesses and partake of the spoils of these. Those in other professions - doctors, lawyers, chartered accountants, journalists, members of the teaching fraternity- can hardly claim to have higher standards of conduct. The politician can at least plead that he needs large sums of money to practise his vocation; not so, others who point the accusing finger at him.

The politician is seen as not only corrupt but incompetent. One is struck by the general lack of appreciation of the abilities of politicians and the contributions they make. Few people are aware that debates in parliament are often of high quality. So are the reports of various parliamentary committees. Question hour can be very illuminating. Those who habitually denounce politicians would be well-advised to visit parliament's website and browse through the material posted there.

Cynicism about politicians reflects a lack of awareness of their nation-building activities, their ceaseless interactions with constituents, their attempts to address grievances, the efforts they put in towards developing their constituencies if only so that they can get re-elected. Indian society needs to be educated about the political process. Alas, the Indian media is not up to the job; it is largely responsible for perpetuating the stereotype of the politician.

It would make sense to have students serve as interns with politicians and for professionals to be deputed to government. They will get a sense of the energy levels of politicians; their ability to take quick decisions; and their grasp not only of problems in their constituencies but of broader issues of development and national security. Academics too could profit from interaction with politicians. The chief minister of a state, who has to cope with a baffling diversity of problems in an area the size of a European country, would have valuable lessons in management to offer B-schools.

This is not meant to be one long eulogy of the Indian politician. It is intended to make a short point. There is little substance to the notion that politicians lack the ability or the character to respond to national problems, including corruption, and that social activists or other professional groups are better-placed to do so. To demonise the politician is not only to betray ignorance of the Indian political system, it devalues one of most precious assets, our democratic process itself.

April 14, 2011

14

Affirmative Action

Quotas: Why Commonsense won't do

When the irresistible force of social aspiration collides with the immovable object of social discrimination, sparks must fly. Quotas in education and in jobs arouse strong passions all around. The underprivileged see these as crucial to raising their economic status. Politicians, who must respond to social aspirations, agree and are now pushing for quotas in the private sector.

Those opposed to quotas see these as undermining merit, stoking social divisions and benefiting only a tiny upper crust. They say they favour the goal of reservation, which is to uplift large sections of the population. But quotas are not the way to achieve this goal. How do they know? Because that is what "commonsense" tells them.

But commonsense is not the best guide to decision making. We have better tools available for analysing affirmative action, the tools of economics. As a recent survey paper shows, economic analysis throws up conclusions that are counter-intuitive and that indeed serve to debunk myths about affirmative action. (Affirmative action and its mythology, *Journal of Economic Perspectives,* Summer 2005).

One myth, resurrected in the debate on reservations in India, is that affirmative action can involve goals set by employers while avoiding quotas imposed by government. As the authors point out, this is a dubious distinction. Goals set by employers make sense only when a regulator levies rewards or penalties based on the outcomes. If the penalties for producing "bad results" are severe, firms or educational institutions will see themselves as facing rigid quotas. If the penalties are light, then the quotas will be seen as flexible. But, in either situation, there is an implicit quota against which the employer is judged.

Another myth is that affirmative action undercuts incentives. When people from a targeted group know that the qualifying standards are lower, they have no motivation to do better. Says who? It could well be that by creating opportunities that were previously out of reach, affirmative action enhances incentives for skill acquisition. Whether this happens or not is an empirical issue, it cannot be determined a priori.

A third and much touted myth is that it is enough to create equality of opportunity for disadvantaged groups. This in itself will eventually lead to equality in outcomes for various groups. Not true, the authors say. This is because an individual's entire background will be a determinant of his success. First, less successful parents are less able to contribute to an individual with various forms of social and cultural capital. Secondly, children of less successful parents will live in communities with inferior public goods.

So, even if an individual from a disadvantaged group has the same innate ability as somebody from a privileged group and suffers no discrimination, he is less likely to be successful. This knocks the bottom out of a commonly held position- do not have quotas, just make sure there is enough financial support for all.

Consider another argument that opponents of reservation in jobs are particularly fond of. Do not go for reservations in higher education or in jobs because that undermines merit in institutions or the competitiveness of firms. Go for affirmative action much earlier in the developmental cycle of an individual- say, by extending support at the point of basic education.

This sounds reasonable but, as the authors point out, which approach works better is an empirical issue. To take an example, suppose we want to increase the share of minority faculty in an educational institution. Do we do this by lowering the standards for faculty applicants? Or by lowering admission standards for minority students in graduate programmes? If we opted for the latter, we would enhance skills of some students. But other minority students may not develop similarly and they may leave the programme.

So affirmative action in the graduate programme would make

sense only if a sufficiently large group completes the programme. On the other hand, lowering standards for faculty recruitment would be preferable only if the cost of having underqualified faculty is not too high. Which is a better solution is not obvious - the costs and benefits of the two alternatives have to be weighed.

The paper has more in this vein. It makes clear there are no ready answers to issues of affirmative action. The answers have to be found by applying the tools of economic analysis. If politicians are not buying the arguments against reservation and are bent on widening its scope, you can't blame them. "Commonsense" tells them that nothing else will work.

February 9, 2006

Forward with Ambedkar

B R Ambedkar, whose birth anniversary falls on April 14, is known as the leader of the Dalits and one of the architects of the Indian Constitution. What is less known is that he was the tallest intellectual among the leaders thrown up by the independence movement, a man whose idea of India remains relevant today.

Ambedkar's educational qualifications alone would mark him out from his peers. He obtained his doctorate in the social sciences at Columbia University in the US. He then proceeded to London, where he registered for a bar-at-law degree as well as an MSc and a doctorate at the London School of Economics. He had to cut short his studies and return to India when his scholarship ran out.

Having saved up a little as a professor at Sydenham college, Ambedkar returned to London four years later to complete his DSc in economics. While waiting for his thesis to be processed, he spent a few months at Bonn University reading economics. In the meantime, he had started studying French and German on his own. Partly, all this was about making a point: for Dalits, higher education is the route to empowerment.

Ambedkar's wide-ranging academic background provided the basis for an astonishing mass of scholarly output. A website lists 56 books and monographs published by Ambedkar. These cover a host of topics: the origins of caste and untouchability, Hinduism, Marxism, Buddhism, the Indian currency and banking, the partition question, linguistic states and the British constitution, to name only a few.

And all this in the midst of a hyper-active political career that included membership of the Viceroy's executive council and a stint as cabinet minister in independent India.

To read Ambedkar is to encounter a forensic and original mind. An example is his analysis of the origins of untouchability. Ambedkar rejects the notion that untouchables belonged to a subjugated race or that they were associated with inferior occupations. He posits that untouchability arose from the confrontation between Hinduism and Buddhism. The Buddhist opposition to animal sacrifice resonated well with the then agrarian communities and posed a serious challenge to Hinduism. Hindus upped the ante by imposing a taboo on beef-eating even though they had been beef-eaters themselves for long. People who subsisted on dead animals could not go along with the taboo and stood condemned forever in consequence.

Ambedkar is often portrayed as a man who sought to divide Indian society by negotiating separately with the British on behalf of the Dalits as Jinnah did for the Muslims.

Such a portrayal does him scant justice. First, in trying to safeguard the interests of Dalits, Ambedkar was merely reacting to the profound divisions created by the practice of untouchability, whereby Hindu society had condemned millions to an inferior status.

Secondly, Ambedkar saw the struggle for a better deal for Dalits as part of the incomplete project for the creation of an Indian nation. India, he felt, was not yet a nation. It was merely a set of peoples- Hindus, Muslims and Dalits- living together in a geographical area. Liberty or independence by itself could not mark the completion of the Indian project, it merely marked the beginning. It was only when Indian society embraced the ideas of equality and fraternity as well that India could develop a sense of nationhood. This would require, among other things, challenging the varnsashrama dharma that lay at the core of Hinduism.

Ambedkar subscribed to the ideal of a socialistic society but he did not see communism as the route to salvation. He disliked the violence and totalitarianism inherent in communism, he was disappointed that Indian communism was blind to caste and, importantly, he was alive to the role of competition in fostering economic growth. A socialistic society, he felt, must be created not through coercion exercised by the state but by Indian society accepting its responsibility towards the underprivileged. The clamour today for reservations in the private sector shows that Indian society is still far from fulfilling this responsibility.

Gandhi's use of Hinduism as a uniting principle for India served the purpose of achieving liberty for Indians. Nehru laid the political and economic foundations of the Indian nation-state. The time is now ripe for the creation of a genuine social democracy along the lines of what obtains in much of Europe, one in which religion is confined to its appropriate sphere and economic growth becomes more, not less, inclusive. For the realisation of such an ideal, Ambedkar emerges as the authentic Indian icon of the twenty-first century.

April 6, 2006

Costs and Benefits of Quotas

Making transparent the costs and benefits of quotas should help evolve a policy that is acceptable as much to disadvantaged groups as to those who see themselves as losers.

The shrill denunciation in certain quarters of the HRD ministry's proposal to extend OBC reservation to central universities, including elite institutions, is notable for its disregard for fact. Prejudices are aired and assertions made without any reference to the body of theory and evidence that has accumulated on the subject of affirmative action (AA).

AA can take many forms. Prescribing quotas is one of them. Like any social intervention, AA carries costs and benefits. AA policy must be based on an estimate of the costs and benefits of AA in a given context. Thomas Weisskopf, a professor of economics at the University of Michigan, provides a framework for cost-benefit analysis in his definitive work on the subject (*Affirmative action in the United States and India, Routledge*).

The central objective underlying AA, Weisskopf points out, is better integration of society's leadership. This is, of course, essential for democracy and for greater harmony in society. But - and this is often overlooked - there are significant efficiency gains as well.

Leaders from under-represented groups serve as role models for their groups and help spur performance among peers. In jobs that require dealing with disadvantaged groups, leaders from those groups could contribute better than those from outside. Social capital is created in under-represented groups. There are gains from diversity.

It is vital to grasp that efficiency in society does not result from selecting the best academic performers alone. It can result from a variety of other sources of the sort mentioned above. It is this recognition that has driven AA in the US, where AA is neither mandated nor authorised by the Constitution.

There is a disarming line that those opposed to quotas are apt to take. They say they are all for reaching benefits to the disadvantaged. But this is better done through ways other than caste-based quotas. Weisskopf addresses some of the propositions commonly heard.

1. Use socio-economic, rather than caste, criteria: why should a poor Brahmin lose his seat in an educational institution to an affluent OBC? This argument misconstrues the objective of AA. AA is not about reducing socio-economic inequalities. It is about reducing inequalities between various groups in society. Using AA to reduce inter-group disparities does not in any way preclude efforts aimed at reducing socio-economic inequalities.
2. Quotas mainly benefit the privileged in the target groups. This is true but, again, AA is not intended to reduce inequalities within the target groups either. It is intended to produce adequate representation for the target groups as a whole.
3. Intervention is best done, not in higher education or in jobs, but at the primary level and through superior economic assistance. The difficulty is that resources required for the latter approach are much larger. AA in higher education and jobs is less costly and the results are better monitored.

Opponents of AA are on surer ground when they point to the costs it imposes. A big cost is dilution of quality in academic institutions. There is evidence that those selected through AA continue to under-perform in their academic careers. This forms the basis for vehement opposition to AA - "merit is sacrificed" - but several caveats are in order.

First, cut-offs for entry may be lower for AA candidates but these could still be high in absolute terms where the applicant pool is as large as in India. Secondly, the majority of AA candidates do graduate, which means that they meet the quality requirements of the concerned institutions.

Thirdly, the gap between AA candidates and others narrows over time as AA candidates selected tend to be from the second or subsequent generations and have had the advantages of a superior environment (the 'creamy layer'). Fourthly, the gap between AA candidates and others is considerably less in post-university career achievements than in the university. For all these reasons, the dilution in quality is far less than is commonly supposed.

April 24, 2006

India Inc Must Rethink HRD

Most of India's leading companies and business groups have long stopped visiting the top IIMs- they cannot compete for talent with foreign consulting firms and investment banks. Many of the leading manufacturing companies are persona non grata at the IITs - students there prefer MNCs and software firms. The top software firms used to recruit from IITs and regional engineering colleges. In recent years, as their need for recruits has run into thousands, they have fanned out into lower and lower tiers of engineering colleges.

What do these facts tell us? Simply that India Inc has been progressively lowering its qualifying standards when it comes to the search for talent. Yet, IT firms are going great guns and Indian industry too has done pretty well for itself. Clearly, India Inc does not operate on the principle that only the best in class from the top schools can deliver. And not doing so has not hurt India Inc.

Why, then, is Indian business so fearful of creating quotas for disadvantaged groups? Perhaps its fears have to do with a mistaken notion of how quotas are practised. When quotas are instituted, seldom do we have absolute quotas, that is, a number that must be filled irrespective of qualifying criteria. What is more common is that the criteria are lowered for disadvantaged groups.

So, if the cut off is, say, 70 per cent for the general pool, it could be 60 per cent for those who qualify for quotas. It can be nobody's case that somebody who gets 70 per cent is meritorious while another who gets 60 per cent is devoid of merit. This is the first principle that must be understood when we talk about quotas in the private sector: there is no escape from qualifying criteria, only the criteria will be less stringent for targeted groups.

The notion that quotas must involve huge compromises on talent that will undermine competitiveness is thus utterly mistaken. On the contrary, quotas have the potential to enhance efficiency in the corporate sector in at least two ways. The first is through bringing the judges have refrained from expressing a view. More bruising battles loom.

May 4, 2006

Index

C

V

W

Y